Ami Bouganim

SITES & SOURCES

The Book of Jerusalem

The Department for Jewish Zionist Education
The Jewish Agency for Israel

The second volume of Sites and Sources, which focuses on Jerusalem, is a translation of a book that was originally published in French by Pathways Editions with the support of Nativ Policy and Planning Consultant. Once again, I'd like to thank Annette Hochstein for her contribution to the creation and the publication of this book and now, for her permission to publish it in English.

The English version was carefully and meticulously translated by Dania Valdez and edited by Shmuel Peerless. This book would not have been published had it not been for the constant assistance and insistance of Mariana Kronfeld and the support of my colleagues in the Jewish Agency's Department of Jewish-Zionist Education.

Acknowledgement

We would like to thank Chaim Hefer for his kind permission to reprint the Paratrooper Cry.

SITES & SOURCES

The Book of Jerusalem

Research & Development Unit
The Department for Jewish Zionist Education
The Jewish Agency for Israel

אתרים ומקורות
ספר ירושלים

היחידה למחקר ופיתוח
המחלקה לחינוך יהודי-ציוני
הסוכנות היהודית
© Ami Bouganim
Gama Design

ISBN 965-7118-26-3

Printed in Israel 2005

TABLE OF CONTENT

GOD'S ATELIER

God, this city! What humility, what pretension! The beautiful city is so courted and so coveted that it does not know to which litanies to listen or to which advances to yield. Those of the rams' horns (the shofar), those of the bells or those of the muezzins. Sometimes serene, almost celestial; sometimes troubled, so terrestrial. Bathed in a dangerous brightness, detailing the contours of both meaning and non-meaning, the city precipitates genius or insanity among its people. Inspiration becomes revelation, revelation becomes inspiration: "The air in Jerusalem", declares Yehudah Amihai, the most magnanimous of its poets, "is saturated with prayers and dreams."

For three thousand years, this city, nonetheless, has been the earthly setting, troubled and stormy, which reflects the heavens. The most crowded of theaters of divine passion in whose back stages all sorts of sects throng and collide – Jews, Christians, and Moslems – who, more dead than alive, await a throbbing resurrection, echoing the reprimands of prophets, the cries of saviors, the eloquence of poets. The terrestrial city jostles at the entrance of the celestial city and, according to the Talmudic protocols, God Himself declares: "I will not ascend to the celestial Jerusalem without passing through the earthly one."No less than Wiesel, who in general is more sensitive than anyone else and also more vulnerable, declares: "I am at home in Jerusalem when I am not there." Perhaps this is his way of avoiding getting involved in the sacrilegious, political uproar that revolves around the city for better or for worse. Those who are among the lovers of Zion, who preach Zionism and who understand only the earthly passion for this city, will severely judge that type of religious evasion: "Whoever loves Jerusalem", declares Amihai, "in tour guide books or in prayer books is like someone who loves women in pornographic magazines."

Jerusalem is an ever-vigilant city, perched on mountains, between heaven and earth. On Mount Moriah, men's faith has constantly been tested, since the time of Abraham, the Father of the Faithful, who took his son, Isaac, there to offer him as a sacrifice to the One God. The debris of the Jewish Temple is scattered upon it, beneath the Dome of Islam. There lies an enormous rock that the Jews believe is the base of the universe, and the Muslims, the place where the Prophet would rise – a rock for which men would not cease to kill each other, around which, perhaps, one day they will unite. On Mount Scopus, a university, dedicated to piercing new openings towards the sky, is more entrenched than open. The Mount of Olives, with hollowed out tombs, covered with sanctuaries, adorns the architecture of the Passion of Christ throughout the centuries. The Mount of Perdition is irreparably tainted by the pagan sanctuaries built by King Solomon, the wisest of kings, who was sensitive to the religious fervor of his foreign wives. The Mount of Bad Counsel houses a monastery, which was established as if to make amends for a wrong recommendation that, nevertheless, resulted in a God rising from the dead. On Mount Zion, a marvelous dream of "the death of the Virgin" hovers with the complacency of part of humanity. Mount Herzl is covered with military tombs, laid out and lined up as if for inspection by history and oblivion. The Mount of Remembrance where another six million dead, reduced to ashes, find a memorial for the outrageousness of their sacrifice. Moreover, the city is enclosed by the valley of Hinnom (Gehenna) – where the sinister echoes of the victims of Moloch still resonate, weighed down by the prophecy of Jeremiah, which continues to threaten turning it into the valley of the Massacre – and by the valley of Judgment where a multitude of dead will indefinitely await their resurrection.

[•]

The city is built over *tehom* – the abyss – where, according to a Muslim legend, the souls of the dead are stranded. It is a city of peace to the poets, of war to the soldiers. All sorts of tombs cover it, the vestiges of a homicidal history. Its most morbid zealots do not permit relieving it of its dead, even if it is to house the living in their places. And as soon as an archeologist or a mason touches a tomb, the cries of pain and of mourning of its guardians, who see themselves as the watchmen of memory and eternity, reverberate. It is, nevertheless, the city most dug up, most excavated, and most subjected to violence: "Ruins everywhere", noted Flaubert in the mid-19th century, "it breathes sepulchers." The sacred texts relate that its rocks would preserve the memory of kings, prophets, pilgrims, perhaps even of a God. Guides say that its sites are nothing less than the vestiges of divine settings decimated by absurd human disputes.

Its relation to death is even more disturbing and more disconcerting. Built upon cemeteries, it does not tolerate death within its walls overnight, demanding that human remains be buried the same day that the person dies. But above all, it houses the tomb of a God, accused of his death for a long time and considered to be a city of deicide by some Christian descendents. The sky is covered with the dust to which it has been reduced as punishment for one of the most serious and most unpardonable crimes ever committed against the divinity. Chateaubriand stated: "This punishment, so prolonged and almost supernatural, bespeaks an unparalleled crime that no chastisement can expiate."

Then there is its proximity to a Dead Sea…

[•]

The city considers itself nothing less than the center of the universe: "The universe", declares the Talmud, "was created from Zion." But this world has had so many centers attributed to it, in so many sanctuaries, that, henceforth, it would settle for this generalized "navel-ization". However, it is the only city to claim One God, in every sense of the word, as its creator, its owner, its master, its guardian and its lover. One God Who haunts the clashing, rival settings of the three religions, all of which claim an ecumenical concern, while fighting for the exclusivity of God as much as for the credulity, the feelings or the intelligence of men.

Although driven towards the same heaven, they have killed each other over misunderstandings and vulgar differences in their reading of the texts. "A Babel of religions", the French writer, Pierre Loti, declares. Church bell towers, minarets of mosques, domes of synagogues dominate a kind of vast, divine archeological construction site, surrounded by hostels and hotels, where pilgrim tourists stay and often roam among the ruins of a flashing and recurring, strange, divine drama. It is a parchment, upon which men engrave their confused versions of this drama. It is true that God's presence lies in waiting on every street, on every page, in every paragraph: "Anything", writes Amihai, "can be the beginning of a new religion."

Furthermore, the city has been placed, against its will, within the civilization of museums and towers, overflowing everywhere with holy history. Waiting for an architect who will give it an earthly appearance without running counter to its celestial pretensions, the heavens will inevitably repudiate those who would try to mark the stone with the strange mix of pride and humility, of despair and hope, of wisdom and credulity that distinguishes this crossroads of Judaism, Christianity and Islam. The city, nevertheless, will make the best of the architectural decision to clothe itself with stones: perhaps because these stones would not be Jewish or Christian or Muslim; because they would not be partial to one or the other; in this divine disarray, they would be stripped of meaning. In spite of the perpetual imminence of catastrophe and of Salvation, they would not deviate from their patience for eternity and according to Jewish Law, they would not retain impurity, preserving a wise neutrality in every dispute concerning the sacred. Although sensitive to the tones of the light, they add a note of silence and of severity to the din of the city and to its solemnity as well. That of a mausoleum perhaps: "The stone of Jerusalem", continues Amihai, "is the only stone that suffers; a network of nerves runs through it."

Its people also have a divine air. Sometimes humble, sometimes dignified, sometimes haughty, sometimes in rags. The air of prophets, of wise men, of anchorites, of preachers, of beadles, plunged in a dream, a vision, a text. They do not really live, but are content to meditate, considering it a sacrilege to interrupt their prayers, their meditation, their reading. Priests, visionaries, fanatics, with the same expression, claiming to belong to some religion, some church, some synagogue or some mosque. Their beards are galvanized by the same piety. The look in their eyes is tormented by the same fear, animated by the same passion, won over by the same grace. God's dignitaries or perhaps His vagabonds, without question, they are constant figures in this interminable divine production that wavers between tragedy and comedy. This city shelters the Savior within its walls – unaware, confused by all the contradictory expectations, not knowing which to honor, intimidated, perhaps, by previous failures.

Visitors are inevitably converted to pilgrims and are struck with vertigo at the entrance of this bazaar of the unknown, assailed by eternal memories. The most Jewish among them knock against that Wailing Wall, which ricochets their prayers and obstinately opposes their desire for national restoration. Perhaps humanity's most muted monument that, nevertheless, would echo the lamentations of God, grieved by the downfall of men, irreparably forced into a kind of religious begging. The most Christian succumb to the sadness and the melancholy of the sites that witnessed the death of Christ, dragging themselves along a painful path to the paradoxical tomb of a God. Conversion lies in wait at every corner of the sky. Or is it only fanaticism? All sorts of unusual disorders, from inviolable meditation to the most incurable alienation, which, moreover, would give rise to strange vocations: the Messianic vocation to save the world that does not tolerate refutation; the architectural vocation to leave its signature in stone by building a sanctuary on piling, a university with the wings of a dove, a subway upon aqueducts, a Papal Residence... The literary vocation to finally produce a new gospel. All sorts of dark and bright schemes that are characteristic of what a poor, too earthly psychiatrist of the heavens would call the "Jerusalem Syndrome"...

In spite of the restorations made during the last century, this city maintains the appearance of a construction site. Due to what Loti called its "accumulation of humanity's past", it evades every attempt to penetrate it...

CHRONOLOGY

About 1350 B.C.	Ursalim, a Jebusite city under Egyptian rule.
About 1006 B.C.	King David conquers Jerusalem, making it the capital of his kingdom.
About 970 B.C.	King Solomon extends the territory of the city, fortifies its walls and builds a temple consecrated to God.
About 710 B.C.	King Hezekiah digs the Shiloach Tunnel.
About 586 B.C.	The Babylonians conquer Jerusalem, destroy its Temple and deport its elite.
586 – 538 B.C.	Under Babylonian domination, Jerusalem is deserted.
538 – 333 B.C.	The exiles return to Jerusalem under the Persians. A second Temple is built on the ruins of the first.
333 – 164 B.C.	The Greeks occupy Jerusalem, attempt to hellenize the Jews and prohibit their religious practices (198-168). The Temple in Jerusalem is pillaged and desecrated (169). The Hasmoneans revolt against the Greeks (167).
164 – 62 B.C.	Jerusalem, the capital of the Hasmonean kingdom.
63 B.C.	The Romans enter Jerusalem, which remains under Jewish dominion, while submitting to Romans.
37 – 4 B.C.	Herod the Great rules over Jerusalem with the support of the Romans. He expands the city and rebuilds the Temple.

6 – 324 A.D.	**The Romans govern the country.**
6	Judea becomes a Roman province whose capital is Caesarea.
30	The trial, crucifixion and resurrection of Jesus Christ.
66	The country revolts against the Romans.
70	The Romans occupy and destroy Jerusalem. Its inhabitants are massacred and its Temple is burned down.
131 – 135	Bar Kochba leads a new Jewish revolt against the Romans. The Romans put it down and seize the city again.
135	A Roman colony, Aelia Capitolina, is built upon the ruins of the city.
324 - 638	**The Romans-Byzantines govern the country.**
335	The dedication of the Holy Sepulcher Church.
614	The Persians seize Jerusalem.
628	Heraclius recaptures Jerusalem.
638 – 1099	**Jerusalem under Arab rule.**
638	The Caliph, Omar, enters Jerusalem and authorizes the resettling of Jews there.
691	The beginning of the construction of the Dome of the Rock on the Temple Mount.
1030	The Arabs authorize the Christians to restore the Church of the Holy Sepulcher.
1099 – 1187	**Jerusalem under the domination of the Crusaders.**
1099	The Crusaders occupy Jerusalem, massacre its inhabitants and make it the capital of the Latin Kingdom of Jerusalem.

1187 – 1229	**Jerusalem under the domination of the Muslim Ayyubides.**
1187	Saladin conquers the city, drives the Christians out and authorizes the resettlement of the Jews.
1229 – 1250	Jerusalem undergoes a period of political instability.
1250 – 1516	Jerusalem under the domination of the Mamluks.
1517 – 1917	**Jerusalem under Ottoman rule.**
1537 – 1541	Suleiman, the Magnificent, builds the walls of Jerusalem.
1700	Rabbi Judah, the Pious, settles in Jerusalem with his disciples, establishing an Ashkenazi community.
1831 – 1840	The Egyptians, in rebellion against the Ottomans, occupy Jerusalem.
1840	The Ottomans reign again in Jerusalem. European powers open consulates and create diverse institutions, contributing to the development of the city.
1860	The first Jewish neighborhoods outside the walls of the Old City are built.
1917 – 1948	**Jerusalem under the British Mandate.**
1917	General Allenby enters Jerusalem.
1918	The corner stone of Hebrew University is laid in Jerusalem.
1947	On November 29th, a plan to partition Palestine between the Jews and the Arabs with the stipulation that Jerusalem would be internationalized is put to a vote in the U.N.
1948	The British leave Jerusalem on May 14th.

1948 –1949	**The city is the scene of battles during the War of Independence.**
1948	The Old City falls into the hands of the Jordanians on May 28th.
1949	The city is divided between the Israelis and the Jordanians. The Western part of the city is declared the capital of the State of Israel.
1967	The Israelis besiege the Old City. Jerusalem is reunited under Israeli rule.
1977	Jerusalem receives Anwar El-Sadat, the Egyptian president with whom a peace treaty will be concluded.
1980	Jerusalem, "in its intirety", is declared the eternal capital of the State of Israel.
1987	The city is torn apart by the First Intifada.
1993	Mutual recognition between the Israelis and the Palestinians.
2000	The city is virtually divided by the Second Intifada.

THE BEGINNINGS

Jerusalem is perched 700 meters above sea level, between the mountains of Beth El in the north and those of Hebron in the south. The Judean Mountains sprawl towards the southwest, slanting towards the coastal plain. On the other side, the Judean Desert stretches towards the southeast, descending towards the Jericho Plain, the Jordan Valley and the Dead Sea, which are all located below sea level.

Since the middle of the 4th millennium, there is a small earthen mass that is fed by the Gihon Spring that flows through the Kidron Valley, away from the highway axes between the coastal plain and the desert. It is mentioned for the first time in the text of Curses in an Egyptian statuette dating back to the 19th century B.C. It reappears under the name of Urusalim in the archives of the Akhenaton palace in Tell El-Amarna, dating back to the 14th century. It is then the seat of a king – Abdi Heba, the servant of the goddess Heba – the vassal of the Egyptian pharaoh who rules over the region. In the letters from Tell El-Amarna, Abdi-Heba solicits the aid of the pharaoh against the Habirus – perhaps the Hebrews – who are a threat to his power.

The first name of the city would have been Irusalem, the contraction, perhaps, of the two words *yarah* and *Sahlim* – a city consecrated to the god, Shalim, according to the Semitic tradition. The Bible speaks about it for the first time in the chapters of Genesis, which are devoted to the patriarchs. Abraham, who was still called Avram, meets Melchizedek, the king of Salem:

Abraham and Melchizedek

Melchizedek, the king of Salem brought out bread and wine: he was a priest of the Most High God. He blessed him saying: "Blessed be Avram of the Most High God, possessor of heaven and earth! And blessed be the Most High God Who delivered your enemies into your hand!" And Avram gave him a tithe of everything.

Genesis 14: 18 - 20

Melchizedek was the king-priest of a city consecrated to one god whose name bore the ending *zedek*. Later, during the time of Joshua, Moses' successor as the leader of the Hebrews, the king of the city was still called Adoni-Zedek – perhaps the Biblical name of Abdi-Heba. Be that as it may, the city evidently extended on the eastern slope, slanting towards the south of a hill surrounded by mountains, bordered on the east by the Kidron Valley and by the central valley or the Tyropoeon Valley on the south and the west. Further to the west, the Hinnom Valley – the Gehenna – the site of pagan worship until the 8th century, encircled the hill that becomes known as Mount Zion, before joining the Kidron Valley.[1] The city, which was entirely situated outside of the present day walls of Jerusalem, did not exceed a width of 100 meters in the north and was even more narrow in the south.

Early on, the summit of the hill upon whose slope the city extended was considered to be Mount Moriah where, according to Hebraic tradition, Adam resided after his expulsion from Paradise, and to which God led Abraham when He asked him to sacrifice his son, Isaac:

Mount Moriah

...God tested Abraham and said to him: "Abraham!" He said: "Here I am." And He said: "Now take your son, your only son, Isaac, whom you love, and go to the land of Moriah and offer him there for a burnt offering upon the mountains that I will show you." And Abraham rose early in the morning, saddled his ass and took two of his young men and his son, Isaac, with him. He split the wood for the burnt offering and set out for the place that God had told him. On the third day, Abraham lifted his eyes and saw the place from afar. And Abraham said to his young men: "Stay here with the ass while I and the young man continue further to prostrate ourselves and then return to you."

Abraham took the wood for the burnt offering and laid it upon Isaac, his son, and he took the fire in his hand and the knife and the two of them went together. And Isaac spoke to his father: "My father!" And he said: "Here I am, my son." He then said: "Behold the fire and the wood, but where is the lamb for the burnt offering?" And Abraham replied: "My

1. These three valleys are the most well known in the mountainous region where Jerusalem was established. The Cedron Valley – Kidron in Hebrew – runs from the neighborhood of Mea Shearim along wadi el-Joz, slants towards the south, separating the Old City from Mount Scopus and the Mount of Olives, following its course up to the Dead Sea. See the Jehosophat Valley, p.149. The Tyropoeon Valley or the Central Valley begins in the Morasha neighborhood, crosses the Damascus Gate, divides the Old City from north to south in two parts along ha-Gai Street, goes through the Dung Gate and casts itself into the Kidron. The Gehenna Valley – Gai ben-Hinnom in Hebrew – begins around French Square and extends to Jaffa Gate where it slants towards the south, skirting Mount Zion and then following its course towards the east to cast itself in turn into the Kidron.

son, God will provide for Himself a burnt offering." So they went together to the place that God had indicated.

Abraham built an altar there, laid out the wood, bound his son, Isaac, and laid him on the altar upon the wood. Abraham stretched out his hand and took the knife to slay his son when an angel of the Lord called out to him from heaven, saying: "Abraham, Abraham!" And he said: "Here I am." He replied: "Do not lay your hand on the lad, do not do him any harm because now I know that you fear God for you did not withhold your son, your only son from Me."

And Abraham raised his eyes and saw a ram behind him, caught in the bushes. He took the ram and offered it as a burnt offering in place of his son. (...) And the angel of the Lord called out to Abraham a second time and said: "I have sworn to myself", the Eternal declared, "that because you have done this and have not withheld your son, your only son, I will bless you greatly and I will exceedingly multiply your seed as the stars of the heaven and sand upon the sea shore. And your descendents will possess the gates of their enemies and through your seed all the nations of the earth will be blessed because you have obeyed my voice."

Genesis 22: 1 - 18

The destiny of humanity will be played out in a certain manner in this setting. The attachment to the One God, to whom all would be sacrificed, will mobilize men. At least the adherents of the three monotheistic religions, who all claim Abraham as the Father of the Faithful, consider Mount Moriah one of the foremost site of its faith. According to Jewish and Muslim traditions, it is situated on the Temple Mount where the Dome of the Rock stands today. Christian tradition situates it on the Golgotha where the Church of the Holy Sepulcher now stands.

[•]

In the book of Joshua, the Jebusite king of the city is the head of the league of Amorite sovereigns who are defeated by the Hebrews at Givon. In spite of his death, the Hebrews do not occupy the city. It falls between the tribes Benjamin and Judah when Canaan is partitioned among the twelve tribes. At the time, the city is still called Jebus. The Bible later names it *Yerushalayim* – a Talmudic commentary will call it *ir-shalom*: the city of peace. Another name, that of Zion, first appears in the book of Samuel (Samuel 2: 5 –7). Through the course of time, prophets and poets will bestow it with a multitude of names to express their veneration: City of God, Holy City, City of Justice, City of the Faithful, Beautiful City, etc. Almost three thousand years later, Yehudah Amihai will write: "The city plays hide-and-seek with its names."

THE CITY OF DAVID

King David (1000 – 972 B.C.) unites the Hebrew tribes under his authority. In search of a location for his capital, he decides to eliminate the Jebusite enclave that separated the territory belonging to the tribe of Yehuda, from which he descended, from the rest of the tribes. The conquest of the city is described in an obscure passage in the book of Samuel:

The capture of the city

The king and his men went to Yerushalayim to the Jebusites who inhabited the land. They spoke to David saying: "Unless you remove the blind and the lame, you will not enter here", meaning that David would not enter. Nevertheless, David seized the stronghold of Zion, which is the city of David. On that day, David said: "Whoever goes through the tunnel and smites the Jebusites, the lame and the blind (who became odious to David) – hence, the saying: 'The blind and the lame will not enter the house.'" So David dwelt in the stronghold and called it the city of David. And David built all around as far as Millo.

2 Samuel 5: 6 - 9

The commentators are divided over their interpretation of this passage. Some maintain that the procession of the lame and the blind arose from a magic ritual intended to stir up the enemies' fear; others claim that it was a diversion tactic. Be is as it may, according to some researchers, the conquest of the city mobilized only a handful of men, who penetrated the city through the tunnel mentioned in the passage. According to others, the city was seized in the manner of Jericho, with drums, bugles and trumpets, and the tunnel in question – *tzinor* in Hebrew – designates a musical instrument.[1] In any case, the inhabitants did not suffer from the fall of the city, nor did their king, Arevnah, since we meet him again selling David the threshing-floor for wheat located north of the city

1. Historians compared it to a shaft – Warren's Shaft, named after of the archeologist who discovered it in around 1860 – evidently constructed between the 10th and the 8th century B.C., at David's Tzinor. See the Shiloach Pool p.39.

21

– Mount Moriah – where both the Tabernacle is set up and king Solomon, David's successor, builds the Temple.

One of David's first decisions is, in fact, the transfer of the Ark of the Covenant in which the Tablets of the Law were kept from Kiryat Yearim to Jerusalem. Upon the advice of the prophet, Nathan, he then builds a sanctuary, making Jerusalem the religious and political center of all the tribes. The city of David extended on the slope descending from Mount Moriah at the southern junction point between the valleys of Kidron to the east and that of Tyropoeon to the west. Furthermore, David fills in some ravines to permit the extension of the city to the northwest.

Thereupon, David commits a crime of passion. Going out for some air on the terrace of his palace, he falls in love with the beautiful Bathsheva. Unfortunately, she is married to Uriah, the Hittite, who is serving in his army. David makes arrangements to have his rival placed on the frontline so that he will die in battle. Although posterity will pardon him, David's romantic-military intrigues incite Nathan's indignation, who reproaches his baseness in a remarkable scene – a classical scene in which the prophet challenges all political authority, listening only to his religious conscience, denouncing the abuse of power committed by the monarch:

The poor man's lamb

The Eternal sent Nathan to David and he said to him: "There were two men in one city; one rich and one poor. The rich man had many flocks and herds, but the poor man had nothing except one small ewe lamb, which he had bought. And it grew up with him and his children. It ate of his bread and drank from his cup and lay on his bosom and was like a daughter to him. A traveler came to the rich man, who spared his own flock and his own herd to take and prepare for his guest, and took the poor man's lamb and prepared it for the man who had come to him." And David's anger was greatly inflamed against that man and he said to Nathan: "As the Eternal lives, the man who has done this deserves to die and he will pay fourfold for the lamb because he did this and had no pity. "

And Nathan said to David: You are that man! Thus says the Eternal; the God of Israel: 'I anointed you king over Israel and I delivered you out of the hand of Saul; I gave you your master's house and your master's wives into your arms. I gave you the house of Israel and of Yehudah and if that had been too little, I would have given you as much again. Why have you despised the commandment of the Lord and done evil in his sight? You have slain Uriah, the Hittite, with the sword and taken his wife as your wife. You have slain him with the sword of the children of Ammon. Therefore, now the sword will never depart from your house because you have despised me and have taken the wife of Uriah, the Hittite, to be your wife.'"

2 Samuel 12: 1 - 10

The curse of the prophet Nathan will be realized in the interdiction to David of building the Temple in Jerusalem:

David's punishment

And David assembled all the princes of Israel, the princes of the tribes, the captains of the companies that served the king by divisions, the captains over the thousands, the captains over the hundreds, the stewards over all the property and herds of the king and of his sons together with the officers [of the palace], the mighty men and all the men at arms. Then David, the king, stood up on his feet and said: "Hear me, my brothers and my people, my heart was set on building a house of rest for the Ark of the Covenant of the Eternal and a footstool for our God and I had made the preparations to build it. But God said to me: 'You will not build a house for My Name because you have been a man of war and have shed much blood!' Yet the Eternal God of Israel chose me before all the house of my father to be king over all Israel forever, for He has chosen Yehudah to be the ruler. And out of the house of Yehudah, the house of my father, and among the sons of my father, He chose me to reign over all Israel. And from among all my sons – for the Eternal has given me many sons – He has chosen Solomon, my son, to sit upon the throne of the kingdom of the Eternal over Israel. And He said to me: 'Solomon, your son, will build my house and my courts for I have chosen him to be my son and I will be his Father. Moreover, I will establish his kingdom forever if he remains constant in observing my commandments and my judgments as on this day.'"

I Chronicles 28: 1 - 7

The commentaries by the rabbis detail the reasons that prevented David from building the Temple:

The burden of power

The day that David slew Goliath, the daughters of Israel celebrated his victory, covering him with jewels made of gold and silver. David decided to save them for the construction of the Temple. The famine had been raging for three years and the people sought his aid, but he refused to listen. Likewise, the Holy One, Blessed be He, said to him: "Because you did not agree to come to the aid of the miserable poor, you will not build the Temple, but your successor, Solomon, will."

Yalkut Shimoni Ruth

The Mount of Olives to the east, Mount Zion to the west and Mount Moriah to the north overlook the city of David that stretches over an area measuring sixty hectares. It covers the archeological site facing the picturesque Arab village of Silwan.[2]

According to the Jewish pilgrimage tradition, and contrary to the opinion of archeologists and historians, the tombs of David, Solomon and their successors are located on Mount Zion. The hall in which the cenotaph stands has a hollowed out niche facing the Temple – perhaps a synagogue dating to the 4th century that one day would be used as a church. Catholic tradition identifies this site as the home of Mark the Evangelist, where the first Christians would gather. In the 15th century, the site, claimed by both the Christians and the Jews, is conquered by the Mamluks who convert it into a mosque and prohibit them from entering it. They had to wait until 1839 for the intervention of the Jewish philanthropist, Moses Montefiore, to be permitted by the Turkish authorities to visit it.

2. The archeological site of the city of David – excavated by Kathleen Kenyon during the 1960s – preserves vestiges of a wall that dates back to the 18th century, B.C. A second wall, built in the 8th century, on part of the same location as the first, surrounded the city until its destruction in 586 B.C. The base of a tower that supported the gate, which the inhabitants of the city used to reach the Shiloach Pool in the Kidron Valley, can be seen. Another area of the archeological site – Zone G –, excavated by Y. Shiloh (1978 – 1985), contains the vestiges of a wall dating to the Second Temple Period (516 B.C. – 70 B.C.), which supports a leaning wall, the vestige of a building dating back to the 10th century. The ruins of a Canaanite citadel as well of some residences were discovered underneath that wall on the side of the hill, dating to the First Temple Period (970 – 586 B.C.) – Ahiel's house identified by some ostracon with the owner's name engraved on it, the House of Medallions where medallions bearing, for the most part, Hebrew names were found, and the Burnt House.

In 1855, the drought in Palestine is so severe that Muslim religious authorities ask the rabbis of the city to join them on the Temple Mount to pronounce prayers destined to "open the sky's floodgates". But it is said that the rabbis do not agree to solicit God's meteorological help except from the enclosure of David's tomb. This religious collaboration will lead to the opening of the doors of the site to Jews, who will be authorized to gather at the tomb in exchange for a fee handed over to the Ottoman authorities, especially on Pentecost that, according to rabbinic tradition, coincides with the anniversary of David's death. They even composed a prayer, which they pronounce at the tomb:

David's Merit

Master of the universe, God of hosts, You who are enthroned among the kerubim, today I prostrate upon the tombs of the members of David's dynasty, who served you with truth and integrity, to offer my supplications. In the same way that you considered the prayers of David, your servant and of his son, Solomon... with your great compassion, please accept this prayer that I pronounce upon their tombs. Grant that by the merit of the kings of Israel, which is the heritage of all Israel, that the members of your people, the House of Israel, wherever they may be, find grace and mercy in the eyes of the rulers and their dignitaries.

Upon leaving David's tomb, immediately to the left, there is access to a series of underground halls. One of them, the Harp Hall, exhibits a collection of books of Psalms, which according to rabbinic tradition, were composed by king David, as were their musical scores:

Psalm of David

To the Chief Musician: a Psalm of David.

The heavens declare the glory of God,
the firmament proclaims His handiwork.
Day to day utters speech,
night to night expresses knowledge.
There is no speech, nor are there words;

where their voice is not heard.
Their harmony extends throughout the world,
their words to the end of the world.
In them He has set a tent for the sun,
that comes out like a bridegroom from his nuptial chamber,
rejoicing like a mighty man to run a race.
His going forth is from the end of the heaven,
and his course to the ends of it,
and nothing can be hidden from his heat.
The Torah of the Eternal is perfect,
restoring the soul.
The testimony of the Eternal is accurate,
making wise the simple.
The statutes of the Eternal are just,
gladdening the heart.
The commandment of the Eternal is clear,
enlightening the eyes.
The fear of the Eternal is pure,
enduring forever.
The judgments of the Eternal are true,
and altogether righteous,
more desirable than gold, than much fine gold,
and sweeter than honey and the honeycomb.
Moreover, your servant is careful to observe them,
for there is great reward for keeping them.
Who can discern one's errors?
Cleanse me from hidden faults.
Preserve your servant from presumptuous sins,
let them have no dominion over me,
and I will be upright, innocent of any transgression.
Let the words of my mouth and the meditation of my heart be
acceptable in Your sight,
Oh Eternal, my strength and my redeemer!

Psalms 19: 1 - 15

Upon leaving the tomb, there are stairs to the right that lead to the hall of the Last Supper – Cenaculum or Cenacle – located above David's tomb, and the Hall of the Washing of the Feet, which was restored by the Franciscans in the 14th century, adorned with two Gothic columns that support a domed roof. This is where Jesus had his last meal on the eve of Easter – Holy Thursday. That meal was preceded by a ceremony that would establish the Eucharist, the sacrament that perpetuates the sacrifice of Christ:

The Last Supper

As they were eating, Jesus took bread, blessed it, broke it and gave it to his disciples and said: "Take, eat, this is my body." And he took the cup, gave thanks and gave it to them, saying: "Drink of it all of you for this is my blood of the New Testament, which is shed for many for the remission of sins. I say to you: henceforth, I will not drink of this fruit of the vine until the day that I drink it, new, with you in my Father's kingdom."

Matthew 26: 26 - 29

The Muslim tombs on the site are those of the illustrious Muslim family, the Adjani, who for centuries demonstrate such devotion in maintaining the sites that they will be worthy of the name, *el Daoud'na* – the Davidians.

THE CITY OF SOLOMON

At the time of David's death, there are no more than 2,500 inhabitants in the city. It will not truly develop until the reign of his successor, King Solomon (965 – approximately 928 B.C.), serving as a crossroads to the caravans that link the Euphrates to Egypt and housing the royal granaries fed by the twelve districts of the kingdom. The style of the court, Solomon's international renown, and the constant presence of military chariots, of mercenaries and of foreign delegations, confer the city with a cosmopolitan character. Furthermore, a sanctuary set aside for the worship of idols stands on a hill at the outskirts of the city – the actual Mount of Contempt or Mount of Perdition. This tolerance for idol worship will be considered the gravest transgression of the wisest of Hebrew kings, to whom the hagiographic tradition of Israel attributes the composition of the Song of Songs, Ecclesiastes and Proverbs. According to a Talmudic commentary, these works illustrate the three stages of the life of a man: youth, whose distinguishing characteristic is ardor, maturity, which is characterized by disillusionment, and old age, whose mark is wisdom:

The ardor of youth

The Song of Songs by Solomon.

That your lips cover me with kisses,
For your kisses are more delicious to me than wine,
Your scent sweeter than perfume,
and your name overcomes me like an aroma –
for this reason so many maidens are in love with you.

So take me away, let's run away!
You, my king, will lead me to your palace,
Where we will know joy and happiness,
praising our revelry more than wine –
There is reason to love you!

I am black and beautiful,
oh daughters of Jerusalem,
like the tents of Qedar,
like Solomon's pavilions.
Do not be mistaken,
my complexion is tanned by the sun.
Taunted by my mother's sons,
I was compelled to look after their vineyards,
neglecting my own vineyard!

Tell me, you whom my soul loves,
where does (your flock) graze,
how do you mark the mid-day break?
Why should I cover myself to look for you
among your companions' flocks?

– If you do not know, oh most beautiful among women,
follow the path of the sheep
and lead your kids to the shepherds' huts.
I compare you, my dear,
to a mare harnessed to Pharaoh's chariots.
Your cheeks framed in pearls,
your neck adorned with necklaces are delightful.
We will offer you chains of gold studded with silver.

– While my king was reclining on his couch,
my spikenard exhaled its aroma.
My beloved is to me
like a sachet of myrrh
that I keep between my breasts,
my beloved is to me
like a cluster of privet
in the vineyards of Ein Gedi.

Behold, you are beautiful, my love, you are beautiful!
You have the eyes of a dove.
You are beautiful, my beloved, so pleasant!
Our couch is verdurous,
the beams of our house – cedars,
the rafters – cypress.

Song of Songs I: 1 - 17

THE CITY OF SOLOMON

The disillusionment of maturity

The words of Kohelet, the son of David, the king of Jerusalem:

Vanity of vanities, says Kohelet, vanity of vanities, all is vanity!

What is man's profit for the toil of his labor under the sun?

One generation passes away and another generation comes, but the earth abides forever.

The sun rises and the sun sets, continually hastening to its place from where it rises again.

The wind blows towards the south and veers to the north, around and around it returns on its round.

All the rivers run into the sea – yet the sea is not full, they return to the place where the rivers flow.

All things grow weary; man cannot speak of it, the eye is not satisfied with seeing and the ear is not filled with hearing.

That which has been is that which will be and that which has been done is that which will be done and there is nothing new under the sun! Is there something about which it may be said: "Look, this is new!" that hasn't already existed in previous worlds. There is no memory of the past and there will be no memory of things to come among those who come after.

I, Kohelet, was king over Israel in Jerusalem and with all my heart I sought and searched out with wisdom everything done under the sun – it is a sore task that God has assigned to the sons of man. I have seen all that has been done under the sun and behold all is vanity and futility.

Ecclesiastes 1: 1 - 14

The wisdom of old age

The proverbs of Solomon, the son of David, king of Israel:

To know wisdom and morality; to perceive the words of understanding; to retain the lessons of wisdom, of justice, of law and of integrity; to give discernment to the simple and to youth, knowledge and discretion. A wise man will listen and increase learning; and a man of understanding will acquire acumen; to understand parables and metaphors; the

words of the wise and their riddles. The fear of the Eternal
is the beginning of knowledge; but fools despise wisdom and
morality. Listen, my son, to the instruction of your father and
do not forsake the Torah of your mother.

Proverbs 1: 1 - 8

Solomon's most important architectural achievement was
a temple – the First Temple – which, like other palatial and
administrative buildings, such as the House of the Lebanon
Forest and the House of Pharoah's Daughter, occupies the
summit of a hill – Mount Moriah, formerly Mount Zion,
which became the Temple Mount – upon whose slope the
city of David spread. Its construction required many years
of work, costly materials and great technological skills. The
materials and the artisans were provided by the Phoenician
king of the coastal city of Sidon: "There is no one among
us", wrote Solomon to the Phoenician king, "who can hew
timber like the Sidonians" (I Kings 5: 20).

The Biblical text describes at length the First Temple in
Jerusalem, which was probably one of the most impressive
monuments of the epoch. It included a square that was
accessible to the people, and a court where the altar and the
Temple stood, which only the priests could enter. The latter
appeared to be a long building, divided in three parts: a porch
or vestibule – *oulam;* a sanctuary – *heichal* – that housed the
items required for worship; and the Holy of Holies – *devir* – the
most sacred place in the Temple where the Ark of the Covenant
was kept. The court was supposed to have had a circular basin
of purifying water – the Sea of Bronze – 5 meters in diameter
and 2.5 meters high, supported by 12 bronze bulls, fashioned in
groups of three, facing the four cardinal directions: north, south,
east and west. Two brass columns – named Yakine and Boaz
– topped by capitals, framed the entrance. Outbuildings – *yatsai*
– surrounded the building.

Solomon's Temple

And the house that King Solomon built for the Eternal was
sixty cubits long, twenty cubits wide and thirty cubits high.
The porch before the temple of the house was twenty cubits
long along the width of the house and ten cubits wide before

the length of the house. And for the house, he made windows wide without and narrow within. Against the wall of the house, he built galleries all along the walls of the building – of the Temple and of the Holy of Holies – like lateral wings. The lowest chamber was five cubits wide, the middle was six cubits wide and the third was seven cubits wide, for he made narrow steps outside in the wall all around so that the beams would not be fastened into the walls of the house. The house was built of stone prepared before it was brought there so that no hammer, no ax nor any other tool of iron was heard when the house was being built. The door for the middle chamber was in the right side of the house, and they went up on winding stairs into the middle chamber and out of the middle into the third. He built the house and finished it, and covered the house with beams and boards of cedar. And then he built the side structure against the house, five cubits height, clothing it with timber of cedar.

I Kings 6: 2 - 10

The placement of the Ark of the Covenant in the Holy of Holies takes place during a ceremony that gathers together the dignitaries of the kingdom. Following the sacrifices, the king delivers a speech and pronounces a prayer:

The dedication of the Temple
And Solomon stood before the altar of the Eternal in the presence of all the congregation of Israel and spread out his hands towards heaven and said: "Eternal God of Israel, there is no God like You in the heaven above or on the earth below Who keeps the covenant and loving kindness with His servants who wholeheartedly walk before You, Who has kept His promise to Your servant, David, my father, which Your mouth proclaimed and Your hand has fulfilled today. Therefore, Lord, God of Israel, keep the promise that You made to him, saying: "No man will be excluded in my sight from the throne of Israel provided that your children preserve their way to walk before Me as you have walked before Me." And now, Oh God of Israel, keep the promise that You made to Your servant, David, my father. For will God indeed dwell on earth? Behold, the heaven and the

33

heaven of heavens cannot contain You. How much less this house that I have built? Hear Your servant's prayer and his supplication, hear the cry and the prayer that your servant prays before You today that Your eyes be open upon this house day and night, upon the place which You have said: "My name will be there", and that You hear the prayer that Your servant will address towards this place. Listen to the supplication of Your servant and of Your people, Israel, when they will pray towards this place, hear them in Your dwelling place in heaven and when you hear them, forgive them.

I Kings 8: 22 - 30

Popular Israeli tradition continues to embellish the legends about the site of the Temple:

The field of brotherhood

Once two brothers had shared the field where the house of our holiness and our glory was to be built. One was single, the other married and the father of many children. They lived together peacefully, content with the produce of the field that they had inherited from their father, cultivating it together with the sweat of their brow. At the end of the harvest, they divided the sheaves of grain in two equal parts, which they left in the field for some time.

One year, when he was getting ready for bed, the single brother said to himself: "I live alone without anyone but myself to feed, as opposed to my brother who must provide for his wife and his children; my portion should not be equal to his." He surreptitiously rose like a thief in the night to take some of the sheaves from his share to add them to his brother's.

That very night, the married brother told his wife: "It is unjust to share the wheat in two equal parts when my situation is better than that of my brother for God has blessed me with a wife and children while he lives alone with no other comfort or consolation than that provided by the produce of the field. Come with me to secretly take some of the sheaves from our heap and put them in his."

The next morning, to their astonishment, the two brothers saw that their heaps had not changed, but they said nothing. The following night, they carried out the same plan and then again on the third night and the fourth, each morning seeing that their shares remained the same – until the night that they met each other, carrying their sheaves to once again perform their good deed. Upon discovering their secret, they fell into each other's arms, hugging each other and thanking God for having made them brothers. And it is at the place where they met each other that God wanted to build a house that would bear His name.

Another legend drawn from the Zohar, the masterpiece of Kabbalistic literature composed in the 12th century, situates the Holy of Holies at the center of the universe:

The center of the universe

When the Holy One, blessed be He, created the world, He took a stone from under His throne and threw it into the tehom *– the abyss. One of its ends penetrated it and the other remained outside – and it was at this point in the center that the universe expanded towards the right, towards the left and in every direction.*

This is where the Holy of Holies is located.

That stone, a mix of fire, of water and of wind, which will later be introduced into His creation, rises above the abyss and from time to time, some waters gush forth, filling it.

This stone is called Shetiyya *(foundation) for the universe was founded upon it.*

The earth would spread from this point in three movements. The first produced all that is pure and bright on earth. The second, taking over the first without being as pure nor as bright, produced the fine and subtle things from the purest sand anywhere in the world. The sand of things that produced the third movement of propagation is the most common and the most obscure and is encompassed by the waters of the oceans that surround the land...

The Temple, the sanctuaries, the outbuildings, the institutions and the entire city within the walls are contained in the ray of the first movement of propagation. The land of Israel, which received sanctity as a heritage, is contained in the second ray of propagation. The third ray of propagation contains the rest of the earth where the other peoples reside as well as the sea that surrounds it.

The explicit name of God, whose knowledge would permit the initiated to penetrate the mysteries of creation, and the plans of the Creator are engraved upon this stone – *even ha-shetiyya*. This would be the stone that even to this day is mounted under the Dome of the Rock in the middle of the esplanade of the Temple. It would be displaced by the *tohu ve-vohu* that reigned in the abyss before creation would again overtake the world…

[•]

Solomon commits the blunder of building his palace as well as the pagan sanctuaries of his wives near the Temple, inciting the prompt reactions of the prophets who unceasingly denounce the violations of the spiritual power by the temporal power. The prophet Ezekiel expresses this denunciation in the following passage:

The prophet's word

And the glory of the Eternal came into the Temple through the gate facing the east. And a spirit lifted me and brought me to the inner court and, behold, the glory of the Eternal filled the Temple. I heard someone speak to me from the Temple and a man stood by me. And He said to me: "Son of man, [this is] the place of my throne and the place of the soles of my feet where I will dwell in the midst of the children of Israel forever. Henceforth, the house of Israel will not profane my name again, neither they nor their kings through their harlotry nor by the burial of their kings in their high places. They set the thresholds of their doors near my thresholds, their doorposts near my doorposts with only a wall between Me and them, defiling My name with their abominations that they have committed. Therefore, I have consumed them in my anger. Now let them distance themselves from their harlotry and the sepultures of their kings and I will dwell among them forever.

Ezekiel 43: 4 - 9

THE CITY OF EZEKIEL

A schism among the twelve tribes of the Hebrews follows the death of King Solomon in 932 B.C. They divide themselves into two kingdoms, that of Israel in the north and that of Yehudah in the south, which maintains Jerusalem as its capital. The decline is first manifested in the status and the role of the latter, which only recovers a little of its religious influence and its political ascendancy when the two enemy tribes conclude a peace treaty in the 9th century. At the same time, it opens its doors to the influences of idol worship, particularly under the reign of Athalie (842 – 834 B.C.), incurring the vehement reproach of the prophets, including Isaiah who prophesizes during the reign of King Uzziyahu or Uzziyah (789 – 738 B.C.). He reproaches the city for the religious and social compromises that it made:

The rebellious city

The vision of Isaiah, the son of Amoz, which he saw concerning Yehudah and Jerusalem in the days of Uzziyahu, Yotam, Ahaz, Hezekiah, the kings of Yehudah:

Hear, oh heavens! Lend me an ear, oh earth! The Eternal has spoken:

I have reared and brought up children and they have rebelled against me. The ox knows his owner and the ass his master's crib, but Israel knows nothing, my people lack discernment. Oh sinful nation, a people laden with iniquity, seed of evildoers, children that act corruptly! They have forsaken the Eternal, they have provoked the anger of the Holy One of Israel and they have abandoned Him. Where could you still be struck, you who persist in revolt? Every head is sick; every heart is faint. From the soles of your feet to your head, there is nothing sound. There are only wounds, bruises and putrefying sores, which have not been cleaned or bound or soothed with oil. Your country is desolate; your cities are burned with fire. As for your land, strangers devour it in your presence and it is desolate, as if overthrown by strangers.

The daughter of Zion has been abandoned, like a hut in a vineyard, like a shack in a vegetable field, like a besieged city. If the Eternal, Lord of hosts, had not left us a very small remnant, we would have been like Sodom and should have been like Gomorrah.

Isaiah 1: 1 - 9

In addition to his reproaches, Isaiah, nevertheless, predicts the future of the city as the universal, religious center:

The city of peace

The vision of Yehudah and Jerusalem that Isaiah, the son of Amoz, received: It will come to pass in the last days that the mountain of the Eternal's house will be established on the top of the mountains and will be exalted above the hills and all the nations will flow to it. And many people will go and say: "Come, let us go up to the mountain of the Eternal, to the house of the God of Jacob and He will teach us His ways and we will walk in His paths for out of Zion will the Torah go forth and the word of the Lord from Jerusalem." He will judge among the nations and will rebuke many peoples and they will beat their swords into plowshares and their spears into pruning hooks. Nation will not lift up sword against nation; neither will they learn war anymore.

Isaiah 2: 1 - 4

1. The vestiges of the wall, discovered by the archeologist, N. Avigad, during the restoration of the Jewish Quarter in the Old City, date back to this period. The building of this wall upon existing habitations, which was probably Hezekiah's decision in order to protect the city, indicates that from the time of the First Temple, the city extended 60 hectares to the western hill – that will be the site of the upper part of the city below the Second Temple. The dimensions of this wall – 8 meters wide and 3.5 meters high – leads us to guess that it rose to 8 meters in height. The wall formed an angle, perhaps in order to avoid some ravine, extending to the west and to the existing citadel.

King Ahaz (736 – 716 B.C.) attempts to gain the good graces of the Assyrians, the dominant power in the region, by handing over the Temple treasures and encouraging the worship of the heavenly bodies. The more pious King Hezekiah (716 – 688 B.C.) will fight against the practice of idol worship as advised by the prophet Isaiah. He restores and purifies the Temple and rebuilds the walls of the city,[1] incorporating the new neighborhoods in the north and the west in anticipation of an attack by the Assyrians. He also digs a tunnel to divert the waters of Gihon – the Shiloach Pool – that ran through the Kidron Valley and conveyed them to the interior of the city, guaranteeing in this manner a supply of water in case of a siege:

Hezekiah's work

Following these things and these deeds of integrity, Sennacherib, king of Assyria entered Yehudah and encamped against the fortified cities with the goal of conquering them for himself. And when Hezekiah saw that Sennacherib had arrived and intended to attack Jerusalem, he took counsel with his princes and his mighty men of war to stop the waters of the springs that were outside of the city and they assisted him. So a great number of people were gathered together to stop all the springs as well as the wadi that ran through the land, saying: "Why should the Assyrian kings come and find a great amount of water?" And he was emboldened and built up the entire broken wall and raised up the towers and the exterior wall, strengthening the Millo in the city of David, and made an abundant amount of weapons and shields. He set captains of war over the people and assembled them together to him on the road at the city gate and encouraged them, saying: "Be strong and courageous, do not fear or be dismayed by the king of Assyria or by the multitude that is with him because a greater one is with us than is with him. An arm of flesh is with him, but the Eternal, our God, is with us to help us and to fight our battles." And the people were strengthened by the words of Hezekiah, king of Yehudah.

II Chronicles 32: 1 - 8

In the end, the Assyrians, perhaps after having been struck with an epidemic, end the siege and spare the city.

[•]

The intermittent spring – whose Hebrew name reproduces the gushing of the waters – flows in a cave that is accessed through stairs. Five hundred and fifty-three meters long, about one meter wide, with a height that varies from one to four meters, the path of the tunnel dug by Hezekiah winds its way along the natural faults in the rock. An inscription, engraved on the tunnel wall approximately twenty feet from the exit, contributes to solving the technical mystery surrounding how it was dug. Some laborers, beginning at both ends, met mid-way. The inscription declares:

The Shiloach Tunnel

...[the completion of] the work of digging. Here is an account. While [the laborers dug with] hatchets, they moved towards each other, and when there were about 3 meters left to penetrate, voices echoed from one side to the other, for there was a crack to the right... the day of the breakthrough, the laborers began digging [enthusiastically] to meet again, hatchet to hatchet. The water then began to flow from the spring to the pool...

Charles Warren (1840 – 1927), a British officer and archeologist, will lead the first research projects on the site of the City of David. In 1867, he discovers a second method to supply water, which is probably older than that of Hezekiah's tunnel, that some historians compare to the wells that David's men captured to invade the Jebusite city.[2] In its entirety, it includes an entrance, a sloping passage with steps hewn in the rock, a well of almost thirteen meters dug in a limestone passage and a horizontal tunnel that brings the waters from the spring to the foot of the well. The archeological excavations stirred up a vague messianic sense of anticipation among the city's Jewish population, which Warren recalls in the following terms:

2. See the City of David, p. 21.

The third source

These Jews are constantly awaiting the advent of their Messiah, and looked upon my work in Jerusalem as assisting in bringing about the end: they have an old tradition that when the third spring of living water is found, the Messiah will come, but this had so many variations that I could get no clear idea of its proper form or how it might have originated.

All the time that we were working, clearing out a cleft in the rock north of Jerusalem, the traditional wall of Gihon, they used to collect eagerly around and inquire after, and pray for, our success; and were much disappointed when I at last gave up the excavation; for we found it to be a natural cleft in the rock, filled with red clay, with got wider as we descended, until we arrived at 135 feet from the surface. At this depth our work was stopped by a heavy storm of rain which filled up the cleft partially with water, reducing the clay to a state of mud, and producing a general ruin in our shaft, which was supported by a few scaffold poles and planks, here and there. There are several of these clefts about Jerusalem, which penetrate to great depths under the surface; they are natural results of the percolation of rain-water through the limestone rock over a great number of years.

Finding that we still continued in search of water, they would come and sit for hours at the mouths of our shafts, asking as each basketful came up whether water has been found. Sometimes I tried to persuade them to go down, but they seldom could be prevailed upon to do so. On one occasion, on a Saturday, there was a party of them standing about us, and on being asked to go down they said it was their Sabbath; upon this, one of our missionaries proved to the great satisfaction of all that the Sabbath day's journey could be taken underground as well as above, and then one of their number came down with us and went into ecstasies. No sooner did the news spread abroad that we had found a spring of water under the great causeway, close to the Temple, then a general excitement sprang up among them and they crowded down to ascertain if it was a fact. Hundreds wanted to go over the works, but this would have been out of the question, as our excavations would then have been stopped; I therefore told the Chief Rabbi that I could only take a limited number of the more learned men, and not more than twenty at a time, for I was apprehensive lest some accident might occur while conducting them over.

C. Warren, *Underground Jerusalem*

Warren's Shaft is open to the public. The entrance building that dates back to the Ottoman Period exhibits archeological discoveries. The lower floor displays some photographs taken during the excavations as well as some sketches that reconstruct the underground water system. The first sloping passage goes to a second horizontal passage that leads to the opening of the well. The underground tunnel that brings the water from the pool of Shiloach to the bottom of the well is a short segment of Hezekiah's tunnel, which is also known as the Shiloach Tunnel.

3. The village of Silwan, located on one of the slopes of the Mount of Perdition that housed the pagan sanctuaries built by King Solomon for his foreign wives, covers part of the catacombs in Jerusalem, which date back to the First Temple Period. The best preserved tombs are known as the Tomb of Jehu, the Tomb of the King's Servant and the Tomb of Pharaoh's Daughter; all three are located in the north of the village. They would be the sepulchers of dignitaries whose custom was to hew their tombs in the cliff, according to a passage in Isaiah: Thus says the Lord, God of Hosts: "Go see the steward, to Shevna, who is over the house. Say to him: what have you here and who is here that you have hewn out a tomb on high, carving out a habitation in the rock?" (Isaiah 22: 15 - 16).

This tunnel opens into the Shiloach Pool, which is located in the Arab village of Silwan.[3] Seventeen meters long, six meters wide, it was used for ritual immersion during the Second Temple Period. It was also considered to be the setting for one of the miracles performed by Jesus:

The healing of the blind

As Jesus passed by, he saw a man who was born blind. And his disciples asked him, saying: "Master, who sinned, this man or his parents, that he was born blind?" Jesus replied: "Neither the man nor his parents has sinned, but that the works of God may be made manifest in him. I must carry out the works of him that sent me while it is day; night is coming when no man can work. As long as I am in the world, I am the light of the world." When he had said this, he spat on the ground and made clay of the spittle and he anointed the eyes of the blind man with the clay. He said to him: "Go wash in the pool of Siloam"… He went on his way and washed and came back seeing.

John 9: 1 - 7

A mosque rises today upon the vestiges of a Byzantine church.

[•]

The fall of the kingdom of Israel (721 B.C.), which was destroyed by the Assyrians, restores to Jerusalem its place as the religious center. Around 700 B.C., it is three to four times more extensive than during the time of King Solomon, with a population of approximately 24,000 inhabitants. It primarily covers the western hill, from which the upper city will later develop. Its more cultured classes continue to demonstrate a penchant for pagan customs, especially during the reign of King Menashe (688 – 642 B.C.), who is compelled to appease the Assyrians and their allies:

Foreign abominations

Menashe was twelve years old when he began to reign and he reigned fifty years in Jerusalem. And his mother's name was Hefziva. And he did evil in the sight of the Eternal, following the abominations of the nations whom the Eternal had cast out before Israel. He rebuilt the high places that Hezekiah, his father, had destroyed and he raised up altars for the Baal and made an Ashera as did Ahab, king of Israel. He worshipped all the hosts of heaven and served them. And he built altars in the Temple of the Lord in spite of the words of the Eternal: "In Jerusalem I will establish my name." And he built altars for all the hosts of heaven in the courts of the Temple of the Lord. And he made his son pass through the fire, observed signs, used enchantments and dealt with mediums. He did much evil in the eyes of the Eternal to provoke His anger.

II Kings 21: 1 - 7

The leaders of Jerusalem will somehow manage to come to an understanding with the dominating powers, submitting here, revolting there, depending on the political circumstances. In 597, the king, Joachin (608 – 598 B.C.), is forced to submit to the Babylonian monarch, Nebuchadnezzar. The Biblical text recounts the surrender of the city and the deportation of its elite:

The surrender of Jerusalem

At the time, the servants of Nebuchadnezzar, king of Babylonia, rose up against Jerusalem and besieged the city. And Nebuchadnezzar, king of Babylonia, rose up against the city and his servants besieged it. Joachin, king of Yehudah, went out to the king of Babylonia, he and his mother, his servants, his princes and his officers, and the king of Babylonia took him prisoner in the eighth year of his reign. He carried away all the treasures of the house of God and the treasures of the king's palace and cut into pieces all the vessels of gold that Solomon had made for the Temple, as the Eternal had predicted. And he carried into exile all Jerusalem, all the princes, all the mighty warriors, ten thousand exiles and all the craftsmen and smiths. None remained except for the poorest class of people in the land. And he carried away Joachin to Babylonia and the king's mother, the king's wives, his officers and the mighty of the land. Those he took away in exile from Jerusalem to Babylonia... And the king of Babylonia made Mattanya, his father's brother, king in his stead and changed his name to Zidkiyyahu.

II Kings 24: 10 - 17

4. Traces of its destruction can be seen on the foundations of a tower – perhaps the Middle door to which the prophet Jeremy refers – dating to this period and located under a home in the Jewish Quarter known as the Burnt House. Some pottery and some arrow heads, probably Babylonian, were discovered at these sites. A second tower from the Second Temple Period rises next to the first. The drawings on the stairs that lead to the towers reconstruct the conquest of the city of Lakhish by the Assyrians. At the exit of the site, there is a model of the city during the First Temple Period, with its walls and its methods of supplying water.

Ten years later, the Babylonians are once again at the foot of the walls of Jerusalem, resolved to put down the revolt by Zidkiyaahu (597 – 587 B.C.), who had joined the Egyptians. The city was seized after a short period of resistance – the destruction of its Temple on the 9th of the month of Av (586), will remain engraved in the Jewish collective consciousness as a day or mourning[4]:

The destruction of the Temple

It came to pass in the ninth year of his reign, in the tenth month, on the tenth day of the month that Nebuchadnezzar, king of Babylonia, came, he and all his army, against Jerusalem. They camped against it and built a siege wall all around it. The city was besieged until the eleventh year of the reign of king Zidkiyyahu and on the ninth day of the month, the famine prevailed in the city and there was no bread for the people of the land. And the city was breached and all the men of war fled during the night through the gate between the two walls by the king's garden in the direction of the Arava. The Chaldeans had surrounded the city and its army pursued the king and overtook him in the plains of Jericho and all his army had scattered and abandoned him. So they took the king prisoner and brought him to the king of Babylonia in Rivla where they sentenced him. And they slew the sons of Zidkiyahhu before his eyes, bound him with brass fetters and carried him to Babylonia. In the fifth day, on the seventh day of the month, which was the nineteenth year of the reign of Nebuchadnezzar, king of Babylonia, Nevuzaradan, the captain of the guard, a servant of the king of Babylonia, came to Jerusalem and burnt down the Temple, the king's palace and all the houses in Jerusalem, in particular the great houses of the dignitaries. And the entire Chaldean army pulled down the walls of Jerusalem under the orders of the captain of the guard. Nevuzaradan, the captain of the guard exiled the rest of the people that were left in the city and the fugitives that were turned over to the king of Babylonia as well as all the others. The captain of the guard left only the poor in the land to work as vinedressers and field workers.

II Kings 25: 1 - 12

For almost fifty years, the city remained deserted while the exiles from Zion in Babylonia would express their nostalgia in their Psalms, which are attributed to David:

The exiles' nostalgia

By the rivers of Babylonia,
there we sat and wept,
as we remembered Zion.
We hung our lyres
upon the willows in its midst,
for our captors asked us for a song
and our oppressors – for songs of joy,
saying "Sing us a Song of Zion".

How can we sing the Eternal's song
in a foreign land?
If I forget you, oh Jerusalem,
let my right hand forget her cunning.
If I do not remember you,
let my tongue cleave to the roof of my mouth,
if I do not set Jerusalem above my highest joy!...

Psalms 137: 1 - 6

The exiles do not cease to cherish the hope of returning to Jerusalem. The first Messianic yearnings for deliverance and renewal will arise in exile. The prophet Ezekiel, a contemporary of the destruction of the First Temple and the captivity, announces the arrival of a redeemer, who is supposed to enter Jerusalem through a shut gate:

The announcement of a redeemer

*He then brought me back by way of the outer gate of the
sanctuary, which faces east, and it was shut. And the Eternal
said to me: "This gate will remain shut, it will not be opened
and no one will enter through it because the Eternal, the God
of Israel, entered through it and therefore, it will remain shut.
The prince, being the prince, will sit there to eat the bread of
the Eternal. He will enter this gate and will exit it."*

Ezekiel 44: 1 - 3

5. The Gate of
Mercy, see p.167.

This passage from the book of Ezekiel will nourish the legend
that even today surrounds the Gate of Mercy in the eastern
wall of the Old City.[5] According to Christian tradition, Jesus
entered Jerusalem through this gate, which is also known as
the Golden Gate, on the Feast of the Palm Branches. The
Muslims also foretell the entrance of the mahdi through this
gate that opens on to the Josaphat Valley where the Final
Judgment is to take place. It was sealed in the 16th century
by the Muslim religious authorities – to prevent the Messiah
of the Jews from entering the Temple Mount.

EZRA & NEHEMIAH

In 539 B.C., the Persians seize the Babylonian Empire. In 538, Cyrus the Great proclaims an edict authorizing the Jews to return to their land and to rebuild the Temple in Jerusalem. The prophets, Haggai and Zechariah, urge the exiles to return to Judea:

The return of the exiles

Thus says the Lord of hosts: "Old men and old women will yet again dwell in the streets of Jerusalem, every man with a staff in his hand because of his age. And the streets of the city will be filled with boys and girls playing..."

Thus says the Lord of hosts: "Behold I will deliver my people from the countries in the east and from the countries in the west. I will bring them to dwell once again in Jerusalem and they will be my people and I will be their God in truth and in righteousness."

Zechariah 8: 4 - 8

The return of the exiles will spread over a long period, stirring up the hostility of the colonists settled in the region by the Babylonians, especially the Samaritans. The rebuilding of the Temple, moreover, will not be completed until 515. The completion of the work and the reinstatement of the religious service give way to a ceremony instituted by the scribe, Ezra, to whom the establishment of the reading of the Torah as a form of worship is attributed:

The reading of the Torah

Then all the people gathered together as one man in the open place that was before the Gate of Water and they spoke to Ezra, the scribe, to bring the book of the Torah of Moses, which the Eternal had commanded to Israel. And Ezra, the priest, brought the Torah before the congregation of both men and women and all those who could understand to hear on the first day of the seventh month. And he read there facing the open place before the Gate of Water from morning until midday before the men and the women and anyone who could understand. And the ears of all the people were attentive to listening to the Book of the Law. Ezra, the scribe, stood upon a platform of wood, which had been made for that purpose, [...] Ezra opened the book in the sight of all the people and when he opened it, all the people stood up. Ezra blessed the Eternal, the great God, and lifting up their hands, all the people answered: "Amen! Amen!" And they bowed their heads and worshipped the Eternal with their faces to the ground... The Levites explained the Torah to the people as the people stood in their places. They distinctly read in the book, in the Torah of God, and explained its meaning so that everyone understood the reading.

Nehemiah 8: 1 - 8

The city remains practically deserted for a long time with its broken down walls and its burned gates. In 445, Nehemiah, a Jewish dignitary who was well known in the Persian court, arrives in Judea as governor. He immediately begins rebuilding the city, taking a series of measures to prevent and to discourage attacks by hostile peoples and tribes. His testimony in the book bearing his name reconstructs the atmosphere in which the work of rebuilding the walls was carried out:

The restoration of the walls

And it came to pass that when Sanballat and Tobia, the Arabians, the Ammonites and the people of Ashdod heard that the restoration of the walls of Jerusalem was advancing and that the breaches were being filled, they were very angry and conspired all together to attack Jerusalem and to cause havoc there. We prayed to our God and set up surveillance over them to watch them day and night... Therefore, I stationed the people in the lower places behind the wall among the rocks. I stationed them according to their families with their swords, their spears and their bows. I inspected them and rose to tell the nobles and the leaders and the rest of the people: "Do not fear them, remember the Lord, Who is great and awesome and Who fights for your brothers, your sons and your daughters, your wives and your houses."

And it came to pass when they heard that we had been informed and that God had ruined their plan, we returned to the wall, everyone to his task. From that time onwards, half of my servants did the work and the other half held the spears, the shields, the bows and the armors; and also the dignitaries were behind all the house of Yehudah. Those who built the walls and those who carried the burdens did their work with one hand and held a weapon in the other. Each builder had his sword girded by his side as he built while the one who blew the shofar was at my side. I said to the nobles and the leaders and to the rest of the people: "The work is great, extending over a large area, and we are scattered the length of the wall, separated one from the other. Wherever you hear the sound of the shofar, rally to us there. God will fight for us." We carried out the work in this way with half of the people holding the spears from dawn until the appearance of the stars. At the time, I also said to the people that each man and his servant lodge in Jerusalem to guard it at night and to work during the day.

Nehemiah 4: 1 - 16

A ceremony takes place at the completion of the work:

The dedication of the wall

At the time of the dedication of the wall of Jerusalem, they sought the Levites in their dwellings to bring them to Jerusalem, to inaugurate it with gladness, thanksgiving and song, with cymbals, harps and lyres. And the singers gathered together from the districts surrounding Jerusalem as well as from the villages of Nefotai, from the house of Gilgal and the fields of Geva and Azmavet, for the singer had built villages for themselves around Jerusalem. The priests and the Levites purified themselves and purified the people, the gates and the wall.

I then brought the princes of Yehudah up on the wall and appointed two large companies that gave thanks and followed them in a procession. One went to the right towards the Dung Gate... led by Ezra, the scribe... The other company went to meet them and I followed them with half of the people upon the wall above the Tower of the Furnaces... The two companies who gave thanks stood near the house of God... and the singers sang loudly... and on that day, they offered great sacrifices that day and they rejoiced for God had made them rejoice with great joy; the women and the children also rejoiced and the joy of Jerusalem was heard from afar.

Nehemiah 12: 27 - 43

1. The perimeter of the City of Nehemiah corresponded, more or less, to that of the City of David.

Nehemiah takes measures to ensure populating the city once again, especially by requiring the dignitaries in every region to build houses within its perimeters.[1] Religious and political decrees are issued, which would considerably determine the character of Judaism for a long time. Judges, entrusted with teaching, explaining and practicing the law are appointed over the entire territory. Mixed marriages are forbidden and the observance of the Sabbath is established. The scribes assume some of the responsibilities and privileges that until then belonged to the priests. Nehemiah also institutes an annual tax amounting to a third of a shekel to ensure the maintenance of the Temple service. Until the accession of the Hasmoneans, Judea operates as a theocracy under the authority of a civil governor appointed by the Persians and of a High Priest who was a descendant of Zadok.

In 332 B.C., all of Judea submits to Alexander the Great who will not interfere in its internal affairs except to settle disputes between the Israelites and the Samaritans. Jerusalem will not begin to feel Greek domination until after his death, at which time the Ptolemies in the south and the Seleucids in the north struggle for dominion over it. Ptolemy I of Egypt seizes the city and deports some of its inhabitants. Once he firmly establishes his power, he, in turn, grants Judea a great degree of autonomy. Jerusalem will actually be governed by a high priest who combines religious power with political power and by a council of elders. The priests, entrusted with the Temple service, form a privileged class while the scribes, entrusted with the interpretation and teaching of the law, continue to assume the pedagogic and judicial roles in the city. In fact, power will be in the hands of the great and wealthy families of the dignitaries who, in general, are close to the court and open to Hellenistic culture and customs.

THE HASMONEANS

In 198 B.C., the Greek Seleucids who reign in Syria wrest control of Jerusalem from the Ptolemies in Egypt. They are well received by the Jews who join them in the siege against the Egyptian garrison occupying the city. Antiochus III even signs a charter, which grants the inhabitants of the city great autonomy, the freedom to live according to the laws and customs of their ancestors and an exemption from taxes for a three year period. The Jewish historian, Josephus Flavius, attributes this letter to him:

The liberality of Antiochus III

King Antiochus, in Ptolemy, greetings. The Jews are so friendly towards us that as soon as we entered their country, they came to welcome us with their leaders, receiving us in their cities with full honors, feeding our troops and our elephants, and they joined us against the Egyptian garrison that had occupied the fortress in Jerusalem. We also consider it our duty to express our gratitude to them by giving them the possibility of again populating their city, which had been devastated by so much misfortune, and of calling upon the former inhabitants, who have been widely dispersed in many places, to return.

We also order the following: First, out of respect for their religion and their piety, that they be allotted the twenty thousand pieces of silver required to purchase the animals for their sacrifices, wine, oil and incense... It is also our desire that they be supplied with all that they need to restore the doors and for any repair in the Temple and that the wood that is taken for this purpose from Judea, its neighboring provinces and from the Lebanon Mountain, be exempted from taxes and, likewise, all the other materials required for the restoration of their Temple.

Furthermore, we permit the Jews to live in accordance with their laws and customs. We, moreover, exempt their governors, their priests, their scribes and their cantors from the tribute established per person in the amount of a gold crown, which is customarily offered to the king, as well as from all the other taxes. In addition, in order to again populate the city of Jerusalem as quickly as possible, we exempt everyone that is currently living there as well as those who will return to live there during a month of hyperberetee and in the future, we will reimburse them one third of all the tributes as compensation for the losses they suffered.

Above all, it is our wish that all citizens who had been taken prisoners and are currently being held as slaves be liberated together with their children, and that all their property be restored to them.

J. Flavius, *Jewish Antiquities, XII, 3*

The hellenization of the upper classes continually intensifies, creating a rift between the Hellenist movement and the traditionalist movement, which is at first led by the high priest Onias III. The important and wealthy families will attempt to limit his power, provoking protests and disturbances within the population and forcing Onias to solicit the intervention of the Syrians to reestablish order.

In 175, Antiochus IV, nicknamed Antiochus Epiphanes, rises to power in Syria. He replaces the high priest, Onias, with his brother, Jason, in exchange for a heavy tribute. As soon as he is appointed, Jason undertakes the construction of a gymnasium at the foot of the Temple, stirring up strong reactions within the traditionalist circles, which are all the more shocked when the Greeks place the gymnasiums under the patronage of the two gods, Hermes and Hercules. Jason's supporters convert the city into a "polis", endowed with all the rights and privileges of a Greek city, but without having the courage to dissolve the council of the elders. Jason pushes his slavishness so far as to even name the city Antiochus after his patron, provoking new protests and riots. Disappointed by his protégé's timid measures, Antiochus dismisses him and replaces him with Menelaus to whom the second book of the Maccabees attributes "the temperament of a cruel tyrant and the fury of a savage beast". His enemies will accuse him of promoting Hellenistic customs and of concealing the pillage of the Temple by the Seleucids. Taking advantage of his absence, one of his brothers, who had been left in charge of managing affairs, attempts in turn to seize the treasures of the Temple. A first revolt erupts, which Antiochus harshly represses.

From then on, Antiochus will be unceasingly set against Judea. Upon returning from a campaign in Egypt, he pauses in Jerusalem only to take the gold altar of the Temple, its oil lamps and various ritual objects. One year later, in 170, rumors announcing his death prompt the former high priest, Jason, to mobilize a thousand men to seize control of the city. Antiochus, who is more alive than ever, tears himself away from his campaigns and marches towards Jerusalem to crush the revolt. The insurgents disband and another Greek garrison, charged with the surveillance of the city, establishes itself in a fortress built on a hill adjacent to that of the Temple – the Acro. Jerusalem looses its privileges and is relegated to the most humiliating rank possible for a city under the Greeks. Antiochus dedicates the Temple to Dionysus and orders the building of a sanctuary in honor of Zeus Olympus. Furthermore, he proclaims a series of decrees forbidding Jewish customs – decrees that represent one of the first attempts in history to destroy the religious and cultural singularity of the Jews. There are echoes of Antiochus' outburst against Judea in the following passage by Josephus Flavius:

Antiochus' decrees

His insatiable greed drove him to even further profane our faith by stripping the Temple of its riches. He seized the vessels consecrated to God, the gold candlesticks, the table upon which the bread offering was placed and the censers. He even carried away the scarlet tapestries of fine linen and pillaged the secret treasures, leaving practically nothing of value. His crowning blow was to forbid the Jews from offering their customary sacrifices as prescribed by Jewish law.

After having pillaged the entire city, he had some of the inhabitants killed, took ten thousand as prisoners together with their wives and children, burned down the beautiful buildings, destroyed the walls and in the lower part of the city, he built a fortress with large towers overlooking the Temple where he stationed a garrison of Macedonians who were joined by some of the most wicked and irreverent Jews, for whom there was no evil that they would not inflict on the inhabitants.

He also had an altar built in the Temple upon which he had pigs sacrificed, which was one of the things most opposed to our religion. Then he compelled the Jews to renounce worshipping the true God and to worship idols, commanded the building of temples to them throughout the cities, and gave the order that a day not go by without sacrificing pigs. Furthermore, he forbade the Jews to circumcise their sons, threatening severe punishment and ordering the people to be careful in the observance of all his laws and orders, resorting to force in case the need would arise to impose them on the recalcitrant.

The majority of the people obeyed him, willingly or out of fear. Nevertheless, his threats could not prevent the virtuous and noble from observing the laws of their ancestors; the cruel prince subjected the most indomitable to a horrible death by torture. He tore them apart with the lashes of a whip. Not content with crucifying them, driven by his appalling inhumanity, he crucified their wives and their circumcised children next to them while they were still breathing. He, moreover, ordered the burning of their books of the Holy Scriptures, unforgiving towards those in whose homes any were found.

J. Flavius, *Antiquities of the Jews, XII, 7*

At the end of three years of guerilla warfare, the Hasmoneans – some insurgents who united around the high priest Mattathias and his sons Yehudah, Eleazer, Jonathan and Simon – succeed in seizing the Temple Mount. They immediately proceed to purify the sanctuary and in December, 164 B.C., they reinstate the sacrifices. Josephus Flavius recounts:

The consecration of the Temple

After having gained such great victories over the generals of Antiochus' army, Yehudah persuaded the Jews to go to Jerusalem to offer thanks to God, which they owed Him in accordance with their laws, to purify His Temple and to offer sacrifices. They found the gates of the Temple burnt and its enclosure overgrown with wild plants, which had grown since it had been entirely abandoned. Such great desolation would draw sighs and tears among the insurgents, and after having dispersed his troops around the fortress, Yehudah set down to the task of purifying the Temple.

Once this job was completed, he had a candlestick, a table and a gold altar, all new, installed as well as new doors upon which he hung curtains. He ordered the destruction of the altar that had been defiled and had a new one built with stones that had not been polished using a hammer. On the twenty-fifth of Kislev... the candlestick lamps were lit, the altar was censed, loaves of bread were placed on the table and sacrifices were offered upon the new altar – on the same day, three years before, Antiochus had so shamefully desecrated and ravaged the Temple...

Yehudah celebrated the restoration of the Temple with all the people for eight days, offering solemn sacrifices, indulging in every possible and imaginable libation. There were public festivities everywhere. The air resounded with the songs and canticles sung for the glory of God. The joy of seeing the reestablishment of the ancient customs of our ancestors and the renewal of the practice of our religion after so many years and when we had lost all hope was so great that it was proclaimed that an eight-day festival would be celebrated every year. It has been celebrated ever since and is called the Festival of Lights because, it seems to me, of the happiness that befell us – the pleasant light that dissipates the darkness of our long suffering and that illuminated a period during which we no longer dared to hope.

J. Flavius, *Antiquities of the Jews, XII, 11*

The rabbis will celebrate the event by investing it with the miracle of the vial of oil:

The miracle of Hanukkah

Upon seizing the Temple, the Greeks defiled all the oils. When the Hasmoneans repossessed it, all they found was one vial bearing the seal of the high priest, which was sufficient for only one day. But a miracle occurred and the oil contained in the vial permitted lighting for eight days. The following year, they proclaimed a day of festivities to praise God and to thank Him.

TB Sabbath 21b

To this day, the festival of Hanukah commemorates this event at the beginning of the winter. It is celebrated for one week during which the eight branches of the candlestick are progressively lit upon pronouncing blessings and singing the following praises:

The celebration of Hanukah

We kindle these lights to commemorate the miracles, the relief, the feat of arms, the liberation, the wonders, the consolation that You have granted through the intermediary of Your holy priests to our ancestors at that time. During these eight days of Hanukah, we consecrate these lights, which we do not have the right to utilize but only to contemplate, thanking You for Your miracles, Your liberation and Your wonders.

The Hasmoneans, however, do not succeed in ousting the Greek garrison, which is backed by some Hellenistic collaborators. The Seleucids, moreover, will not resign themselves to dealing with them, except under the pressure of the internal conflicts that force the diverse parties to fight for their support. In 152, Alexander Balas finally gives his blessing to the appointment of Jonathan to be governor and high priest. He is authorized to take possession of the city, with the exception of the Acro, which will continue to house a Seleucid garrison until Simon destroys it in 141.

From then on, Jerusalem will experience a period of calm and prosperity for almost eight decades, especially under the reign of John Hyrcanus (135 – 105) and of Alexander Yannai (103 – 76). It becomes the capital of a vast kingdom that extends over the territories of Palestine and Trans-Jordan. It is also the religious center of the Jews who are dispersed throughout the world, who pay an annual tribute of a half shekel. The city develops in every direction and in every domain. The upper city, where the Seleucids had established their markets, is the site of the secular services and institutions. This is also where the Hasmoneans build their palaces and open cultural centers. The upper city will gradually become the residential district of the wealthy society while the lower city, located in the Tyropoeon Valley, will become the residential district of the common people.

The rift between the Sadducees, the descendents of the prominent Hellenized families and the relatives of the priests, and the Pharisees, the descendents of the scribes who are more traditional and sympathetic to the common views, continually widens. The latter will contest the right of the Hasmonean monarchs to hold both spiritual and temporal power. The few archeological vestiges remaining from that period are recognized by the Hasmonean stone, which is characterized by a hump in the middle that is framed by a border.

There is an initial uprising against the Hasmoneans during the reign of Alexander Yannai. As his successor, his widow, who was perhaps Salome Alexander, will somehow succeed in restoring civic order, but after her death, the lower classes again will become restless. Hyrcanus II and Aristobulus II unleash a war of succession and the Romans place their stake on Hyrcanus II. Aristobulus II does not give up and braving the Romans, he seizes the Temple. In 63 B.C., Pompey, the commander of the Roman troops, is compelled to take possession of the sanctuary. He will enter the Holy of Holies, the most sacred place in the Temple, taking care not to touch its treasures. Josephus Flavius left us his version of these events:

Pompey in Jerusalem

The largest Roman tower, jolted by machines, collapsed, pulling down a wall nearby, and the Romans rushed to enter through the breach... Immediately, there were corpses everywhere. The Romans killed some of the Jews while others chose to kill each other and to set their houses on fire, preferring death to such horrible desolation. Twelve thousand Jews and a few Romans perished and Absalon, Aristobulus' uncle and father-in-law, was taken prisoner.

The sanctity of the Temple was violated in a strange manner for if until then, the gentiles had never entered the sanctuary nor had even seen it, Pompey, himself, together with some of his followers, entered and saw what only the priests were permitted to see. They found the table, the gold candlesticks and gold cups, a large quantity of scents and a consecrated treasure of approximately two thousand talents. His piety, however, prevented him from touching any of it and he did nothing on that particular occasion that was beneath his moral standards. The following day, he ordered the officers of the Temple to purify it in order to offer sacrifices to God, and entrusted Hyrcanus with the office of high priest as much to show his gratitude for the assistance he had provided him as for having prevented the Jews from supporting Aristobolus.

J. Flavius, *Antiquities of the Jews, XIV, 8*

The Roman general leaves the management of the affairs of the country to Hyrcanus and his Idumean advisor, Antipater, who will become the actual ruler. He also appoints his two sons, Phasael and Herod, governors of Jerusalem and of the Galilee. In 40 B.C., the city falls into the hands of the Parthians who install Mattathias Antigone, the son of Aristobulus, upon the throne. Three years later, the Roman troops, reinforced by Herod's men, recapture Jerusalem. The last Hasmonean monarch had only reigned for three years.

THE CITY OF HEROD

Soon after the Romans return, cleverly managing his relations with its leaders, Herod is named king (37 – 4 B.C.). The extensive construction that he carries out will assure him true archeological glory two thousand years later. At the beginning of his reign, Jerusalem is delimited by a wall that runs along the present David Street to the north, curving to the south to include all or part of Mount Zion as well as the City of David, and joining the surrounding wall of the Temple at the southeast end. The topographical conditions demarcate three areas: the upper city in the west, encompassing the present day Jewish and Armenian Quarters as well as part of Mount Zion, the Temple Mount in the east, and between these two areas, the lower city.

Herod has no illusion about his popularity. He knows he is hated as much for his foreign origins as for his collaboration with the Romans. Some of his Greek-Roman style constructions – a hippodrome and a theater where gladiators kill each other – alienate the religious parties. He is concerned only with protecting himself from the threats that hang over his head and with consolidating his power. His architectural megalomania will rank him among the greatest builders of Ancient times.

In 20 B.C., Herod initiates the work of remodeling the Temple, which continues for more than forty years, well after his death. The esplanade is enlarged, particularly to the south, taking the form of a trapezoid. To this day, the mount where the mosques stand still retains this shape. It measures 462 meters long on the eastern side, 491 meters long on the western side, 281 meters wide on the southern side, and 310 meters wide on the northern side. The esplanade is framed by four gigantic retaining walls – the present day western Wailing Wall is a segment of the western enclosure that ran along a paved road. The walls are built of heavy stones, most of which weigh two to eight tons. One of them, which is still visible today at the southwest corner, measures 12 meters long, 3 meters high and 4 meters wide, and is estimated to weigh almost three hundred and fifty tons.

Herod's architectural concern was such that he was not content with simply polishing the stones, but he also framed them with borders that created a play of light. According to some Talmudic masters, he even envisioned gold plating the wall: "Forget it", the sages would discourage him, "they are more beautiful as they are, evoking waves" (Sukkah 51b).

The western enclosure comprised three gates – maybe four. One of them was to the north of the Wailing Wall, which was accessed by a bridge that connected the upper city to the Temple esplanade, spanning the Tyropoeon. An imposing arch – Wilson's Arch, named after the archeologist who discovered it – marks its emplacement in the wall. A second gate – the Kipponos Gate according to the Talmud, better known as the Berkeley Gate – was located at the level of the paved passage that ran along the length of the surrounding wall. Its lintel can be seen at the end of the area reserved for women in front of the Wailing Wall. A third gate was located further to the south. A staircase, in the southwest corner, provided access from the Tyropoeon Valley to the house of study – *beit ha-midrash* – that housed the Sanhedrin, which was like a supreme court, while its permanent location – *lishkat ha-gazit* – was being renovated on the other side of the esplanade. The remains of this third gate in the wall are identified as Robinson's Arch. A raised terrace above the house of study in the southwest corner was used to sound the horn to announce the Sabbath.

Wilson's Bridge or Arch opened on to colonnades that bordered the esplanade where the Pharisaical rabbis presented their commentaries of the law to their disciples. The row of columns formed a central artery where commercial activities were conducted, such as the exchange of money. A regal basilica along the southern side housed the Temple services. The Romans destroyed it and its ruins lay on the vast archeological site that stretches out at the base of the enclosure. There were two flights of stairs on this site that led to the Hulda Gates – the Double Gate and the Triple Gate – one was reserved for those who entered and the other for those who exited. Ritual baths between the two flights of stairs permitted visitors – the tens of thousands of pilgrims who thronged to the Temple on Succoth, Passover and especially Shavuot – to purify themselves before entering the Temple.

According to Josephus Flavius, the restoration work undertaken by Herod would represent one of the most important architectural enterprises of the epoch. The construction of the surrounding walls, which were built to withstand considerable pressure, required great technical skills – particularly, the eastern enclosure that abruptly descended towards the Kidron Valley. Rising to 45 meters above the ravine at the southern end, it was supported by arches, which today are known as King Solomon's Stables. More than ten thousand men worked under the supervision of the one thousand priests on the work sites. The only way Herod would overcome the reservations to his plans expressed by the traditionalist circles was by pledging to gather all the necessary materials in advance and to not touch the old masonry as long as the new one had not been completed, so as to not disturb the religious service. Once the work was completed, the surface of the Temple constituted one sixth of the city. The following description by Josephus Flavius continues to be considered the authoritative report among researchers:

The galleries around the Temple

We built a double gallery, supported by white marble columns made from a single piece of marble, measuring twenty-five cubits in height. Their cedar wood paneling was so meticulously fashioned, so well joined and so well polished that the columns did not require painted or sculptured adornment to be a visual delight. The galleries, which measured thirty cubits wide and six stadiums long, all led to the Antonia Fortress. The open space was paved with a diverse assortment of stones...

J. Flavius, *The Jewish War V, 5, 2*

A first lower wall – the *soreg* – on which warnings forbidding the Gentiles entrance to the Temple were written in Greek and in Latin, surrounded the Temple. Fourteen stairs led to a second wall. The Temple was comprised of two sections: a first court where the women gathered to pray and which included four rooms located in the four corners: *lishkat ha-nezirim*, which was reserved for the Nazirites, *lishkat ha-etzim*, where the priests prepared the wood, *lishkat ha-metzoraim*, which was reserved for the lepers and *lishkat ha-shemanim*, where the oils were treated:

The women's court

The chapel that was reserved for the women was set apart by a wall and was accessed by two doors, one on the south and one on the north. This chapel was opened not only to the women of our nation who resided in Judea, but also to all those who piously came from other provinces to offer homage to God. The wall on the west side of the chapel did not have a door. Between the two doors that I mentioned, on the side of the interior wall, near the treasury, there were galleries supported by large columns. Although they were not decorated with very much ornamentation, they were no less beautiful than the galleries on the parvis...

J. Flavius, *The Jewish War V, 5, 2*

Fifteen steps, corresponding to the fifteen scales in the songs of the Levites, led to the Nicanor doors – named after their donor, a Jew from Alexandria. They opened to a second court – the court of Israel – where a large altar stood upon which sacrifices were offered:

The altar

The altar, located in front of the Temple, was fifty cubits long and fifteen cubits high. The southern side was difficult to reach and was built without a single blow of a hammer. A very beautiful, cubit high balustrade encompassed the Temple and the altar, separating the people from the priests...

J. Flavius, *The Jewish War V, 5, 6*

Twelve stairs led to the Temple, which was composed of three connected halls: the *oulam*, where two tables stood, one made of marble and one made of gold; the *hekhal* or sanctuary whose walls were inlaid with gold, where the candlestick (the *menorah*), the table for the loaves of bread and other furniture stood; and the *devir* or Holy of Holies that was completely empty – lacking the tablets of the law that were lost when the First Temple was destroyed, which according to a rabbinic legend, were retrieved by their divine benefactor – and that only the high priest entered once a year on Yom Kippur:

The Temple

The Temple, a sacred site consecrated to God, was centrally located. Twelve steps led to it. Although its frontispiece measured one hundred cubits high and one hundred cubits wide, it did not exceed sixty cubits in the rear. The front part comprised large areas measuring twenty cubits, like two arms that opened to receive and embrace those who entered. The first portico, which was seventy cubits high and twenty-five cubits wide, did not have any doors; like the sky, it was visible and open to everyone. The portico was golden as was everything that could be seen in the interior of the Temple, and the glare was almost blinding.

The interior was divided into two large units, one higher than the other. The upper unit to the front was ninety cubits high, fifty cubits long and twenty cubits wide. The inner door was covered with gold leaf and, as I said, the wall surrounding it was also golden. Gold, grapevine-shaped festoons, indicating the greatness of man, were carved at the top. The unit in the back was lower. Its doors, which were also made of gold, measured fifty cubits high and sixteen cubits wide. There was a Babylonian covering of the same dimensions in which azure, purple, scarlet and linen were combined so artistically that one could not help but admire it. The four materials represented the four elements as much by their colors as from where they came; scarlet represented fire; the linen, the earth that produced it; azure, the air; and purple, the ocean from where it was drawn. The nature of the heavens was represented on this superb covering, but without the zodiac signs.

From there, we had access to the back unit of the Temple, which measured sixty cubits in length, sixty cubits in height

*and twenty cubits in width. It was divided lengthwise into
two unequal parts; the first one, which measured forty cubits,
contained such splendid items that one never grew weary of
looking at them: the candlestick, the table and the altar of
incense. The candlestick was composed of seven branches
holding seven oil lamps that represented the seven planets.
The twelve loaves of bread placed on the table designated the
twelve signs of the zodiac as well as the rotation of the year.
The thirteen sorts of spices that were put in the censer, some
of which came from the sea, which is impossible to inhabit
and cultivate, but gives its fruit, signified that everything
comes from God and belongs to God.*

The Holy of Holies.

*The other part of this unit, the innermost section measured
twenty cubits. Closed off with a curtain, it was empty. It
was not only forbidden to enter it, but you could not even
risk looking at it. It was called the sanctuary or the Holy of
Holies. Three-story buildings surrounded it, through which
you passed to reach the large portal from every direction.
The upper unit was more narrow and did not include
comparable buildings...*

The façade

*Everything on the façade of the Temple was ravishing, a
splendid and awesome sight to behold. For it was completely
covered with gold leaf that was so thick that as soon as the
day began to break, it was as dazzling as the sunrays. As for
the other sides, which were not covered with gold leaf, the
stones were so white that from a distance, this superb mass
appeared to be a snow-covered mountain to those who had
never seen it before.*

*The roof of the Temple was covered with very pointed, gold
spikes to prevent the birds from resting on it and soiling it.
Some of the stones used to build the Temple were forty-five
cubits long, five cubits wide and six cubits high.*

J. Flavius, *The Jewish War V, 5, 4 - 6*

Herod also undertakes fortifying the Hasmonean fortress with towers that permitted the surveillance of the esplanade. Situated on the eastern hill that was adjacent to the Temple Mount – Baris – he called it the Antonia Fortress in honor of the emperor, Marcus Antonius. Josephus Flavius recounts:

The Antonia Fortress

As for the Antonia Fortress, it was situated in the corner that was formed by the two galleries of the Temple that faced the west and the north. King Herod had built it upon a rock that rose to a height of fifty cubits; inaccessible from every direction, it was more magnificent than any other construction. The rock was inlaid with marble from the ground to the summit, not only to make it beautiful but also to make it slippery so that no one could climb it or come down it. He had surrounded the fortress with a wall measuring only three cubits high – the fortress rose forty cubits above the wall. While it had an imposing exterior, the interior was composed of lodgings, baths and halls that could accommodate a large number of people such that it could have easily passed for a magnificent palace. Furthermore, the services provided there were as well organized and convenient as those in a small city.

Built in the shape of a huge tower, it was studded at equal distances with four towers, three of which were fifty cubits high and the fourth, which was situated at an angle facing the south and the east, measured seventy cubits, and thus, overlooked the Temple esplanade. At the point where the galleries intersected, there were winding staircases to the left and to the right. When the Romans ruled Jerusalem, armed men patrolled there to prevent riots during the holidays. Thus, just as the Temple could be considered to be the city's citadel, the Antonia Fortress could be considered the Temple's citadel – the garrison that occupied it was responsible for its surveillance, but also for maintaining control of both the city and the Temple.

J. Flavius, *The Jewish War V, 5, 8*

It is in this fortress that, according to Christian tradition, Jesus appeared before Pontius Pilate, the procurator of Judea. The

Via Dolorosa begins at the site of the Antonia Fortress, not far from the Lions Gate. Some vestiges can be seen beneath the churches that line the Via. A huge, underground hall beneath the basilica of the Sisters of Zion or the Women of Zion – the Lithostrotos – was the exact place where Pontius Pilate pronounced the verdict condemning Jesus to death by crucifixion. A model of the fortress is on display in the basilica.[1]

1. The Via Dolorosa, see p.199.

[•]

Herod transfered the seat of civil power from the former palace that was built on the ruins of the Acro to a new complex erected at the northwest end of the city on the site of a Hasmonean fortress – where the citadel known as the Tower of David stands today. Three towers protected the complex: the Phasael Tower was the highest of the three, rising to 45 meters, and was named after Herod's brother who committed suicide when the Parthians captured the city; the Hippicus Tower, named after a friend, rose to a height of 40 meters; the Mariamne Tower, which was especially beautiful and delicate and rose to a height of 25 meters, bore the name of his wife, a descendent of the Hasmoneans, whom he had passionately loved and had brutally murdered in a fit of jealousy. The complex was surrounded by a wall, studded with watchtowers that enclosed extensive gardens and two units, which were named *Caesareum* and *Agrippeum* in honor of the emperor and one of his generals. The complex could accommodate hundreds of prominent guests. Herod evidently resided in a palace located on the present site of the Armenian Garden. Josephus Flavius writes:

Herod's extravagance

In the north, there was a royal palace that extended between these towers, whose magnificence and beauty exceeded any possible description, and whose architecture and construction discouraged any competition. A thirty-cubit high wall, studded with equidistant towers of the finest architecture, enclosed it. The interior was so extensive that the halls intended for festivities could accommodate hundreds of the divans used to lie on to eat. The variety of the types of marble was incredible as was the variety of rare objects that had been gathered there. The length and width of the beams that supported the roof of this marvelous building invariably drew great admiration. Gold and silver sparkled all over the ornate paneling and in the wealth of furniture. The porticos were supported by columns of awesome beauty and nothing could have been lovelier than the open air spaces that spread between them, landscaped with all sorts of plants, beautiful promenades, clear fish ponds, fountains with bronze statuettes from whose mouths the water flowed and, surrounding these waters, aviaries where pigeons cooed.

J. Flavius, *The Jewish War V, 4, 4*

This building would continue to serve the successive powers in Jerusalem. At first, it is the residence of the Roman procurators visiting the city – perhaps also serving as Pontius Pilate's court. Converted into a fortress by the insurgents during the Great Revolt against the Romans, it is severely damaged, especially with the destruction of its towers. The Romans, the Byzantines and the Arabs stationed their men there and also set up many of the services that they required. One tradition from the 6th century compares it to the fortress mentioned in the passage in the book of Samuel:

The Tower of David
But David seized the fortress of Zion, which is the City of David... David moved into the fortress, which he named the City of David...

II Samuel 5: 7 - 9

The Muslims assume this tradition, naming the city "the *mirhab* (a prayer niche in a mosque) of David, the prophet." The Umayyads caliphs set it up as a square *castrum* with a tower at every corner. The Crusader kings of the Latin Kingdom of Jerusalem use it as a fortress with projecting towers that overlook a trench, establishing it as their residence and engraving a drawing of it on their royal seal, together with that of the Holy Sepulcher Church and the Dome of the Rock. In 1239, the Muslim prince of Kerak demolishes the citadel and in 1335, the Mamluks rebuild it. The masonry, as seen today, dates back to the 16th century. Since then, it has continually undergone modifications and additions, including the erection of a minaret in 1635 that 19th century travelers will compare to the Tower of David. The archeological excavations undertaken beginning during that period uncover the foundations of a tower that traces back to John Hyrcanus (134 – 103 B.C.), as well as the vestiges of a second wall, restored in 66 A.D. on the Hasmonean foundations, some Frank vestiges, etc.

Today, the complex houses a museum that uses the most sophisticated audio-visual resources to reconstruct the history of the city from its origins to the end of the 19th century. Concerts and plays are also performed there. Renee Sivan, a French archeologist, reconstructs the deliberations that preceded setting up the citadel to house the Museum of the History of Jerusalem:

The Jerusalem Museum

A proposal had been made to make the citadel a kind of guide to the Old City, "a visitors' reception center". Others thought that the citadel would be the ideal site for temporary exhibits about subjects related to the city of Jerusalem. The proposal that the citadel become a historic-ethnographic museum organized by periods and exhibiting a collection of objects, documents and costumes was confronted with the problem of the lack of balance between the various historic periods. For certain periods, there was a wealth of objects and documents; for others, the lack of graphic documentation was almost total.

The complex design of the building (small, non-interconnected rooms) and the difficulty posed by the visualization of history would lead to a new concept: the thematic museum that would present various subjects related to the city of Jerusalem – the stone, the water, the bread, the art, the development of the city, etc. – autonomous subjects through which the history of the city and of its inhabitants, its religious importance, its spiritual dimension, etc. could be presented. A museum where the authentic object and its creative representation would work together to communicate the desired message.

Towards the end of 1984, this concept led to a new idea: the illustrated museum – not a historic testimony, but an illustrated history. That is, not a museum that "shows", but a museum that narrates. Not a museum that uses authentic objects as a means of expression, but a museum that creates images. A museum without a collection, without a warehouse, without a laboratory. A permanent exhibit, an educational program, a room for temporary exhibits and an information center.

On April 13, 1989, the Museum of the History of Jerusalem was opened to the public. This museum is not a traditional museum. The permanent exhibit does not include a single original piece, such as archeological objects or historic documents. The historic sequences are presented through reconstructions or representations such as models, dioramas, holograms, reproductions, animated films, computerized images, etc. Under the direction of the museum's scientific staff, various artists or artisans specifically created representations of the subjects presented (including the City of David, the capture of Jerusalem by the Romans, the Dome of the Rock, the coronation of the Crusaders' king, etc.). All the representations on exhibit were inspired by archeological findings as well as by literary and graphic sources related to the period being represented, thus assuring their credibility.

R. Sivan, *Dossiers d'Archéologie*

The tower (10 meter diameter) that stands today was built in the 14th century on the emplacement of the Tower of Phasael or on that of the Tower of Hippicus.

[•]

After Herod's death and the deportation of his son, Archelaus, in 6 B. C., Judea becomes a Roman province, governed by procurators in Caesarea. However, during a short period between 41 and 44, it is ruled by Herod Agrippa, a descendent of both Herod and the Hasmonean Dynasty. He undertakes the construction of a third wall around the city. The procurators at first avoid coming to Jerusalem and only dispatch detachments at the time of the pilgrimage festivals – Sukkot at the beginning of autumn, Passover at the beginning of spring, and Shavuot at the beginning of summer – when thousands of pilgrims from all parts of the country and from every community in the Diaspora gather in Jerusalem. The government of the city remains in the hands of the high priest and of the Sanhedrin – the judicial-religious authority that is dominated by the leaders of the Pharisees. The estimated 120,000 inhabitants of the city come from various countries and speak Hebrew, Aramaic and Greek. A city in constant turmoil, agitated by public disturbances, frequented by ascetics and prophets, welcomes Jesus of Nazareth during the Passover celebrations in the year 30. The Evangelists describe his arrival in the city:

Entering Jerusalem

And when they drew near Jerusalem and arrived in Bethphage at the Mount of Olives, Jesus sent two disciples saying: Go to the village that is before you and you will immediately find an ass and a colt tied with her; free them and bring them to me. And if any man should say anything to you, you will reply: "The Lord needs them", and he will immediately let them go. All of this was done to fulfill the words of the prophet: "Tell the daughter of Zion: Behold your king is coming to you, meek and riding an ass and a colt, the foal of the ass."

The disciples went and did as Jesus had commanded them. They brought the ass and the colt and laid their clothing on them and Jesus sat on them. And a very great multitude spread their garments on the path; some cut branches off the trees and strew them on the road. The crowds that went ahead of him as well as those who followed him cried out: "Hosanna to the son of David! Blessed is he who comes in the name of the Lord! Hosanna in the highest." When Jesus entered Jerusalem, the entire city was filled with excitement, saying: "Who is this?" The multitude replied: "This is Jesus, the prophet of Nazareth in the Galilee."

Jesus then entered the Temple of God and cast out all those who sold and bought in the Temple, and overthrew the tables of the moneychangers and of the merchants of doves. He said to them: "It is written: My house will be called the house of prayer, but you have made it a den of thieves." The blind and the lame came to him in the Temple and he healed them.

When the high priests and the scribes saw the wondrous things that he did and the children crying out in the Temple: "Hosanna to the son of David", they were sorely displeased and they said to him: "Do you hear what they are saying?" But Jesus replied: "Yes. Have you never read: Out of the mouths of babies and suckling infants, you have perfected praise?" He then left them and left the city to go to Bethany where he spent the night.

Matthew 21: 1 - 17

THE REBEL CITY

Relations with the Romans would continually deteriorate. Josephus Flavius relates one of the first incidents in the escalation of violence that would lead to the destruction of the city:

Pilate's tactless blunders

Pontius Pilate, the procurator of Judea (26 – 36), sent troops from Caesarea to their winter quarters in Jerusalem, bearing the effigy of the Emperor on their banners, which is so opposed to our laws that no other procurator before him had ever ventured such an act. The troops entered Jerusalem during the night so that they would go unnoticed until the following day. A large group of Jews immediately went to Caesarea to find Pilate, and for many days adjured him to withdraw the banners from the city. He refused under the pretext that he could not do so without offending the emperor. Because they continued to insist, on the seventh day, he secretly mobilized his warriors and ordered them to be on alert. He then installed himself in his court, which was intentionally set up on that day in the field where army maneuvers were conducted, and was the most suitable place to hide his men. The Jews continued to insist and so he ordered his soldiers to surround them, threatening to kill them if they persisted and refused to leave the premises. As soon as he uttered these words, they all lay down on the ground offering their throats, and in this way, demonstrated that their respect for their laws was dearer to them than life. Their perseverance and ardent zeal for their religion would inspire such high admiration that Pilate ordered the withdrawal of the banners from Jerusalem to Caesarea.

J. Flavius, *The Jewish War XVIII, 4*

The divisions within the population continue to grow and the tension is exacerbated. Quarrels between the prominent families rock the ruling class. Extremist groups who advocate all out war against the Romans do not hesitate to execute their coreligionists who are accused of collaboration and treason. Furthermore, all sorts of visionaries continue to spread gloomy apocalyptic forecasts and to stir up messianic yearnings. Josephus Flavius describes the extreme sense of insecurity that dominates the city:

A city in turmoil

Once Judea had been freed of its pillagers, they again made themselves known in Jerusalem, pursuing their infamous and criminal work more than before. It was no longer only during the night that these hired assassins carried out the most violent crimes, but in broad daylight, especially during the most solemn festivals. They would take advantage of large crowds to stab their victims, mingling their cries with the cries of the passers-by who alerted the public to the crime, and would go unnoticed without even arousing any suspicion. One of their first victims was the high priest, Jonathan, and not a day would go by that they would not commit a crime of this sort.

In the end, the sense of insecurity that reigned in Jerusalem was such that a person felt more endangered in the city than in the middle of the bloodiest of wars. Everyone expected to die at any moment, trembling when anyone approached, no longer trusting even one's own friends. In spite of this, although everyone was constantly on guard, every precautionary measure possible could not save those that the assassins had decided to kill. They were that cunning and that skillful in carrying out their work.

In addition to this evil, there was another that disturbed this great city. Those who perpetrated this evil were not murderers who shed blood like the first, but the impious and the agitators who took advantage of the people, invoking false religious pretexts to urge them to retire [to the desert?], promising them divine signs that would confirm their imminent redemption. Felix, the governor of Judea, who considered these groups to be kernels of revolt, sent his cavalry and his infantry to fight them, which resulted in many victims.

An even greater evil was rampant in Judea. A false Egyptian prophet, who was obviously an imposter, beguiled the people to such an extent that he mustered thirty thousand men, led them to the Mount of Olives, and together with the people who were particularly attached to him, marched into Jerusalem with the aim of chasing the Romans out, taking possession of it, and establishing himself as ruler. Felix yet again went out against him with some Roman troops and a large number of Jews. The battle was launched: some of those who were following the Egyptian were cut to pieces while he himself fled with the rest.

One would have thought that after so many uprisings and repressions, Judea would have some peace at last. But like a body that is so contaminated that as soon as one member is healed, another one is overcome with the same evil, some charlatans allied themselves with some thieves to incite the people to revolt against the yoke of the Romans, threatening to kill those who continued to choose to endure such shameful servitude. They dispersed themselves throughout the country, pillaging the houses of the wealthy, killing them and burning down the villages. The situation became increasingly worse, day by the day, as they sowed confusion and destruction throughout Judea.

J. Flavius, *The Jewish War II, 13, 3 - 6*

The pilgrim arriving from the north of the country at the beginning of the Sixties during the 1st century would view the city from the heights of Mount Scopus or the Mount of Olives. He would cross the Kidron Valley, contemplating these funerary monuments[1] with both disdain and horror, to arrive at the exterior or third wall that ran along the length of the valley – some hundreds of meters north of the present wall – up to the Psephinus Tower that rose to a height of 815 meters – on the current site of the Russian Complex. From this tower, the wall turned at almost a right angle towards the south up to the Hippicus Tower that stood on the site of the present day Jaffa Gate. This wall was completely new and not yet finished. Herod Agrippa, the grandson of Herod the Great and the last Jewish monarch of Jerusalem, had begun to build it in the 40's.

1. See p.152.

Our pilgrim would pass through one of the gates in the wall, let's call it the Women's Gate, which opened onto the nearby suburb of Jerusalem, Bethseda. Soon, he would pass a second wall off the Wood Market in the Tyropoeon Valley, leaving the Sheep Market on the left and the Sheep Pool, situated one next to the other between the outer wall and the second wall. This wall that Herod had built, constituted a line of defense, connecting one of his palaces to the Antonia Fortress. Having completed a tour of the bazaars and markets that were spread out in the shadow of the Temple's western wall, the pilgrims would pass the first wall. Dating back to the Hasmonean period, it connected Herod's palace to the western wall of the Temple in a straight line along the present day King David Street. He would arrive in the upper city at the actual emplacement of the Jewish Quarter through the Water Gate or Gardens Gate. There he would meander for some time between the luxurious dwellings of the prominent families of the Hasmonean priests. He would scrutinize the three towers that protected the ancient palace of Herod, casting a quasi-ritual curse at the Roman Legion that encamped between its walls. He would then take the stairs that led to the bridge that connected the upper city to the Temple Mount – the remains of this bridge, Robinson's Arch, can still be seen against the wall today. He would pause on the bridge to view the lower city that extended towards the south in the Tyropoeon Valley on the ruins of the city of David as far as the Gate of the Essenes to the Pool of Shiloach, where the waters of the Gihon flowed.

The visitor would pull himself away from the scene in the lower city where merchants and artisans were bustling and would pass the Temple's western wall, which was built with double spaced, heavy Herodian stones. He would wander through the porticos and columns, listening to the lesson by some Pharisee teacher, the inflammatory discourse of a member of one of the Essenian sects that had retreated to the Judean Desert, and would take advantage of the opportunity to exchange money in order to cover the costs of his pilgrimage. He would cross the Gentile's court to reach the Temple Square, scanning the four towers of the Antonia Fortress in passing – especially the southeastern tower that rose to a height of 180 feet – and would cast another curse, this time against Herod, who built it. He would then fulfill his religious obligations before taking interest in the dissensions between the parties who were preparing to push the Romans out of Judea.

Two thousand years later, an hotelier, the owner of the Holy Land Hotel, located in the Bayit ve-Gan neighborhood in the western part of Jerusalem, has the idea of reconstructing, within the hotel, a model of the city as it appeared to the visitor on the eve of its destruction by the Romans. He entrusts this task to a team led by the renowned archeologist, Michael Avi-Yona. The reconstruction begins in 1965 and continues for three years. The 1000 square meter model reproduces the various neighborhoods in the city at a scale of 1:50^e, including the topographical contours, as well as the buildings and the most important monuments.

At the time, the city spread over almost 180 hectares, including 14 hectares of the Temple Mount and 26 hectares of public spaces, and had a population of an estimated 30,000 inhabitants.

[•]

In 64, a new procurator, Gessius Florus, who is appointed without taking into consideration the religious feelings of the inhabitants of the city, takes a series of measures that incite an explosive response. An open revolt erupts in the autumn of 66, following the summary executions that the Romans perpetrated on the streets. A strike paralyzes the religious services at the Temple, and demanding the departure of all the strangers in the city, including the Roman Legions, the priests refuse to offer the compulsory sacrifices dedicated to the emperor.

The disturbances continue, often degenerating into internal struggles between rival parties; the Roman governor of Syria, Cestius Gallus, marches into the city at the head of a powerful army. Perhaps surprised by the resistance, he is driven back and his army is routed. The city will in some way recover its freedom and in a heavy climate of mutual accusations and political assassinations, it will prepare to repulse the Romans. Josephus Flavius, who led the revolt in the Galilee before surrendering to the Romans and rallying the party supporting them, writes:

An insurgent city

The high priest, Ananus, and the leaders in Jerusalem who advocated revolt hastened to raise the walls of the city, to assemble a large number of war machines and to forge a great quantity of arms. All the youths practiced using them, and the feverish activity of such a large enterprise stirred up excitement and agitation everywhere. But with heavy hearts, the wisest and the most judicious foresaw the calamity that threatened the city and its inhabitants, and they could not hold back their tears. Those who fanned the flames of revolt, in contrast, took pleasure in raising their hopes: this miserable city was in such a state that one would have readily thought that it was determined to bring about its own downfall as if it wanted to rob the Romans of the glory of destroying it.

J. Flavius, *The Jewish War II, 22, 1*

The quarrels between the insurgents turn into a civil war. To add to the bitterness, the opposing extremist factions, led by intransigent men, pound each other in Jerusalem in the face of the advance of the Romans in the Galilee. Their reign of terror in the besieged city will not prevent certain Pharisee masters from seeking a solution to this revolt that threatens to end in a blood bath. Rabbinic history-philosophy pinpoints an incident during this dramatic period that would play a decisive role in the evolution of Judaism following the destruction of the Temple: the departure from the city of one of the most prestigious teachers of the period, Rabbi Yohanan ben Zakkai, and his settlement in Yavne, a small village on the coastal plain. The Talmud describes the incident as follows:

Yohanan ben Zakkai

While making the rounds in the city, Rabbi Yohanan ben Zakkai saw that the inhabitants of Jerusalem were boiling straw to drink the juice. He asked himself: "How can men who nourish themselves in this way be able to hold out against Vespasian's soldiers?! There is nothing else to do, but to leave the city."

Rabbi Yohanan's nephew, Abba Siqara ben Batiha, was the leader of one of the factions controlling the city. He secretly sent for him.

When he arrived, Rabbi Yohanan asked: "How long will we continue to make the people die of hunger by conducting ourselves in this manner?" His nephew replied: "What can I do about it? I would be overthrown if I dared to say a word." The rabbi declared: "I see no other solution than to leave the city. Perhaps some good will result from this." "We have decided that no man will leave Jerusalem alive", Ben Batiha warned. – "In that case", the rabbi proposed, "take me out as if I were dead". – "Act as if you are ill for a period and even receive visitors", Ben Batiha advised. "Then place something that smells badly in your house so that they will believe that you are dead. Thereafter, your disciples will place you in a coffin..."

Rabbi Yohanan did everything that his nephew had advised him to do. He then sent for his disciples, Rabbi Eliezer and Rabbi Yehoshua, and said to them: "My children, prepare a coffin for me in which I can hide and take me out of here." Rabbi Eliezer lifted the end of the coffin near the rabbi's head and Rabbi Yehoshua lifted the end where his feet lay; they carried him to the gates of Jerusalem, arriving at sunset. The guards asked: "Who is in there?" "A dead man", they replied. "Don't you know that it is forbidden to leave a corpse within the walls of Jerusalem overnight?" The guards wanted to make sure that the body was that of a dead man by piercing it with their swords, but Abba Siqara, who was nearby spoke out saying: "You will be reproached for having profaned the remains of your master." They wanted to examine the body, but Abba Siqara again spoke out: "You will be reproached for having disturbed your master!" The guards gave the order to open the gate and authorized them to leave.

The disciples took their master to Vespasian's camp where they opened the coffin. Rabbi Yohanan got out of it and went before the general: "Greetings, your Majesty." – "You deserve to die for two reasons", the general exclaimed, "first of all, because you address me as if I were a monarch when I am not, and then precisely because you consider me a king, you have indeed delayed in coming to see me." Rabbi Yohanan replied: "In spite of your denials, you are a monarch. Otherwise, Jerusalem would not have been delivered into your hands…"

Whereupon, a messenger arrived from Rome announcing to Vespasian: "The emperor is dead and the members of the senate have named you his successor." Vespasian was only wearing one boot; wishing to put on the second boot, he could not fit his foot in it; wishing to remove the first boot, he could not take his foot out of it. Vespasian cried out: "What is this?" Rabbi Yohanan replied: "Don't worry, what is happening to you is a sign that you have received good news for it is said: 'Good news makes the bones fat'" (Proverbs 15: 30).

"What remedy do you propose?"
"Have someone with an unpleasant appearance brought before you for it is said: "A broken spirit dries the bones" (Proverbs 17: 23).

Vespasian did what the rabbi recommended and his foot immediately entered his boot: "If you are so wise", he exclaimed, "why didn't you come to see me sooner?"…

Finally, Vespasian said to Rabbi Yohanan: "I must leave the country, but before I leave, I would like to grant you one of your requests. What do request? Rabbi Yohanan said: "Grant me Yavne and it sages…

TB Guittin 55a - 57a

Upon becoming emperor, Vespasian dispatches his son, Titus, to lead the four legions. The insurgents will not reach an agreement until the Romans are at the walls of the city. Jean de Giscala's men are entrusted with the defense of the lower city and of the Temple Mount, while Simon Bar Giora's men are entrusted with that of the upper city. The Romans prepare to breach the exterior wall – the third wall – harassed by the insurgents whose forays demonstrate as much audacity as courage, according to Josephus Flavius:

The insurgents' audacity

Thus, all the parties put aside their hostilities, forming a single body, and posting men on the ramparts and along the walls. They continually hurled an incredible quantity of torches and arrows against the besieging army's machines and against those pushing the battering rams. The most determined even went out on forays of small groups, sabotaging the Romans' machines, demonstrating such audacity and hardiness that all they lacked was the science of warfare to be true warriors. Titus continually appeared on the premises to offer his assistance wherever there was a need, positioning some horsemen and some archers around the machines to repulse the assailants, while men perched on the towers persistently flung javelins to provide cover for the activity of the battering rams. But the wall that the Romans were attempting to breach was so strong that it withstood their blows. The Fifth Legion's battering ram only succeeded in loosening a corner of one tower that rose over the wall, which resisted being brought down.

The insurgents spaced their forays to lead the Romans to believe that they had succumbed to fatigue and to fear, thus encouraging the Romans to disperse to carry out their tasks. Then choosing the favorable moment, they went out through the concealed gate in the Hippicus Tower, setting the work of the besiegers on fire and even venturing into their camp... Their audacity prevailed over the Roman's discipline. They killed those who were on the premises and repulsed those who hastened to the rescue. The battles took place around the machines. Using every possible means, some attempted to burn them, while others attempted to prevent them from doing so. Confusion reigned on both sides and many of those on the front line of this brutal clash lay lifeless on the ground. The vigor and the disdain for death that the Jews continued to display would not only earn them the recognition on that day of being more valiant than the Romans, contrary to all expectations, but would even give them a certain advantage over the soldiers recruited in Alexandria who attempted to contain them.

J. Flavius, *The Jewish War V, 6, 5 - 6*

The Romans breach the first wall near Herod's palace and occupy Bethseda. Titus then attacks the second wall, which he breaches at the end of long and difficult battles. Thereafter, he orders the construction of a wall of siege around the first wall in order to starve the population, while the Romans bombard the city with stone cannon balls. At the beginning of the month of August, the Antonia Fortress is captured and a few days later, the Temple galleries, where the insurgents had retreated, are in flames. According to Josephus Flavius, Titus did not intend to burn down the Temple. Although challenged by some, historians have preserved his version of the events:

The destruction of the Temple

Having withdrawn to the Antonia Fortress, Titus was determined to have his army attack the Temple the following morning, the 10th of the month of August: it was the eve of the fatal day designated by God long ago to carry out his sentence of condemning this holy place to be burnt down at the end of long years of revolt as in the past, on the same day, at the hands of Nebuchadnezzar, the king of Babylonia...

Without having received the order and without even realizing that he was committing a grave sacrilege, driven by God, one might say, a soldier, perched on one of his companions, hurled a torch through the gold window into the vestibule that led to the buildings situated around the northern side of the Temple. The fire ignited immediately and faced with such extreme misfortune, the Jews began to cry out in horror. They rushed in from all directions to attempt to extinguish the fire; seeing the Temple burning before their very eyes, nothing could stop them, not even death. The Temple, more than anything else, urged them to preserve their lives only to enable them to protect it.

While Titus had taken a break from the battles and was resting in his tent, he was notified. He immediately went to extinguish the fire, followed by his officers and behind them, the legionnaires, who were shouting out and making such a commotion. The confusion was so great that it could have been said that an enemy had surprised an immense army, routing it and leaving it in disorder and without command.

*Titus shouted with all his might and signaled with his hands
to urge his men to extinguish the fire, but the uproar made
it impossible to hear him, and the zeal as well as the rage
that drove the soldiers in this war did not allow them to pay
attention to the signs that he was making. The impetuous
legionnaires, who entered in throngs, could not be restrained
by orders or by threats. Driven only by their fury, they pushed
each other so fiercely that many were thrown down and
trampled, while others fell on the ruins of the still burning
and smoking porticos and galleries. Although victorious,
their fate was no less sad than that of the vanquished. When
all these warriors reached the Temple, they no longer wanted
to hear the orders that their commander shouted, and those
in the back urged those in front to set it on fire...*

*Wherever you turned, all you saw was confusion and
carnage. A great number of unarmed people who were
incapable of defending themselves were killed. The areas
around the altar were covered with body parts, cast on this
holy site, which was not intended to receive slaughtered men
in lieu of sacrifices, and rivers of blood flowed along the
stairs.*

J. Flavius, *The Jewish War VI, 4, 5 - 6*

The Romans invade the lower city and the Tyropoeon Valley,
but must renew their siege of the upper city where the most
indomitable insurgents had withdrawn. The latter will hold
out until the end, giving rise to an outburst of violence that,
one month later, will result in the total destruction of the city,
the massacre of some of its inhabitants and the deportation
and enslavement of the remainder. The capture of three of
the towers of Herod's palace, which overlooked Jerusalem,
hallowed, in a certain manner, the crushing of the revolt that
in Jerusalem alone had taken more than five months. Flavius
recounts:

The debacle of a city
*Upon taking possession of the towers, the Romans hoisted
their flags over them with cries of joy. The severe hardships
that they had endured during this war made them savor all*

the more the pleasure and the happiness of having concluded it so gloriously... The soldiers who were dispersed throughout the city indiscriminately killed whomever they encountered and burned down all the houses with people hidden inside. Those who risked pillaging the houses found them filled with the cadavers of entire families who had starved to death, and they ran away empty handed, horrified by the sight. Their compassion for the dead did not make them more humane to the living: they killed everyone that they met, and the number of bodies piled one over the other was so great that the avenues and streets were blocked, and the blood that bathed the city extinguished the fire in many places. If the manslaughter let up during the evening, then the fire intensified during the night.

J. Flavius, *The Jewish War VI, 8, 5*

The city was destroyed, with the exception of the Western Wall of the Temple and the three towers of Herod, which had been spared to protect the Tenth Legion that had established itself upon the ruins. Two thousand years later, traces of this destruction can still be seen in many places: for example, in the Archeological Park of the Wailing Wall, where stones and columns lay along the southern wall of the Temple in the irremediable chaos that archeologists tried in vain to sort out; in the Herodian House, a vast and luxurious residence in the upper city that obviously belonged to one of the wealthiest families in Jerusalem, which has been partially restored. This residence, which covers an area of 600 square meters, is composed of a series of dwellings that open to a central court. The presence of ritual baths attest to the owner's respect for Jewish Law in general and, in particular, for the laws of purity. In the Burnt House, the residence of the priests of the Bar-Kathros clan, traces of the fire can be seen on the wall and the mark of the skeleton of an arm of a woman, who had obviously been caught by surprise by the fire, remains on the kitchen floor. During the excavations between 1969 and 1983 that preceded and accompanied the restoration of the Jewish Quarter, the archeologist, Nahman Avigad, unearthed these houses there. Avigad wrote the following in *Les Dossiers d'Archéologie*:

The price of freedom

Some of the other houses bore witness to the quality of the apartments. A noteworthy example is a restored living room of an apartment complex called the "middle block". A very fine mosaic, which was partly destroyed, covers the floor of this spacious room. The central panel is framed with checkered, triangular motifs in the form of small waves. The center is filled with intersecting lines forming swastikas. Originally Greek, this motif is found in Jewish, decorative art. When this room was discovered, the floor was still hidden under the ashes that remained from the fire that had ravaged the house. Once they were removed, a coin was discovered, stuck to this floor; it was a bronze coin from the first war of the Jews against the Romans, bearing the inscription "Year II – the Liberty of Israel", that is, dating to the second year of this war in 67 A.D.

N. Avigad, *Les Dossiers d'Archéologie*

If we are to believe Flavius and the rabbis, the Second Temple was destroyed on the 9th of Av, the same date that the First Temple was destroyed five centuries before. Since then, the 9th of Av – *tisha b'Av* – is commemorated by all the communities of Israel as a day of mourning and lamentation. The medieval Jewish poet, Yehudah Halevi (between 1075 and 1141), will echo the desolation in which Jerusalem foundered as well as the nostalgia harbored by its exiles all over the world:

Zion

Zion, don't you wonder what has been the lot of your exiles,
who unceasingly enquire about you,
the miserable remnants of your flocks?
From west to east, from north to south,
from far and near, from all places,
receive their greetings of peace,
as well as that of the man, the prisoner of your desire,
who sheds his tears like dew upon the Hermon,
asking for nothing more than to pour them out on your hills.
Crying like a jackal for your desolation,

singing to you like a lyre
as soon as I begin to dream of the return of your exiles.
What I wouldn't give to wander on your sites
where God revealed Himself to your visionaries and your heralds!

That I may have wings to transport me far away,
to lay the pieces of my heart among your hills, which have
been parceled out!
I would prostrate, face down upon the ground,
I would kiss your stones and caress your dust.
I would go to the tombs of my ancestors
and would grieve at Hebron upon the tombs of your greatest
[that of our Patriarchs].
I would traverse your forests and your Carmel
and would pause at your Gilad to contemplate the mountains
along your rivers,
Mount Abarim and Mount Hor,
where the two great lights rest [Moses and Aaron],
your luminaries, your masters.
Your air is sap for souls,
the grains of your dust are myrrh,
the waters of your rivers are honey...

Happy is he who merits being present
at the dawning of your day,
followed by the fullness of your sunrise.
He will see the prosperity of your chosen
and will savor the joy of recovering
the days gone by of your youth.

Y. Halevi

AELIA CAPITOLINA

Jerusalem remains in ruins for more than sixty years. Not until 129 does the emperor Hadrian, the great artist and the great persecutor, decide to create a Roman colony on its site. On behalf of Hadrian, the governor of Palestine participates in a ceremony during which the furrows for the new walls are dug – a ceremony that is immortalized on the coins of the new colony. Its Roman name will be Aelia Capitolina, uniting that of the dynasty reigning in Rome – Aelius – and that of the Roman Capitoline Triad: Jupiter, Juno and Minerva.

The creation of a pagan colony upon the site of the holy city will obviously precipitate another revolt by the Jews, united under the leadership of the prominent Pharisee master, Rabbi Akiba, and under the military command of Bar Kohkba. The Roman garrison in the city as well as its inhabitants – colonists who, for the most part, are Roman war veterans – are forced to evacuate the places occupied by the insurgents (132 – 135). The latter will even attempt to rebuild the Temple. In the end, this revolt will also be crushed in a blood bath. Hadrian decides to rename Judea *Palestina*, its former name, which designated the southern coastal plane. Furthermore, he promulgates harsh decrees in lieu of reprisals, in particular, forbidding the circumcised entrance to the colony under pain of death. From then on, his men will be able to continue their work without hindrance.

The city is rebuilt, modeled after the Roman colonies throughout the world. It will take the shape of a square, as preserved to this day by the Old City, with twists here and there along the original outline. A main road lined with colonnades – Decumanus – traversed it from west to east, from the present day Jaffa Gate to the Temple Mount, along the actual David Street and its continuation, Chain Street. A second principal road lined with colonnades, from north to south – the Cardo from the Latin cardinal – with a width of approximately 22.5 meters, connected the existing Damascus Gate – then called the Neapolis Gate before becoming the Saint-Etienne Gate – to the present day Zion Gate[1]. The first

1. The Cardo continued to serve the Crusaders before sinking under almost 4 meters of debris following the recapture of Jerusalem by the Arabs. It was partially cleared and restored only in 1980, when it recovered a little of its commercial activity. A part of the enclosure wall that surrounded the city under King Ezekias was also cleared. See p.276. Both are located in the Jewish Quarter of the Old City.

gate opened onto a paved square where a Roman column, which obviously bore a bust, had been set – a gate the Arabs would name Bab al-Amoud or the Gate of the Column. At their intersection, the two roads formed arcades – Tetra pylon or tetra-portico: the four quarters that constitute the Old City today, the Muslim, Christian, Armenian and Jewish Quarters that correspond more or less to the four sections delimited by these two roads. The forum of the Roman city was located along the Decumanus, not far from the intersection of the two roads and at the present site of the Mouristan bazaar.

2. According to Christian tradition, Pontius Pilate was under this arch when he saw Jesus and exclaimed: "So this is the man!" See p.113. The arch in question may have led to the forum – known by the name of Lithostrotos – whose pavement can be seen today in the cellars of the Convent of the Sisters of Zion.

A second artery proceeded from the Damascus Gate to pass along the Tyropoeon Valley to the Dung or Detritus Gate. It continued through staircases that led to a public fountain bordered by twelve arches – *Tetranymphon* – located not far from the Pool of Shiloach. The most important pagan temple in the city, which is dedicated to Aphrodite or Venus, was built on the Golgotha – the actual site of the Holy Sepulcher Church – raised on a mound of packed earth that filled the caves. In addition, the city was the site of numerous monuments, public baths, a theater, a library and two triumphal arches, including the one christened Ecce Homo[2] on the existing Via Dolorosa. A temple dedicated to the god of health, *Esculapius*, rose above the pools used to purify the victims destined to be sacrificed or the Bethseda Pools, which were renowned for the healing qualities of their waters[3] during the period of the Second Temple. Another sanctuary in honor of Jupiter that stood on the Temple Mount stood outside of the colony; walls would not be built around it until the end of the 3rd century.

3. The two pools, which are surrounded and separated by colonnades, were unearthed during the excavations conducted in the courtyard of the Church of Saint Anne. They collected the waters of the tiny valley – the Bethseda Valley – that ran up to the supporting wall of the Temple Mount.

[•]

In 324, the emperor, Constantine, converts to Christianity, followed by many members of his court. This conversion arouses the Roman-Byzantine authorities' interest in Jerusalem. At the Nicaean Council, Bishop Macaire laments the condition of the Christian sites. In 326, Helena, Constantine's mother, who had also converted to Christianity, visits Palestine for the first time and to a certain extent draws up a map of the holy sites of Christianity.

The destruction of the temple of Venus makes possible the discovery of the cross that was used to crucify Jesus, which was buried in a crypt under the sanctuary. Constantine orders the construction of numerous churches, including the church of the Holy Sepulcher (325 – 335), which would become one of the highlights of Christian pilgrimages. A rotunda – the Anastasis or the Resurrection Rotunda – is erected around the sepulcher, which had been hollowed into a rock that had been detached from the massif by leveling it all around. The three doors of the rotunda open on to an interior courtyard – atrium – where the evened rock of Calvary rises, overlooking a cross surmounted by a baldachin. A chevet of a basilica with five naves on the eastern side – the Martyrion – is built over the pit where Christ's cross and that of the two thieves were discovered. The eight doors of the Martyrion lead to an exterior courtyard, under the open sky and are surrounded by porticos, the most important of which leads to the Cardo. Constantine the Great solemnly inaugurates the sanctuary on September 17th, 335.[4]

4. Only very few vestiges of this first church, which the Persians destroyed in 614, can be discerned in the existing complex whose broad outline dates back to the masonry of the Crusaders. See p.120.

Since then, the city assumes a Christian appearance. The interdiction of visiting the city that weighed heavy on the Jews is renewed, except on the 9th of Av (July – August), which commemorates the destruction of the First and Second Temples, and at which time they are permitted to gather on the hill of the Temple to pray and lament. When Julian, who had returned to the ancient Greek religion, accedes to the throne, he limits the creation of Christian institutions. In 363, openly demonstrating his goodwill towards the Jews, he entrusts the rebuilding of the Temple to one of his relatives. But as soon as the work is initiated, an earthquake interrupts it. The death of Julian, who is killed during a campaign against the Persians, will hinder it irreparably. His friendship with the Jews will alienate the Christians for all time. One of the most famous travelers of the 19th century, the French writer, Chateaubriand, describes his initiative as follows:

Thirty-seven years later, Julian gathered the Jews in Jerusalem to rebuild the Temple there, but without success: The men worked on this project with hods, spades and shovels; the women carried dirt in the skirts of their most beautiful dresses; but fireballs leaped out of the partly hollowed out foundations, dispersing the workers and preventing the realization of this enterprise.

R. Chateaubriand, *Itinerary from Paris to Jerusalem*

The Christianization of the city is resumed with the renewal of Christian pilgrimages. In 378, a first church, the Chapel of the Ascension, is built on the summit of the Mount of Olives – on the site where Jesus appeared to his disciples before ascending to heaven forty days after his resurrection. In 385, Theodosius I builds a church at Gethsemane. The first monks settle in the desert on the outskirts of the city. The city's population grows to 50,000, perhaps 80,000 inhabitants, most of whom are Christian.

In 438, the empress, Eudocia, permits the Jews to settle in the city. She herself moves there (444 – 460) after leaving her husband, Theodosius II, nevertheless, maintaining the title of Augusta. Spending her time in prayer, she is no less involved in the controversy about the nature of Christ – the controversy regarding Monophysitism (451), which divides Christendom – and sides with Juvenal, the bishop of Jerusalem. At the conclusion of this controversy, Juvenal receives the title and rank of Orthodox Patriarch with authority over the churches in Palestine and in Arabia. At the same time, Monophysitic churches are established, which support its thesis about the nature of Christ – the Armenian, the Coptic, the Syrian-Jacobite and the Ethiopian churches – which are all represented at the holy Christian sites in the city.

5. The stake is housed in the Church of the Dormition, which was built upon the ruins of the Church of Zion, and was considered "the mother of all churches" at the time. See p.192.

Under the auspices of Eudocia, sanctuaries are built at the sites of the peregrination, the miracles and the passion of Christ in a grandiose attempt to translate the Gospels into architecture, engraving their accounts in stone. To site one example, Saint Peter's Church is built not far from the Pool of Siloam (Shiloach) upon one of the sites presumed to be the house of Caiaphas, the high priest who handed Jesus over to the Romans. It enshrines a stake[5], which the pilgrims are told is the one used to attach Jesus to whip him:

The house of Caiphas

And those who had laid hold of Jesus led him away to Caiphas, the high priest, where the scribes and elders were assembled. But Peter followed him from a distance to the high priest's palace, which he entered and where he sat with the servants to see the outcome. Now the high priests and all the elders of the Sanhedrin sought a false witness against Jesus in order to put him to death; but none was found although many false witnesses appeared there. Finally, two false witnesses came and said: "This man said: 'I can destroy the Temple of God and rebuild it in three days.'" The high priest rose and said to him: "Have you nothing to say? What do these witnesses have against you?" But Jesus remained silent. The high priest said to him: "I adjure you to the living God that you tell us if you are Christ, the Son of God: Jesus replied: "You said it. Nevertheless, I say to you that thereafter, you will see the son of man sitting on the right hand of power, coming in the clouds of heaven." The high priest rent his clothes and said: "He has spoken blasphemy. What need do we have of more witnesses? Now you have heard the blasphemy. What is your opinion?" They answered: "He is guilty and deserves death." Then they spat on his face and hit him while others slapped him.

Matthew 26: 57 - 67

The construction of buildings outside of the city, such as Saint Stephen's Monastery on the north that is on the present site of Saint Stephen's Basilica and the Siloam Church on the south,[6] required the displacement of the walls. The southern wall, which was built on the foundations of the Second Temple, encompasses the City of David and Mount Zion. The city hosts thousands of pilgrims and immigrants from the four corners of Christendom, who roam through the same scene of the Passion of Christ in search of a relic or a revelation, both exalted and overwhelmed at the same time. Withdrawing to the desert surrounding the city in atonement for their sins, some find the silence of discernment and the promise of an eternal peace in religious retreat.

6. The Siloam Church was built near the pool bearing the same name on the site where Jesus performed miracles. See p.42. Stairs lead from the pool, which is covered and surrounded by columns, to the basilica. A second staircase leads from the basilica to the city. The actual pool (4 by 6 meters) is only a fourth of its original size.

7. The reconstructed Monastery of the Cross, situated today in a valley in the western part of the city, was turned over to the Greek Orthodox in the 19th century. The altar in the church stands over the emplacement of the Tree of the Cross.

8. The ruins of the church spread along the two sides of the existing southern wall on the side of the Battei Mahasseh in the Jewish Quarter. Its particularly impressive foundations lie hidden in cavities that were used as cisterns to collect rainwater. One of the walls bore the following inscription: "This project was carried out through the benevolence of the most pious of our emperors, Flavius Justinian, under the supervision and attention of the most holy Constantine, priest and Father Superior in the year 13."

During Justinian's reign (527 – 565), the Samaritans revolt. The churches and the monasteries located outside the city, including the Monastery of the Cross,[7] which the Georgians built in the 5th century on the site of the tree whose wood was used to carve the cross, are partially destroyed. The map of Jerusalem at the time resembled the one presented by the Madaba mosaic on a scale of approximately 1:1600e, which the bishop of the city ordered in Trans-Jordan to pave the floor of his church. The Cardo passed near the Church of the Holy Sepulcher, skirting the Saint Sophie Church and opening on to the largest Christian sanctuary in the city, the new Mother of God Church – the Nea – built around 540, which accommodated hundreds of faithful, and was destroyed in the 7th century in an earthquake.[8] The numerous Christian pilgrims who often resided in the city for long periods, lodging in the inns, the monasteries and the hospices, were enchanted by their visits to the holy sites as confirmed by Antonin Martyr's testimony (566 – 70):

The miracles of the Cross

Upon prostrating and kissing the ground, we entered the holy city and traversed it, reciting prayers, to arrive at the tomb of our Lord. The sepulcher holding the remains of our Lord Jesus Christ is hollowed out in natural rock. A candle like the one we placed on its border, burns day and night... Upon leaving the tomb, visitors take some of the dirt with them, carrying away the blessing of the site. The stone that sealed the tomb can still be seen at the entrance. The natural rock, carved in Golgotha, is hidden under gold ornamentation and precious stones. The tombstone is as large as a millstone and is also covered with many ornaments: iron bars, bracelets, chains, necklaces, diadems, earrings, belts, emperors' gold crowns set with precious stones and a large number of ornaments offered by empresses. The entire tomb... is encrusted with silver and an altar is set up inside under suns of gold...

Eighty steps separate the sepulcher from Golgotha. It is accessed from the side by the same stairs used by our Lord. Traces of blood can be seen on the rock at the emplacement of the crucifix. The altar upon which Abraham prepared the sacrifice of his son Isaac is on the other side...

The holy Cross is made from walnut wood. When it is taken out of its chamber to the atrium for the service, a star appears in the sky that covers it. Throughout the time that we worship before the Cross, the star does not move and many earthenware jars full of oil are brought in to be blessed. If the jars happen to touch the wood of the Cross, the oil they contain begins to boil and unless someone touches them quickly, they risk spilling over. When the Cross is returned to its place, the star is also withdrawn and as long as the Cross is locked away, the star will not reappear.

In 614, the Persians assemble to take possession of the city with the help of its Jewish inhabitants. Its Christian inhabitants are massacred – almost 34,000 – most of the churches are destroyed and the Patriarch is deported with the holy Cross. At first, the Persians entrust the government of the city to the Jews, but three years later, they expel them and appoint a governor who authorizes the monk, Modestus, to restore the Christian sanctuaries, including the Church of the Holy Sepulcher. Soon after, the Byzantines vanquish the Persians, the Cross is retrieved and in 629, the city is once again in the hands of the Christians. The Gate of Mercy is opened on this occasion to celebrate the recovery of the Cross.[9]

9. The Gate of Mercy, see p.167.

AL-QUDS

Following Mohammed's death in 632, the Arabs launch a holy war to spread the new religion throughout the world. In 634, they invade Palestine. Three years later, they besiege Jerusalem. Having despaired of receiving the aid of the Christians, the Patriarch surrenders to the court in the spring of 638. The city will obviously be surrendered according to the same terms specified in the surrender agreements concluded by the conquering Arabs with the Jewish and Christian populations, the so-called protégés: the inhabitants lives are spared and their religious sites are protected in exchange for a surrender tax.

There are many versions describing the circumstances of the arrival in Jerusalem of Omar (634 – 644), the successor of the prophet, Mohammed, and the reasons that prompted him to clear the Temple Mount to erect the first Muslim sanctuary on the actual site of the Dome of the Rock, or perhaps on that of the Mosque of Al-Aksa.[1] In any case, Jerusalem will quickly be considered a holy city to Islam as well, worthy of the name "Holy" – Al-Quds in Arabic. In fact, the Temple Mount will be designated the place where Mohammed rose to heaven. This tradition is based on the interpretation of a passage in the Koran that declares:

The distant sanctuary

Glory to He Who led His servant during the night from the holy sanctuary to the distant sanctuary, whose walls we have blessed, so that we could demonstrate some of our (miraculous) signs. He is the One Who hears, the One Who sees.

Sura 17

The first mosque referred to in this passage is in Mecca; the second is in Jerusalem. According to one of the versions of the account of Omar's entry, he was drawn to the sacred rock – *even ha-shetiyya* in Hebrew, – which was enthroned in the

[1]. Upon declining the offer of the Patriarch of Jerusalem to pray inside the Church of the Holy Sepulcher, Omar would fulfill his religious obligation near the church. The mosque bearing his name would be built on the site where he prayed.

Holy of Holies, the most sacred site in the Temple where the Jews gathered to pray:[2]

Omar's conquest

2. The Founding Rock, see p.101.

We know from Shaddad ibn Aus, who accompanied Omar when he entered the noble sanctuary of the holy city on the day that God delivered it to him, that Omar passed through Mohammed's Gate, crawling on his hands and knees, followed by those accompanying him, until they reached the parvis (of the sanctuary). He looked all around and glorifying the Lord, he declared: "By God – in Whose hands my soul rests – this is truly David's mosque that the Prophet referred to when he said: 'I was led to it in the night.'" Omar visited the southern part of the Haram, advancing towards the west. He then decreed: "We will build a mosque here."

According to Al-Walid ibn Muslim, we know from a sheikh – the son of Shaddad ibn Aus, who heard it from his father, who heard it from his grandfather – that as soon as the surrender agreement was concluded, Omar asked the Patriarch of Jerusalem to take him to David's mosque. The latter agreed to do so. Omar took the lead, walking with his saber girthed and followed by four thousand companions who had accompanied him to Jerusalem, also with their sabers girthed, as well as the rest of us, Arabs who had come to the holy city with no other weapon than our sabers. The Patriarch was our guide, walking ahead of Omar and his companions whom we followed. We entered the city in this manner. The Patriarch first led us to the church bearing the name of Koumana (the Church of the Holy Sepulcher), announcing: "This is David's mosque." Omar pensively looked all around before retorting: "You are lying for the Prophet described the mosque of David to me and this place does not correspond with his description." The Patriarch took us to the Church of Zion, again announcing: "This is David's mosque." The caliph again rejoined: "You're lying!" The Patriarch continued his stratagem until he brought us to the city's noble sanctuary, to the gate that we would name the Gate of Mohammed. The garbage that covered the noble sanctuary also covered the gate steps and was even strewn on the street, filling the entrance to the ceiling. The Patriarch said to Omar: "It's impossible to go any further unless we get down on our hands and knees." Omar replied: "So be it, on our hands and our knees!" The Patriarch had to get down on all four ahead of Omar whom we followed; we crawled in this manner until we reached the parvis of the city's noble sanctuary. Once there, we stood straight up. Omar looked all around and after much thought, he declared: "By the One in Whose hands my soul rests! This is the place described by God's Prophet."

We know from another source, in this case, Hisham ibn Ammar – who heard it from Al-Haitham ibn al-Abbassi, who himself claims to have heard it from his grandfather, Abd Akkah ibn Abou abd Allah – when Omar became caliph, he visited Syria. He first stopped over in the village Al-Jabiyya where he dispatched a man from the tribe of Jadila to the holy city. Soon after, Jerusalem surrendered. The caliph entered the city accompanied by Kaab (a Jew) whom he asked: "Abu Itzhak, do you know where the rock is?" – Kaab replied: "You will have to cross so many meters from the wall that stands in the Jahannem wadi and dig a little to find it." He added: "Today it is nothing more than a pile of debris." They dug up the designated place and discovered the rock. Omar then asked Kaab: "In your opinion, where should we build the mosque, the Kibla?" – "Build it there, behind the rock, in such a way that the site may house two Kibla, that of Moses and that of Mohammed", Kaab responded. – "So you persist in supporting the Jews, oh Abu Itzhak," Omar noted, "but the mosque will stand over the rock." And this is how the mosque was built over the Haram.

Al-Walid later recounted that according to Kulthum ibn Ziyyad, Omar asked Kaab: "In your opinion, where on this holy site should we build the temple of the Muslims?" – Kaab replied: "To the north near the Gate of the Tribes. – "On the contrary", retorted Omar, "we are entitled to the south of the sanctuary." Having heard it himself from his father, Al-Walid continued: "Omar headed towards the front, towards the southwest, where he began to gather the rubbish with his own hands and to cram it into his coat; those of us who were with him immediately did the same. He then took his coat and went and threw out its contents in the wadi called the

Jahannem wadi (the wadi of Gehenna). Following his lead, we repeatedly gathered more rubbish until we had finished clearing the site where the mosque stands today."

A. Jamal ad-Din, Muthir al Ghiram

The majority of the inhabitants of Jerusalem remain Christian in spite of the interest that the caliphs of the Umayyad Dynasty in Damascus took in it. Its founder, Muawiyya, who is proclaimed the caliph of Jerusalem in 661, builds a second sanctuary on the Temple Mount. In 692, one of his successors, Abd al-Malik builds a magnificent cupola over one of the two sanctuaries – the Dome of the Rock, which is erroneously called the Mosque of Omar. His goal was obviously to establish a Muslim pilgrimage center that could compete with that of Mecca, the seat of his political rival. Nonetheless, the holy city gradually becomes less important, particularly with the promotion of Ramla as the capital of southern Palestine. It does not even maintain a garrison that is large enough to keep order and assure the safety of the Christian pilgrims. Furthermore, during the final years of Umayyad rule, the city experiences political agitation. Moreover, it suffers earthquakes that damage the Dome of the Rock. During the 10th century, the Arab geographer, Mouqadassi, a native of Jerusalem, writes:

The Dome of the Rock

At dawn, when daylight first shines upon the mosque and the sunrays are reflected by the gold leaf, the building is a marvelous sight to see. Its beauty is unlike any that I have ever seen in any Islamic country; neither have I heard of a building dating to the pagan era that could rival the Dome of the Rock.

Today, the faithful access the Temple Mount – *haram ash-sharif* or the noble sanctuary – through gates made in the Western Wall which is venerated by the Jews: From north to south, *Bab el-Ghwanimeh, Bab el-Hedid, Bab el-Kattanim* (the Gate of the Cotton Merchants), *Bab el-Mastarah* (the

Gate of the Latrines) and *Bab el-Silseleh,* (the Gate of the Chain). The most widely used gate is that of the Maghrebins, which is accessed from the actual esplanade of the Western Wall and leads to archways that date back to the period of the Mamluks.

The Dome of the Rock is more a memorial than a mosque. The octagonal building, built on a platform in the middle of the esplanade, is erected on three concentric circles of pillars and columns, a first circular colonnade surrounding the rock that supports the dome and two octagonal colonnades. The geometric arrangement of the complex is so elaborate and so harmonious (the rotunda and the dome are of equal height – approximately 20 meters, and the height of the building – 54 meters – and its diameter – 52 meters – are almost equal), and the interior is so sumptuously and so elaborately decorated, that as the French writer, Pierre Loti, noted during a visit in the month of Ramadan (April 1894), one has the impression of entering a palace, the seat of a rock, where the light of day arises: "and one is almost terrified by what appears: something dark and shapeless in the semi-darkness of this magnificent place; something that rises irregularly like a large, black wave, frozen; a wild rock, the top of a mountain..." Four gates open from the sanctuary on to the parvis towards the north, *Bab el-Jennah*, the Gate of Paradise, towards the east, *Bab el-Silseleh*, the Gate of the Chain, towards the south, *Bab el-Kibla*, and towards the west, *Bab-el Gharb,* the Gate of the West.

The second monument dominating the *haram ash-sharif*, the El-Aksa Mosque – the distant – with the silver dome, occupies its southern part. Also built by the Umayyad caliph, Al-Walid (705-715), it is located on the site of the Christian basilica, which the Crusaders thought was the site of the Temple of Solomon. It has been renovated repeatedly following earthquakes and measures 80 meters by 55 meters. Much larger than the Dome of the Rock, divided into seven naves, it can accommodate up to 5,000 worshippers. Its carved wooden pulpit and its central mosaic date to the 12th century; both were gifts offered by Saladin. The *minrab*, which is built on beautiful marble columns, also dates to that period.

Under the Crusaders, the mosque is first converted into a royal palace. In 1128, it houses a church, entrusted to the care of the Templars. Today we can still see traces of their stay: the interior Zacharia Chapel and the remains of an exterior monastery. In 1187, Saladin restores it to Muslim worship. In 1938 - 1943, it receives marble columns from Carrare from Mussolini and a cupola from King Farouk of Egypt. In 1951, King Abdallah of Jordan, accused of goodwill towards the Israelis, is assassinated on its steps. In 1969, an Australian fanatic ignites a fire to precipitate the coming of the savior. In 1977, it welcomes the Egyptian president, Anouar el-Sadat, who came to convince the Israelis of his desire for peace. In 2000, Ariel Sharon's visit to the Temple Mount triggers the uprising of the Palestinians, known as the El-Aksa Intifada.

A variety of other monuments are dispersed on the *haram ash-sharif*: the Dome of the Chain, which is situated at the entrance of the Dome of the Rock, is a square building surmounted by a concentric crown that the Crusaders named the Chapel of Saint John, the Lesser; delicately chiseled fountains, including Sebil Qait Bey, named after the Mamluk sultan who built it in 1487; some pulpits – *minbar* in Arabic – elaborately carved and dating to the period of the Mamluks; some smaller mosques, including Solomon's Throne, situated on the site where the king placed his throne in order to watch over the construction of the Temple; the tombs of saints and of illustrious personalities, such as Hussein ibn Ali, the king of Hedjaz (1916 – 1924), the father of Abdallah, the founder of the Hashemite Dynasty in Jordan; some Koranic institutions such as a theological school that dates back to the 18th century. There are vast, underground, vaulted halls that the Templars used as stables that are known ever since as King Solomon's Stables. An underground passage beneath the mosque leads to the Double Gate in the southern enclosure wall, which was one of the main entrances to Herod's Temple and perhaps even to that of Solomon. The rampart walk in the southeast corner of the *haram* is the pinnacle of the Temple, which Christian tradition identifies as the scene of the third temptation of Jesus:

The temptation of Jesus

The devil brought him to Jerusalem and set him on a pinnacle of the Temple and said to him: "If you are the Son of God, cast yourself down from here. For it is written: 'He will give the angels charge over you to keep you; they will bear you up with their hands so that you will not dash your foot against a stone.'" And Jesus answered him saying: "It is said: 'You will not tempt the Lord your God.'"

Luke 4, 9 - 12

An Islamic Museum, inside the Mosque of the Maghrebins, reconstructs Muslim life in the city throughout the centuries and displays Koran manuscripts from the Middle Ages, ancient arms, and architectural items taken from the Dome of the Rock and the El-Aksa Mosque...

The rock situated in the Dome of the Rock – *eben he-shetiyya* in Hebrew, *koublet es-sakhra* in Arabic – is considered the rock upon which Abraham bound his son, Isaac, in preparation for his sacrifice to God. It is also from this rock that Mohammed mounted the warhorse that took him to heaven. The Muslims scrupulously guard the exclusivity of their rights to these places. Although forbidden by rabbinic law to visit this site and anxious to prevent the sacrilege of venturing into the Holy of Holies that only the high priest was permitted to enter on the day of the Yom Kippur, the Jews are shocked by the religious expropriation of their most sacred site. There is a cave beneath the rock – that rabbinic legend calls *tehom* – and where, according to Muslim tradition – the souls of the dead are stranded, awaiting their resurrection. It is probably the place from where chaos will spread unless peace flourishes all around. Indisputably, it is the most sensitive and the sorest point on earth, if not the most central, as the great and veiled legend surrounding the city would have it...

[•]

In 750, the Abbassid Dynasty (750 – 1258), with its seat in Baghdad, succeeds that of the Umayyads (660 – 750). Its first caliphs continue to visit Jerusalem and to support its Koranic institutions. But their successors will very quickly loose interest and political agitation and earthquakes will alternately strike it. In 878, Egypt annexes the city together with all the Palestinian territory.

The Jews return to Jerusalem under the restrictions imposed by the Arabs. Pressed by the Christian Patriarch, Omar limits them to sixty families, to whom he allocates the section that extends to the southwest of the Temple Mount, which they occupy until their expansion outside the Old City in the middle of the 18th century. The custom to pray in front of the Wailing Wall dates back to this period.

The tensions between the religious communities will unceasingly rock the city. The Muslims regularly attack the Christians while the Jews collapse under the numerous taxes and the heavy labor imposed upon them. It is only thanks to the subsidies collected by the emissaries, who they send to the Diaspora, that the Jews manage to survive. There are some minor artisans, some merchants and above all, some scribes who are absorbed in writing the scrolls of the law and holy books. The Sanhedrin – the supreme political and religious authority – leaves Tiberias to settle in Jerusalem, but it no longer plays the decisive role it once played in the lives of the religious all over the world.

The city also attracts the Karaites, who come from Iraq and Persia and who do not recognize the authority of the rabbis or of the Talmud – they call themselves the *Abelei Zion*, the Mourners of Zion. They undergo a period of cultural development in the fields of linguistic research and especially of Biblical interpretation. The tensions between the two communities – the Rabbinites and the Karaites – often become disputes. Echoes of their rivalry can be perceived in one of the letters of accreditation provided to the emissaries entrusted with collecting subsidies in the Diaspora. Dated at the end of the 10th century, it reconstructs the general environment in which the Jews lived in Jerusalem:

A letter from Jerusalem

The eternal city, God's faithful, sends you the greetings of the leaders of the academies of Zion who reside in the city, which is the seat of the seventy-one members of the Sanhedrin and their disciples..., an unfortunate city, henceforth a widow, an orphan, abandoned and poor, with only a few exceptional scholars... Although lately many competitors and rivals (the Karaites) have arrived, the city continues to pray, begging the merciful God for its liberation...

We, the members of the Rabbinate community, a destitute community that lives near the site of the Temple, regret to inform you that we are constantly being harassed by the foreigners who have occupied the Temple Mount. We pray: "Oh God, how long will the adversary insult? How long will the enemy continue to blaspheme Your name?" (Psalms 74: 10). We will be somewhat relieved when we will be able to once again freely venture into the areas of the gates of the Temple as in other times, to pour out our prayers for the complete liberation of Jerusalem and the restoration of its Temple... Yes, there is a synagogue on the Temple Mount where our coreligionists assemble during the month of Tishri, lamenting over its stones, rolling in the dust, circling its walls and praying constantly.

It was God's will that the Muslim leaders would have mercy on us. After having invaded Palestine, recapturing it from the Edomites (the Roman Byzantines), the Arabs entered Jerusalem where the Jews showed them the location of the Temple. Since then, the latter live among them, agreeing to maintain the site and to keep it clean in exchange for the right to pray at it gates. They have also secured access to the Mount of Olives where the Divine Presence resides – the Shechina - in accordance with what is written in Ezekiel 11: 23: "And the glory of the Eternal rose over the center of the city and stood upon the mountain, which is on the east side of the city." This is where we pray on the holidays, facing the Temple of God, especially on Hoshana Rabba. We earnestly request God's blessing for all the members of Israel wherever they live. Those who remember Jerusalem will merit experiencing its joy..., which every person can earn by supporting its inhabitants. Life is extremely difficult here; there is very little food and the job options are very limited. Furthermore, our terrible neighbors impose heavy taxes and all sorts of fees. If we do not pay them, we will be denied the right to gather on the Mount of Olives... These

*unbearable tributes as well as the jugs of wine that we must
pour on a regular basis oblige us to borrow money at the
highest interest rates in order to avoid incarceration and
expulsion.*

*Come to our aid. Help us. Save us. It is in your interest for
we also pray for you.*

The Fatimids (909 – 1171) rise to power in Egypt. Thanks
to the intervention of the head of the Egyptian community,
Rabbi Paltiel, who has access to the court of the caliph, Al
Mouazziz (953 – 975), the restrictions against the Jews in
Jerusalem are eased. The Arab writer, Mouqadassi left us a
rather gloomy picture of life in the city:

A basin of scorpions

*Nevertheless, Jerusalem offers a series of drawbacks. It is
said – written, it seems, in Moses' Torah – that "Jerusalem
is a gold basin filled with scorpions". In fact, in no other
place will you find dirtier baths than those in the holy city, or
higher taxes. There are very few people of culture and there
are many Christians and they all lack polite manners. In the
markets, the taxes on all the items are exorbitant; there is a
guard posted at every door and no one is authorized to sell
basic products anywhere other than in the places designated
for that purpose. In this city, the oppressed have no recourse,
the poor are brutalized and the wealthy are envied. The jurist
consults are not consulted and the learned are not taken into
consideration. The schools are not frequented because no
classes are held there. Everywhere, the Christians and the
Jews act in a highhanded manner: the mosque, moreover,
is deserted, without a congregation, without an assembly of
scholars…*

Clashes between the Egyptians and the Bedouin tribes shake
the region. In 1009, the mad caliph, El-Hakem (996 – 1021)
persecutes Jews and Christians and destroys churches and
convents, including the Church of the Holy Sepulcher, which
he demolished with the blows of a pick and hammer, leaving
only some protrusions of Golgotha and parts of the rotunda

of Constantine. It is immediately rebuilt, but in 1033, it collapses in an earthquake. It will remain in ruins until the Byzantine emperor, Constantine XI Monomaque, restores it in 1048. The Christian community also participates in the reconstruction of the city that was partially destroyed by the earthquake. Its members undertake, in particular, raising the section of the wall that connects the Jaffa Gate to the Damascus Gate, assuring in this manner that the neighborhood will remain in their hands to this day. In 1074, the Turkish Seljuks invade the city, once again threatening its Christian inhabitants and sites. Reactions in Europe are especially intense – the conditions are favorable for the launching of a Crusade aimed at reoccupying the holy places…

THE CRUSADER CITY

The Crusaders capture the city on July 15th, 1099 at the end of a five-week siege. The troops from Flanders and those from northeastern France, led by Godfrey de Bouillon, seize the northeast sector, which the Muslims and Jews defended. The troops from Provence, led by Raymond de Saint-Gilles, enter the city from the direction of Mount Zion, while the Normans from Sicily enter from the northwest.[1] The city's inhabitants are massacred in great numbers. Some Jews will be sold as slaves in Europe where they will be bought back by their coreligionists in the Diaspora. The following is the testimony of the monk, Robert:

The attack by the Crusaders

On the second day of the third week, the 13th of June 1099, the French attacked Jerusalem, but they were unable to capture it on that day. Nonetheless, their work was not in vain; they knocked down the outer wall and pitched their ladders against the main wall. Had they been greater in number, this first assault would have been the last. Those who climbed the ladders fought the enemy at length with the blows of their swords and javelins. Many of our men died during this assault; but the losses were even greater on the side of the Saracens. Nightfall put an end to the fighting and permitted both sides to rest. However, the ineffectiveness of this first effort caused our army a great deal of work and suffering; for our troops remained without bread for ten days until our ships had reached the port of Jaffa. In addition, they suffered enormously from thirst; the Pool of Siloam could barely provide the men with enough water and we had to lead the horses and the other animals, accompanied by a large escort, to water six thousand feet from the camp...

Although the fleet that arrived at Jaffa supplied provisions to the besieged, they, nonetheless, suffered from thirst. It was so severe during the siege that the soldiers would dig up the ground and would press the humid clumps against their

1. A tower was erected at the northeast corner of the wall for the surveillance of the approaches to the city called: the Tancrede Tower, to the Christians, who launched an attack against the city from this point; the Tower of Goliath, to the Muslims, who identify this as the site of the battle between David and Goliath.

mouths; they would also lick the rocks that were moist with dew; they would drink fetid water that lay in the fresh hides of buffalo and other animals; many abstained from eating with the hope of mollifying their thirst with hunger...

During that time, the generals had large pieces of wood brought from quite a distance to build machines and some war towers. When the towers were completed, Godfrey placed his to the east of the city; Count de Saint-Gilles set one exactly like it to the south. On the fifth day of the week, once they were set up in this way, the Crusaders fasted and distributed alms to the poor. On the sixth day, which was the 12th of July, the sun rose brightly and the elite warriors climbed the war towers and pitched the ladders against the walls of Jerusalem. Upon seeing themselves besieged by such a large multitude, the illegitimate children of the holy city were stunned and shook with fear. But since their final hour threatened them from every side and death hung over their heads, certain that they would die, their only thought was to exact a high price for what remained of their lives...

While some fought in this way on the walls of the city, others walked in a procession around the same walls carrying crosses, relics and holy altars. For part of the day, it was unclear who had the upper hand, but at the same hour that the Savior died, a warrior named l'Etolde who was fighting in Godfrey's war tower, was the first to jump on the ramparts of the city, followed by Guicher who was reputed to have overcome a lion; Godfrey was the third to jump and all the other knights hastened to follow their leader. Abandoning their bows and arrows, they grabbed their swords. Seeing this, their enemies quit the walls, throwing themselves to the ground in the city, chased by Christ's soldiers who were shouting loudly.

Count de Saint-Gilles, who, on his part, was attempting to move his machines closer to the city, heard the clamor. "Why are we tarrying here", he asked his soldiers? The French were in control of Jerusalem; their voices and their blows resounded there. He then promptly advanced towards the gate near David's Citadel; he called out to those inside the fortress to surrender. As soon as the emir recognized Count de Saint-Gilles, he opened the door and entrusted himself to the faith of this venerable warrior.

But together with the French, Godfrey endeavored to avenge the Christian blood shed within the walls of Jerusalem and to punish the infidels for the outrage that they had inflicted on the pilgrims. No other battle had ever seemed so terrible... Guicher and many thousands of select warriors split the Saracens in half from their heads to their waists or cut them in half at the waist. Not one of our soldiers seemed to be intimidated, for no one resisted. The enemies sought only to flee, but it was impossible for them to escape; rushing headlong in a crowd, they blocked each other. The few who managed to escape shut themselves up in Solomon's Temple where they defended themselves for quite a long time. As the sun began to set, our soldiers invaded the Temple; enraged, they massacred everyone there. The carnage was such that the mutilated cadavers were swept away by the blood that flowed as far as the parvis; hands and arms floated in the blood and were united with bodies to which they did not belong.

During the 7th century, the city becomes the capital of the Latin Kingdom in Jerusalem (1099 – 1187) under Christian domination. In 1115, King Baudoin I, concerned with repopulating the city that had been emptied of its inhabitants, succeeds in attracting Christians from Trans-Jordan – the Syrians – to whom they allocate the ancient Jewish Quarter located in the northeastern part of the city – the present day Muslim Quarter that is crossed by the Via Dolorosa. The Teutons settle in the actual Jewish Quarter, building the Saint Mary of the Teutons Church.[2] The Armenians settle in the quarter where they remain to this day in the southwestern part of the city around the Saint John of the Armenians Church.[3] The main street – the Armenians' Street – evidently ended in a cul-de-sac until 1177, when a gate is opened – the Belcayre Gate – to reach Mount Zion where Christian refugees from the coastal plain find refuge from the attacks by Saladin's troops. The Templars settle on the Temple Mount, converting its two mosques into churches – the Dome of the Rock becomes Templum Domini and the Al-Aksa Mosque, which was likened to Solomon's Temple, becomes Templum Solomonis – and setting up their arsenals, their warehouses, their ateliers and their stables in the Herodian basements.

2. The ruins of the church are preserved in an archeological park.

3. According to Christian tradition, the cathedral stands on the site of the home of James, Jesus' brother, whose bones it received in the 4th century. It also houses the skull of James, John the Baptist's brother, who was decapitated by King Agrippa in 44. The main outline of the actual cathedral dates back to the Crusader Period; it was built and richly decorated thanks to donations from Armenian dignitaries.

They, moreover, erect an impressive wall – the Templars' Wall – to protect the southern side of the Temple Mount. The northwest sector, which housed the forum under the Romans and the Byzantines, is divided among the knights who belonged to various orders. The Hospitallers, whose name was drawn from the medical care that they provided to the pilgrims, open a large hospital in the quarter that is granted to them – the present day Mouristan.[4]

4. Mouristan means hospital in Kurdish. The Muslims continue to use the premises as a hospital. In 1869, this area was entrusted to the Germans who built the Redeemer's Church on the site of the Crusader church, the Latin Saint Mary Church.

The layout of the streets in the city under the Crusaders was similar, more or less, to the layout of the Roman and Byzantine city. Two main arteries ran from north to south. The busiest went from the Damascus Gate – called the Saint-Etienne Gate – to the Zion Gate, which was sub-divided into three passageways that circumscribed three markets. The farthest to the west – nicknamed "the Badly Cooked" – offered all sorts of soups, foods and sauces; the central market, which depended on the work of the Saint Anne Church to bring in revenues, sold all kinds of herbs; the farthest to the east, which was evidently covered, offered a large variety of products. The markets opened on to a square at the intersection of the city's two busiest arteries, which the Latin and Syrian money changers divided among themselves. The street then continued up to the Zion Gate along the path of the Byzantine Cardo, separating into two streets lined with boutiques, Via Portae Sion and Via Arcus Jude, which, in turn, delimited a market of sorts – on the present day section of the Byzantine Cardo that was unearthed in the Eighties. The second north-south artery ran from the Damascus Gate to the Dung Gate – then called the Tanners Postern. Another artery that ran perpendicular to the north-south artery, ran from the Jaffa Gate – then known as David's Gate – through the grains market, then along private residences up to the money changers square, continuing to the Beautiful Gate – *Porta Preciosa* – on the Western Wall, which led to the Temple Mount.

The Crusaders rebuild entire sections of the wall especially during the final years of their rule when the Muslims begin to threaten their domination. They will also restore the gates, including the Damascus Gate – named Porta Sancti Stephani – which is apparently restored a second time between 1229 and 1244. David's Citadel, which the Crusaders call the

Fortress or the Tower of Pisans, is enlarged westward in order to house the king's garrison, the army's granaries and the administration of customs, assuming the lines and the appearance that it has today. The royal palace that was first located on the Temple Mount is established on the site of one of Herod's palaces. The Latin Patriarch who replaces the Orthodox Patriarch is granted the area in the vicinity of the Church of the Holy Sepulcher.[5] The Churches of the Holy Sepulcher are united under one roof, and in 1149 the new complex is inaugurated with great pomp and ceremony. New churches are built or rebuilt everywhere: small parish churches that usually consisted of one nave and an apse, which are later converted into mosques or even into boutiques; middle size churches measuring approximately 20 meters in length, composed of a nave and a transept with three apses; large churches that, in general, commemorated events in the life of Jesus. The Roman style Saint Anne Church[6], located in the northeastern part of the city on the consecrated birthplace of Mary, is adjacent to two pools[7], that of Israel and that of Bethseda, either of which may have been the purifying pool where Christ cured the paralytic. The Saint Mary Magdalene Church, also located in the northeast, is considered the Jacobite center. Many churches are built on Mount Zion, and the Church of Mary's Tomb in the Josaphat Valley, which commemorates the place where, according to apocryphal tradition, the Virgin was temporarily entombed, replaces a 5th century Byzantine sanctuary. It is demolished by the Persians, rebuilt by the Crusaders, and once again destroyed by Saladin. The church had the shape of a cross with Mary's tomb in the center. Some chapels were dedicated to the Virgin's parents and to the wives of the Crusader kings.

5. The Patriarch's residence was converted into a mosque and a Dervish Quarter under Saladin.

6. The Saint Anne Church, see p.88.

7. The pools used to purify the victims destined to be sacrificed in Jerusalem.

THE VIA DOLOROSA

Most of the traditions related to the Christian pilgrimage would arise during this period, including the tradition to retrace the route that Christ took to his crucifixion. The *Via Dolorosa* would, nonetheless, undergo numerous modifications throughout the centuries. Located in the Muslim Quarter of the Old City, it begins at the reception area on the site of the Saint Anne Church and is accessed through the Saint Etienne Gate or the Lions Gate. The *first station*, the place where Jesus was sentenced, is located in a corner on the grounds of the El-Omariyye School, which was built on the site of the Crusader Crown of Thorns Chapel that was destroyed in an earthquake in 1927.

Denounced by Judas, Jesus was first summoned by the Sanhedrin – the supreme political-religious authority of the Jews – that accused him of blasphemy and then by the Roman procurator, Pontius Pilate who like his predecessors would spend Passover in Jerusalem in order to better watch over the city, which was thronged with tens of thousands of pilgrims. He may have resided in the Antonia Fortress[8] that overlooked the Temple:

8. The Antonia Fortress, see p.65.

The sentencing of Jesus

Pilate then took Jesus and scourged him. The soldiers platted a crown of thorns and placed it on his head and put a purple robe on him. They said to him: "Hail, king of the Jews!" And they struck him with their hands. Pilate went out again and said to the Jews: "Behold, I bring him to you that you may know that I find no fault in him." Then Jesus came forth, wearing the crown of thorns and the purple robe. And Pilate said to them: "Behold the man!" When the high priests and the officers saw him, they cried out, saying: "Crucify him! Crucify him!" Pilate said to them: "Take him and crucify him for I find no fault in him." The Jews replied: "We have a law and according to that law he must die for he made himself the Son of God!"

When Pilate heard this, he was more frightened. Returning to the Hall of Justice, he said to Jesus: "From where do you come?" But Jesus did not answer. Pilate then said to him: "You refuse to speak to me! Don't you know that I have the power to crucify you and the power to release you?" Jesus answered him: "You could have no power at all over me if it were not given to you from above; therefore, he that delivered me to you bears the greater sin." Henceforth, Pilate sought to release him, but the Jews cried out, saying: "If you release this man, you are not Caesar's friend! For whoever makes himself a king, speaks against Caesar!"

When Pilate heard these words, he brought Jesus forth and sat in the judgment seat in a place called Lithostrotos – *in Hebrew,* Gabatha. *On that day, preparations for Passover were being made and on the sixth hour, Pilate said to the Jews: "Behold your king!" But they cried out: "Away with him! Away with him! Crucify him!" Pilate said to them: "Shall I crucify your king?" The high priests answered: "We have no king but Caesar!" Then he delivered him to them to be crucified.*

John 19: 1 - 16

An archway, the vestige of an arch of triumph built in the 2nd century in honor of Hadrian, straddles the Way of the Cross. Believing it to be a Herodian vestige, the Crusaders identify the site underneath the arc as the place where Pilate exclaimed: "Ecce homo! This is the man!" Its extension – the northern archway – is integrated in the choir of the Sisters of Zion Basilica. Built on a part of the ruins of the Antonia Fortress, it shelters the underground hall – the Lithostrotos – where Pontius Pilate summoned Jesus. The French writer, Pierre Loti, left us his impressions of the convent during his visit in 1894:

Pilate's Hall of Justice

The Sisters of Zion have one of the most enviable locations in Jerusalem. First of all, the Roman Ecce Homo Arch crosses the Via Dolorosa in front of their convent and continues to a second similar arch, which has been left intact with its rough and reddish, old stones. It makes a strange impression: it is probably the remains of Pilate's Hall of Justice, standing in the middle of the stark white chapel, decorated moreover in a simple and highly distinctive manner.

Upon digging up the ground under the convent, they then discovered other sensational ruins: a Roman guardroom of sorts that, obviously, was used by the soldiers at the Hall of Justice, the beginning of a street with an ancient pavement that ran in the same direction as the Via Dolorosa...

What is unusually striking about these excavations is the preservation of the old pavement and the polish of its reddish stones, which have retained the worn marks of the footsteps, after having been buried underground for centuries... and there is even a game crudely engraved on one of the paving stones that is identical to one we play today! A game that the Roman soldiers had drawn to pass the time while on guard duty...

The game on the ground draws and holds my attention... Now, I can almost see them, Pilate's soldiers, kneeling to play there while Jesus is being interrogated in the Hall of Justice. In my mind, unintentionally, spontaneously, the scenes of the Passion are reconstructed with their intimate realities and with their small and human details; without the proliferation of large crowds, they appear to me there, so strangely present, stripped of the halo with which the centuries have surrounded them, diminished – as things appeared at the time that they occurred – and undoubtedly reduced to their true proportions... the small procession of criminals sentenced to death, dragging their crosses on the old, red pavement, passes before me... it is the dawn of some new cloudy, spring day in Judea; they are passing right here between these walls that had been buried for so long, which my hand presses against; they are passing by, accompanied by a horde of early rising vagabonds, for the most part. Some groups of disciples and women who had anxiously stayed awake throughout the cold night, weeping around the fire, timidly follow them at a distance... The event that had renewed the world and that after nineteen hundred years still draws impassioned multitudes to Jerusalem, bringing them to their knees to kiss the stones, seemed to me at that moment to be an obscure, abominable crime, carried out in haste in the early morning in the middle of a city, barely disturbing its daily routine...

P. Loti, *Jerusalem*

The Convent of the Sisters of Zion is built at the initiative of a converted Jew from Strasbourg, Alphonse Ratisbonne. In 1855, he arrives in Palestine to establish a community and a school, entrusted with the task of converting his ex-coreligionists. In 1857, he purchases the plots of land around the arch.

The *second station* on the Via Dolorosa is at the Chapel of Condemnation, which was placed under the authority of the Franciscans along with the Chapel of the Flagellation and its convent:

The condemnation

Then the governor's soldiers took Jesus into the Hall of Justice and the whole cohort gathered around him. They stripped him and put a scarlet robe on him. And when they had platted a crown of thorns, they placed it on his head and put a reed in his right hand. Bowing down on their knees before him, they mocked him, saying: "Hail, king of the Jews!" They spit on him, took the reed and smote him on the head. After they had mocked him, they removed the robe and led him away to be crucified.

Matthew 27: 27 - 31

The Chapel of the Flagellation, which is built during the Middle Ages, is restored for the first time in 1883 and again in 1927. Three stained glass windows, from left to right, depict Pontius Pilate washing his hands clean of the murder of Christ, the flagellation of Christ and the liberation of Barrabas. The Chapel of the Condemnation is rebuilt in 1903 on the ruins of a Byzantine church. It has some stained glass windows that also portray scenes from the Passion of Christ. The convent, built in 1927, houses a well-stocked library of Christian books as well as a museum. The staircase that Jesus used to descend from the Hall of Justice to the street is now in the Scala Santa of Rome Church. The Greek Church is built in 1906 on part of a site that is also presumed to be the site of Pilate's Hall of Justice. It has niches hollowed out in the rock; one of them is said to be the cell in which Jesus was detained and the other, Barrabas' cell.

The *third station,* the place where Jesus fell down for the first time, is marked by a column, built into the wall of a boutique that was converted into a chapel.

The *fourth station* is the place where, according to the Tradition of the Fathers, Mary met her son as he carried the cross. A 19th century traveler, the French writer, Chateaubriand, dedicates these lines to the meeting between the Virgin and Christ:

The encounter with Mary

Saint Boniface said that the Virgin fell as if half-dead and was unable to utter a single word: Nec verbum dicere potuit. *Saint Anselme affirmed that Christ greeted her with these words:* Salve, mater*! Since Mary was at the foot of the cross, this account of the Fathers is merely very probable; faith and its traditions are not at all incompatible: they demonstrate to what extent the marvelous and sublime story of the Passion is engraved in the memory of men. The elapse of eighteen centuries, the endless persecutions, the eternal revolutions, the ever-growing ruins could not erase nor hide the trail of a mother who came to weep for her son.*

R. Chateaubriand, *Itinerary from Paris to Jerusalem*

The *fourth station* is commemorated by the Armenian Church of Notre Dame of Pamoyson, which was built in 1881 at the site where mosaics of a 5th or 6th century Byzantine church and the ruins of a Frank church were excavated. There is a pair of sandals on one of the mosaics, which a Slav tradition identifies as the place where the Virgin stood.

The *fifth station,* the place where Simon, the Cyrenian, helped Jesus carry his cross, is at the intersection of the Via Dolorosa and El-Wad Street:

The assistance of Simon

And as they led him away, they took hold of Simon, the Cyrenian, who was coming from the country and laid the cross on him to carry it behind Jesus.

Luke 23: 26

The *sixth station* is the place where Veronica, who accompanied Jesus along the route to his crucifixion, wiped the perspiration off his face. The house of Saint Veronica, built in 1883, commemorates this station. The cloth that Veronica used, which preserved the imprint of Christ's face, served to cure the Roman emperor, Tiberius. It was placed in the Saint Peter's Church in Rome.

The *seventh station,* the place where Jesus fell a second time, is at the intersection of the Via Dolorosa and Suq Khan Ez-Zeit Street. It is also said to be the location of the Judicial Gate that Jesus passed through to leave the city to reach Golgotha or Calvary. A Coptic Chapel where one of the columns of the Cardo stands commemorates this fall.

The *eighth station* where the encounter with the weeping women took place is in front of the Greek Orthodox Monastery of Charalampos:

The weeping women

A great company of people followed him, including women who wept and lamented him. Turning to them, Jesus said: "Daughters of Jerusalem, do not weep for me but for yourselves and your children…"

Luke 23: 27 - 28

The *ninth station* is at the place where Jesus fell for the third time, marked by a column inside the Ethiopian Coptic Convent that is built over the Saint Helena Chapel.

The *tenth station* where Jesus' garments were divided is on the periphery of the Church of the Holy Sepulcher:

The division of garments

When they came to the place called Golgotha, which means a place of the skull, they gave him vinegar mixed with gall to drink. Upon tasting it, he would not drink it. After they crucified him, they divided his garments by casting lots.

Matthew 27: 33 - 35

The chapel that commemorates this station, which is not open to the public but can be seen through a skylight, was used by the Crusaders to reach Golgotha.

The *eleventh station* that is marked by an altar commemorates the crucifixion:

The crucifixion

They sat there and watched over him. They had written his accusation and set it above his head: "This is Jesus, the king of the Jews". Two thieves had been crucified with him, one to his right and another to his left. The passers-by reviled him, wagging their heads, saying: "You who destroys the Temple and rebuilds it in three days, save yourself; if you are the Son of God, come down from the cross!" The high priests, together with the scribes and the elders, also mocked him, saying: "He saved others, but cannot save himself! If he is the King of Israel, let him come down from the cross and we will believe him! He placed his trust in God, let God deliver him now if He will for he said: 'I am the Son of God!'" Even the thieves who were crucified with him insulted him in the same manner.

Matthew 27: 36 - 44

The *twelfth station*, marked by the Greek altar of Golgotha, commemorates the death of Jesus:

Jesus' death

From the sixth hour (noon), there was darkness over all the land until the ninth hour (three o'clock). At about the ninth hour, Jesus cried out in a loud voice, saying: "Eli, Eli, la ma azavtani?" That is, "my God, my God, why have You forsaken me?" Upon hearing this, some of those who were standing there said: "He is calling for Elijah!" Immediately, one of them ran and took a sponge, filled it with vinegar, put it on a reed and gave him to drink. The others said: "Wait! Let's see whether Elijah will come to save him!" But Jesus cried out again with a loud voice and yielded his spirit. And behold, the veil of the Temple was rent in two from the top to the bottom; the earth quaked and the rocks crumbled; the graves opened and the bodies of many of the saints were resuscitated. They left the graves after his resurrection and went into the holy city where they appeared before many people. When the centurion and those who were with him watching over Jesus witnessed the earthquake and the things that occurred, they were overcome with great fear and said: "Truly this was the son of God."

Matthew 27: 45 - 54

The *thirteenth station* at the altar of the Madonna marks the place where Pilate delivered the body of Jesus:

The delivery of the body

There were many women there looking on from a distance; they had followed Jesus from the Galilee, ministering to him. Mary Magdalene, Mary the mother of Joseph and James and the mother of Zebedee's children were among them. When it was evening, a wealthy man named Joseph, who was also a disciple of Jesus from Arimathaea, came. He went to Pilate and requested the body of Jesus. Pilate ordered that the body be delivered to him.

Matthew 27: 55 - 58

The *fourteenth station*, the location of the sepulcher – at the Holy Sepulcher shelter – is on the floor beneath the church's rotunda:

When Joseph had taken the body, he wrapped it in a clean linen cloth and laid it in his own new tomb, which he had hewn out in the rock; he then rolled a large stone over the entrance and departed.

Matthew 27: 59 - 60

Since the Middle Ages, the Franciscans, who have contributed greatly to the elaboration of the Christian pilgrimage traditions, cross the Via Dolorosa every Friday afternoon, bearing a heavy cross.

THE HOLY SEPULCHER

The Church of the Holy Sepulcher appears to be an architectural reconstruction of the Passion of Christ at Golgotha – a knoll located outside of the ramparts of Jerusalem that draws its name from the Hebrew *gugoleth* and the Aramaic *golgotha*, which means "skull" and whose Latin translation is Calvary. A visitor to this basilica, which is contested by the Catholics, the Greek Orthodox, the Armenians, the Copts, and the Ethiopians, inevitably strays, losing his way – in spite of the maps and the guides, he does not know how to find his way in this maze of sanctuaries where the faithful wander in every direction, overcome by an uncommon religious zeal. He, moreover, very quickly yields to the vertigo induced by the sacred, overwhelmed by the scent of the incense and the wax, lulled by the incantations, restrained by the most extreme humility – bowing before the mystery. Pilgrims unceasingly offer us their impressions throughout the long centuries. In 1806, Chateaubriand, one of the first to renew the tradition of the pilgrimage at the beginning of the 19th century, writes:

The concert of churches

The Church of the Holy Sepulcher, which is composed of many churches, built on uneven ground and illuminated by a multitude of lamps, is unusually mysterious; the darkness that reigns there is conducive to piety and meditation. Christian priests of various sects live in different parts of the complex. From the heights of the archways, where they lodge like nesting doves, from the far end of the chapels and basements, their canticles are heard at every hour of the day and night; the organ of Latin monks, the cymbals of the Abyssinian (Ethiopian) priests, the voice of the Greek monk, the prayer of the Armenian recluse, a kind of moan of a Coptic friar, reach our ears in turn or all at the same time; you don't know from where all those concerts are coming; you inhale the scent of the incense without perceiving the hand that burns it; you only see the priest passing far behind the columns, lost in the shadow of the temple, on his way to celebrate the most formidable of mysteries at the very place where they had unfolded.

R. Chateaubriand, *Itinerary from Paris to Jerusalem*

The main outlines of the actual sanctuary, which date back to the Crusader Period, unite within the same Roman church: the Rotunda of the Resurrection – the Anastasis Rotunda – a 4th century basilica, retouched and embellished, that stood over the sepulcher hollowed out in the rock, a cloister above the Saint Helena Crypt and the pit of the Finding of the Cross, as well as buildings where the canons of the Church of the Holy Sepulcher lived. The new basilica is consecrated on July 15th, 1149. Since then, it incessantly undergoes remodeling, especially after the fire in 1808, and is the setting of rivalries between the Christian communities that are anxious to assure for themselves the custodianship of the plots of this holy land.

The façade of the Church of the Holy Sepulcher, which has two imposing porticos, dates back to the 12th century. The entrance opens on to a parvis where Philippe d'Aubigny's epitaph is housed, protected by iron bars. D'Aubigny was the preceptor of Henry III of England who participated in the Crusades under Frederic II in 1228, and who requested that he be buried at the entrance of the church in order to merit being tread upon by the pilgrims. A staircase to the right leads to a chapel that the Crusaders dedicated to Mary under the name of Our Lady of the Franks – today it is known as the Chapel of Saint Mary, the Egyptian. It is the *tenth station* on the Way of the Cross. There are chapels and convents dispersed here and there in the parvis. To the left, Saint James of the Greeks Chapel shelters the tombs of Crusaders, Saint John, the Forty Martyrs… To the right are the Greek convents of Saint Abraham on the site where the ram of the sacrifice was caught by the horns, Saint John of the Armenians and Saint Michael of the Copts. During his visit in 1894, Pierre Loti left us his first impressions:

The entrance to the sanctuary

Convents and chapels that form the high, reddish-brown, stone walls, which line the sides of the square, have the appearance of fortresses. At the far end, the dark, crumbling, broken façade of the Church of the Holy Sepulcher rises above the rest, having taken on the uneven appearance of a huge rock; it has two enormous doors from the 12th century that are framed with strangely archaic ornamentation; one is blocked shut; the other, which is wide open, allows you to see thousands of small flames in the dark interior. Songs, cries, discordant, mournful lamentations escape with the scents of incense...

Oh! What an unexpected and unforgettable impression upon entering for the first time! A maze of dark sanctuaries from every epoch, of every style, inter-communicate through openings, porticos and superb colonnades, – or small, concealed doors, basement windows and caves. Some are raised, like high dais where groups of women wearing long veils can be seen in the indefinite background; the others are underground where you mingle with the shadows between seeping, black, rock walls that have remained intact. All this is in partial darkness except for a few large rays that accentuate the surrounding darkness even more; all this is infinitely star-studded with the small flames of the silver or gold lamps that descend from the thousands of vaults. And there are crowds everywhere, moving around in confusion as in the tower of Babel or standing, more or less grouped by nationality, around some gold tabernacles where a service is being conducted...

Psalms, lamentations, songs of joy fill the high vaults or vibrate in the funereal sonority underground; the nasal chants of the Greeks, interrupted by the cries of the Copts... and in all these voices, an intensification of tears and prayers blend their dissonance and unite them; in the end, they become, as a whole, indescribably and extraordinary, rising from the entire place like a great wail of men and the ultimate cry of their distress in the face of death...

P. Loti, *Jerusalem*

Candlesticks frame the Rock of the Unction upon which, according to the Latin tradition, they placed the body of Jesus to be embalmed, and, according to the Greek Orthodox, to be mourned by the Virgin:

The Rock of the Unction

And behold, there was a man named Joseph, a counselor,
who was good and just. He had not consented to their plans
or their deeds. Originally from Arimathaea, a Jewish city,
he also was awaiting the kingdom of God. This man went to
Pilate and requested the body of Jesus. He took it down from
the cross, wrapped it in linen and laid it in a sepulcher hewn
in stone wherein no man had ever been laid. It was a day of
preparation and the Sabbath was drawing near. The women
who had accompanied him from the Galilee also followed
Joseph and saw the sepulcher and how his body was laid.
Then they returned and prepared spices and ointments.

Luke 23: 50 - 56

To the left of the Rock of the Unction, a rounded rock
indicates the place where the women stood.

Christ's tomb is sheltered in the passageway in the rotunda.
It is accessed through the vestibule of the Chapel of the
Angel where a fragment of the rock upon which the angel of
the Resurrection sat is enshrined on a pedestal:

The Chapel of the Angel

At the end of the Sabbath, as the first day of the week began
to dawn, Mary Magdalene and the other Mary came to see
the sepulcher. And behold, there was a great earthquake for
the angel of the Lord descended from heaven and came to
roll back the stone and sat upon it. His countenance was like
lightning and his raiment was white as snow. Fearing him,
the guards trembled and became as dead men. The angel
spoke and said to the women: "Do not fear. I know that you
seek Jesus who was crucified. He is not here for he has risen
as he said. Come and see the place where he lay. Then go
quickly and tell his disciples that he has risen from the dead.
Behold, he goes before you to the Galilee. You will see him
there. I have informed you." They quickly departed from the
sepulcher with fear and great joy, and ran to bring the news
to his disciples. And behold, they met Jesus on their way to
tell the disciples and he said to them: "All hail." They came
to him, held on to his feet and worshipped him. And Jesus

said to them: *"Do not be afraid. Go tell my brothers to go to the Galilee where they will see me."*

Matthew 28: 1 - 10

In the sepulcher, a marble bench covers the place where Jesus' body was laid. On October 29th, 1832, Lamartine writes:

The sepulcher of the ancient world

...we again descended into the church and entered the monument that serves as a rock curtain or envelope for the tomb itself. It is divided into two small sanctuaries: The first one houses the rock where the angel sat when he responded to the women: "He is not here for he has risen"; the second and last sanctuary encloses the Sepulcher that is covered with a kind of white marble sarcophagus, which surrounds and completely hides the crude rock itself that was hollowed out to make the Sepulcher. Gold and silver lamps that are permanently lit illuminate this chapel and incense is burned night and day; the air we breathe is warm and scented. Separated from the first sanctuary by a silk, crimson curtain, we entered it one at a time, individually, without permitting any of the ministering priests of the temple to enter with us. We did not want anyone's attention to disturb the solemnity of the place or the privacy of the impressions that it could inspire in each one of us according to the degree and the nature of one's faith in the great event that this tomb commemorates; each one of us remained there for approximately a quarter of an hour and no one came out with his eyes dry. Whatever form the inner musings, the reading of history, the years and the vicissitudes of the heart and of the mind of man may have given to the religious sentiment in his soul, whether he observed Christianity to the letter, his mother's dogmas, or whether he maintained a philosophical, intellectual Christianity, whether he considered Christ a crucified God or simply the holiest of men, deified by virtue, inspired by the supreme truth, who died in order to bear witness to his Father, whether in his eyes, Jesus was the son of God or the son of man, the Divinity that became man or the deified humanity, Christianity remained the religion of

his memories, his heart and his imagination. Christianity has not vanished into the thin air of the century or of life, and the soul in which it was poured still preserves its initial scent; the appearance of the sites and the visible monuments of its first cult renews the impressions it made in him, causing him to shake with solemn tremors. To the Christian or to the philosopher, to the moralist or to the historian, this tomb marks the boundary that separates two worlds, the ancient and the new; it is the point of departure of an idea that has renewed the universe, of a civilization that has transformed everything, of a word that has echoed all over the world: this tomb is the sepulcher of the old world and the cradle of the new world; no other rock on earth has been the foundation of so vast a building, no other tomb has been so fecund, no other doctrine that has been buried for three days or three centuries has ever broken the rock with which man had sealed it in such a victorious manner, nor has so flatly contradicted death by a resurrection that is so dazzling and so perpetual.

Lamartine, *Voyage to the East*

The Chapel of the Copts is behind the Sepulcher towards the west. Facing it, the obscure Chapel of the Jacobites opens on to the tomb of Joseph of Arimathaea, which is hewn in the rock. The Latin section of the church extends to the north of the rotunda where the convent church of the Franciscan Fathers, a sacristy that preserves Godfrey de Bouillon's sword, a convent, the Saint Mary of the Franciscans Chapel where Christ appeared to the Virgin after his resurrection, and the altar of Mary Magdalene are located.The columns of the Roman church that include some Corinthian columns dating back to the 4th century form the Arches of the Virgin. The Holy Prison is a nook hollowed out in the rock where Christ was incarcerated before being crucified. The Saint Longin Chapel is consecrated to the Roman soldier who pierced Jesus with his spear:

The thrust of the spear
Because it was the day of preparation and the Jews were concerned that the bodies not be left on the crosses during

the Sabbath – for the Sabbath was a very important day –
they requested that Pilate have their legs broken and that
they be taken away. Then the soldiers came and broke the
legs of the first and then of the other who had been crucified
with him. When they came to Jesus and saw that he was
already dead, they did not break his legs. But one of the
soldiers pierced his side with a spear and blood and water
immediately came out.

John 19: 31 - 34

The Chapel of the Division of the Raiment preserves the
account of the division of Christ's clothing among the
soldiers after the crucifixion. It is dedicated to the memory of
the victims of the massacre perpetrated by the Turks against
the Armenians during the First World War. The Chapel
of Insults perpetuates Christ's humiliation by the Roman
soldiers. Between the two chapels, a staircase descends
to the Armenian crypt of St. Helena where Constantine's
mother found the holy Cross. The walls hewn in the rock are
covered with crosses. The roof rests upon arches formed by
four Byzantine columns. The light from the dome above the
altar creates a contemplative atmosphere.

Some stairs lead to the Catholic Chapel of the Finding of the
Holy Cross that is set up in a cistern where the statue of St.
Helena stands, which, together with the altar, was a gift from
Maximilien d'Autriche, the emperor of Mexico.

A staircase leads up to Calvary. There are two chapels located
above: the Catholic Chapel of the Crucifixion, which has
reliefs in brass depicting scenes from the Passion of Christ
that were produced in 1588 by the Dominican, Domenico
Portigiani, and commissioned by the cardinal, Ferdinand de
Medicis, and the Greek Chapel of the Crucifixion or of the
Raising of the Cross, whose altar is above the hole where the
cross was driven into the ground.

An altar between the two chapels – the *Stabat Mater* –
commemorates the site where Saint Mary stood during
the crucifixion. The Greek Chapel of Adam, which draws
its name from the legend claiming that Adam's skull was
preserved at Golgotha, is located underneath Golgotha.
On both sides of the entrance, two benches designate the

emplacements of the tombs of the first Crusader kings – Godfrey de Bouillon and Baudoin I – whose remains were removed in the 18th century, and whose tombs were pillaged by Greek monks in 1808.

The Greek Orthodox Church has custody of the basilica. A cup in the middle of the choir marks the center of the world, the spot of salvation according to the passage in the book of Ezekiel:

The center of the world

Thus says the Lord God: "It will come to pass on that day that ideas will come to mind and you will devise evil plans. You will say: 'I will go to the land of unwalled cities, to the peaceful inhabitants living there in safety without walls and without bars or gates' to take spoil and to plunder, to raise your hand against the repopulated ruins and against a people gathered from the nations, who have acquired wealth and property and who inhabit the center of the world."

Ezekiel 38: 10 - 12

The tower of the German Lutheran Church of the Redeemer that is outside of the Church of the Holy Sepulcher offers an excellent panoramic view of the Old City.

The American writer, Mark Twain (1835 – 1910), although tortured by religious self-doubt, wrote :

A holy remembrance

When one enters the Church of the Holy Sepulchre, the Sepulchre itself is the first thing he desires to see, and really is almost the first thing he does see. The next thing he has a strong yearning to see is the spot where the Saviour was crucified. But this they exhibit last. It is the crowning glory of the place. One is grave and thoughtful when he stands in the little Tomb of the Saviour – he could not well be otherwise in such a place – but he has not the slightest possible belief that ever the Lord lay there, and so the interest he feels in the spot is very, very greatly marred by that reflection. He looks at the place where Mary stood, in another part of the church, and where John stood and Mary Magdalen; where the mob derided the Lord; where the angel sat; where the crown of thorns was found and the true Cross; where the risen Saviour appeared – he looks at all these places with interest but with the same conviction he felt in the case of the Sepulchre, that there is nothing genuine about them and that they are imaginary holy places created by the monks. But the place of the Crucifixion affects him differently. He fully believes that he is looking upon the very spot where the Saviour gave up his life. He remembers that Christ was very celebrated long before he came to Jerusalem; he knows that his fame was so great that the crowds followed him all the time; he is aware that his entry into the city produced a stirring sensation, and that his reception was a kind of ovation; he cannot overlook the fact that when he was crucified there were very many in Jerusalem who believed that he was the true Son of God.

[...]

The Church of the Holy Sepulchre – the most sacred locality on earth to millions and millions of men and women and children, the noble and the humble, bond and free. In its history from the first, and its tremendous associations, it is the most illustrious edifice in Christendom. With all its claptrap sideshows and unseemly impostures of every kind, it is still grand, reverend, venerable – for a good died there; for fifteen hundred years its shrines have been wet with the tears of the pilgrims from the earth's remotest confines; for more than two hundred, the most gallant knights that ever wielded sword wasted their lives away in a struggle to seize it and hold it sacred from infidel pollution. Even in our own day a war that cost millions of treasure and rivers of blood was fought because two rival nations claimed the sole right to put a new dome upon it. History is full of this old Church of the Holy Sepulchre – full of blood that was shed because of the respect and the veneration in which men held the last resting place of the meek and the lowly, the mild and gentle, Prince and Peace!

M. Twain, *The Innocents Abroad*

[•]

The Muslims recover Jerusalem in 1187 in the holy war that they launch against the Crusaders. The Patriarch and the leaders in the city surrender to Saladin after a brief siege (from September 21st to October 2nd, 1187). With the exception of the Syrians, its Christian inhabitants are banished. The supervision of the Church of the Holy Sepulcher is turned over from the Latin Church to the Greek Orthodox. The El-Aqsa Mosque and the sanctuary of the Dome of the Rock are returned to the Muslim faith. Most of the churches are converted into mosques or Muslim institutions – especially *medrassa*, Koranic colleges. The recapture of Jerusalem is so staggering to the Christians that six hundred years later Chateaubriand writes:

Saladin did not even want to enter the Temple mosque, which the Christians had converted into a church, without first having the walls washed with rose water. According to Sanut, five hundred camels barely sufficed to bring all the rose water used on that occasion: this tale is worthy of being Oriental. Saladin's soldiers pulled down a gold cross that was raised over the Temple and dragged it through the streets to the summit of Mount Zion where they smashed it.

The situation in the city deteriorates to such an extent that soon there are only 300 Christians in a total population of 2,000 inhabitants.

Nevertheless, Jews from other Palestinian cities and other communities in the Diaspora return to Jerusalem. The Spanish poet, Yehudah al-Harizi, visits the city soon after the Muslims recapture it, leaving us with a rather peculiar testimony in the form of a picaresque dialogue between two characters:

The Rock of Discord
I presume that you are returning from exile from abroad, he said.

–Yes I am, I replied.

–And since when have the Jews once again inhabited the city?

–Ever since the Muslims recaptured it.

–Why didn't they inhabit it under the Christians?

–Because they accuse us of deicide, of having crucified their god, pursuing us and persecuting us wherever they find us.

–Then tell me about the circumstances of the return of our people to live in the city.

–God, jealous for the glory of His Name and having pity for His People, decreed that the sanctuary would not remain in the hands of Esau's descendents for much longer, and that the sons of Jacob would not be perpetually excluded. Thus in 4950 since Creation (1190), God sustained the spirit of the prince of the Ishmaelites (Saladin), a prudent and courageous man who arrived with his entire army, besieged the city, occupied it and proclaimed throughout the region that he would welcome and receive all the descendents of Ephraim from wherever they would come. So we came from every corner of the world to reestablish ourselves in the city. Since then, we have lived in peace and would be very happy were it not for the endless internal quarrels that divide the different congregations and the spirit of discord that is rampant among them – to the extent that we could name this place the Rock of Discord.

J. Al-Harizi, *The Book of Tahkemuni*

The Crusaders fail in their attempt to regain the city during the Third Crusade and must conclude a treaty with the Egyptians. The agreement divides the city between the Christians and the Muslims, guaranteeing the former a passage to Jaffa. In fact, Muslim domination will be limited to the Temple Mount and Christian rule will extend throughout the rest of the city. The Crusaders efforts to repopulate the city during this second period (1229 – 1244) meets with limited success. In 1240, the leaders from Cairo solicit the aid of Turkish hordes in the fight against those from Damascus. In 1244, the latter attack the city, pillaging it, massacring its Christian inhabitants and devastating the Holy Sepulcher. In 1249, Jerusalem comes under the authority of the masters of Damascus who maintain it until the accession of the Mamluks to power in Egypt in 1260. From 1335, the Franciscans, who live in their monastery on Mount Zion and who are the designated custodians of the holy sites, unceasingly exert pressure on the Muslim authorities to limit the prerogatives of the Eastern churches. The city remains under the domination of the Mamluks until the Turks conquer it in 1516 – 1517.

The fight against the Christians contributes to the development of the Muslim beliefs regarding the virtues of the Holy City and the religious practices related to it. We even witness a vast production of homiletic literature – *fahhail al-Quds* – that praises its cosmological and eschatological merits. These samples are drawn from an anthology compiled in Damascus by Burhan ad-Din ibn al-Fikah al-Farazi, who was born in 1262:

The merits of Jerusalem

It is said in the name of Abu Umama: Allah's Messenger said: The Koran was entrusted to me in three places: Mecca, Medina and Syria – that is, in Jerusalem, as Walid stated:

It is said in the name of Abul-Fath Salim ar-Razi: A commentary of the words from the Most High: "Ask the messengers who we have sent you if we have designated another God to adore besides the Merciful One". When the Prophet was about to undertake a nocturnal voyage, the prophets gathered together in Jerusalem to support him; and the moment he was seized with doubt, God said to him: "Ask them!" But he stopped doubting and did not question them…

It is said in the name of Ayesha: Mecca is truly a city that is highly honored by God Who greatly glorifies its holiness. When He created it, He surrounded it with angels on the same day, one thousand years before having created anything else in the world. He then added Medina and added Jerusalem to Medina. Then He created the rest of the world, one thousand years later, in the one and same act of Creation.

It is said in the name of Khalid ibn Madan: Muawiya ibn Abu Sufyan went up on the pulpit in the mosque in Jerusalem and declared: "Everything that there is between the walls of this mosque is dearer to God than the rest of the world."

It is said in the name of Wahb ibn Munabbih: The inhabitants of Jerusalem are like Allah's neighbors and it is incumbent on Allah not to deal severely with his neighbors.

According to Kaab: There is an open door in the heavens, one of the doors of Paradise through which mercy and compassion pour down upon Jerusalem every morning until the Hour arrives. And the dew that descends upon Jerusalem is a remedy against disease for it comes from the gardens of Paradise.

THE MAMLUKS

At first, the Mamluks are not very interested in Jerusalem, which is linked to Damascus, and they do not concern themselves with rebuilding it or repopulating it. Its walls that were destroyed in 1219 by the order of the Ayyubides sultan to discourage the return of the Crusaders are not raised again. Its citadel will not be rebuilt until around 1310.

The Mamluks, nonetheless, consider Jerusalem to be a religious center and attract theologians of every stream of Islam, building and maintaining Koranic institutions. Colleges – *medrass* or *madrassa* – are built thanks to donations – *waqf* in Arabic – that guarantee their future. The emir, Tankiz, the Syrian governor, proves to be particularly enterprising. In 1329, he builds a Koranic institution at the entrance of the *haram asharif* that bears two names: *Tankiziyyeh* and *El Mah'qammeh*[1]. In 1336, this same emir opens the cotton market where many buildings today display the architectural elements of the Mamluks: the alternation of different colored stones (black and white and especially red and white), portals set back from the street, porch vaults covered with stalactites and facades covered with inscriptions, geometric motifs and heraldic emblems. The city's population does not exceed more than a few thousand; its Jewish community numbers a few hundred.

The Jewish Quarter, in the southwest sector of the city, which did not contain any Christian or Muslim sites of any importance, still doesn't have a synagogue. In 1267, after the Mongol hordes had passed through the region, it welcomes the Spanish scholar, Rabbi Moshe ben Nahman – Nachmanides – who was compelled to flee the ecclesiastic authorities of his country. Upon his arrival, he writes a letter to his son disclosing his first impressions:

A letter from Nachmanides
May God's blessing be upon you, Nahman! May you and your descendents merit seeing Jerusalem in joy! May your

1. The name, *Mah'qammeh* – tribunal in Arabic – comes from the tribunal that the building housed until 1917. According to Jewish tradition, this building stands on the site of the Sanhedrin of the Second Temple Period – *lishkat ha-Gazit.* A second *medrass* – *Ashrafiyyeh* – on the Temple Mount, built in the 14th century, was the residence of the Sufi dignitaries and monks. Destroyed in 1475 and rebuilt in 1482, it will be considered for a long time the third Muslim monument in the city. Its portal is one of the most beautiful of the Mamluk Period.

lot be like that of Abraham, our father! I am writing this letter in the holy city of Jerusalem where I have arrived safe and sound, thank God, the guardian of my destiny... I am preparing to go to Hebron where our Patriarchs are buried to prostrate upon their tombs and to prepare mine.

What should I tell you about this country? It is dry and in utter neglect. In short, the sites are even more despoiled than they are sacred. Jerusalem is the most devastated of all the cities. Judea is in even worse condition than the Galilee. The land remains, nonetheless, blessed.

Jerusalem has a population of around 2,000 inhabitants, including 300 Christians who escaped the sultan's persecutions. There are few Jews; some fled the Tartars and others were assassinated. The governor granted two brothers monopoly of the dyeing business. Religious services are held in their homes including the Sabbath service. We urged them to look for another place to pray and in the end, we found an abandoned house with marble columns and a beautiful vaulted roof, which we converted into a synagogue. The institution of private property is unknown in this city – whoever wishes to appropriate an empty building is free to do so without making enemies. We furnished the house. We then sent for the Torah scrolls that had been placed in safekeeping in Shechem at the time of the invasion of Jerusalem by the Tartars. The synagogue will soon be ready and services will be held on a regular basis. People are continually arriving from all parts, from Damascus, from Aleppo and from the four corners of the country to visit the site of the Temple, to pray and to lament. May He Whose will it was that we witness the destruction of Jerusalem grant us the joy of seeing it rebuilt and of participating in the restoration of His presence in all His glory.

May you, my son, your brothers and your dear ones know the joy of Jerusalem and the consolation of Zion! Your father, Moses, the son of Nahman, blessed be his memory.

Nachmanides, *A Letter*

The synagogue mentioned in this passage was built on the ruins of a church dating to the period of the Crusaders, perhaps on the emplacement where the Ramban synagogue still stands today in the center of the Jewish Quarter in the Old City. Destroyed in 1948 and restored in 1967, the Ramban synagogue is the oldest in Jerusalem.

[•]

In 1376, Jerusalem is joined to an independent province that covers the Judean hills to Hebron. In the city, we witness a resumption of construction projects; directly appointed in Cairo, each governor feels obliged to leave his architectural mark on certain sites, particularly on the Temple Mount – while extorting taxes from the inhabitants to make himself wealthy as quickly as possible. The streets are not safe and poverty is rampant everywhere. The persecution of non-Muslims is a common practice, especially against the Franciscans monks who settled on the Temple Mount in 1334. Towards the end of the 15th century, the city has no more than 10,000 inhabitants, including 100 to 150 Jewish families. Ovadia (ben Abraham) de Bartenura from Italy, the author of a commentary on the Mishna, left us his impressions of his voyage to Greece, Egypt and Palestine. He was in Jerusalem in around 1500:

A desolate city

The distance between Bethlehem and Jerusalem is about three miles. The road is lined with vineyards and fields of olive trees. In a first section, the vineyards resemble those of Romagna, with its equally short and full vine stocks. About three miles from Jerusalem, where the road begins to descend in levels, we perceive the holy city, the stronghold of our delight. We tore our garments for the first time as dictated by the Jewish law. Soon after, we caught sight of the ruins of our sanctuary and of our glory and we tore our clothing a second time. This is how we arrived at the gates of Jerusalem on the 13th of Nisan in the year 5248 [1488]. At noon on that day, we could declare: "Our feet stand at your gates, oh Jerusalem!" An Ashkenazi Jew who grew up in Italy came to meet me. He took me to his home where I was his guest throughout Passover.

Most of the quarters in Jerusalem are deserted and in ruins and there are no longer any walls surrounding the city. I am told that there are approximately four thousand families, only seventy of which are Jewish... mostly poor people, without any possessions. It would be difficult to find anyone who eats his fill. At the time that I write this, whoever has enough wheat to satisfy his needs for a year is considered a wealthy man. There are many widows, young and old, Ashkenazi and Sephardi, as well as people who speak other languages – seven woman to every man.

The Ishmaelites evidently do not harass the Jews. I traveled across the length and breadth of the country and no one "opens his mouth nor says a peep". They are, moreover, gracious towards strangers, especially towards those who speak a foreign language. Even when the Jews assemble (for religious ceremonies), no one bothers them. I think that a wise man with experience in the government of the country could serve to guide and judge both the Muslims and the Jews. But out of all the Jews in these regions, there is not one who would be accepted by everyone.

Today, I found lodgings in Jerusalem. I live near the synagogue in a bedroom adjacent to the synagogue. Five people live in the same courtyard, all women, not a single man except for a blind man whose wife is willing to provide some services to me upon request. I cannot help but thank God for having blessed me all along the road that led me to this place and for preserving me from illness since everyone else who accompanied me became ill. Most of the people who come to Jerusalem from distant lands become ill and are bedridden due to the abrupt changes in temperature, which passes from hot to cold and cold to hot at any moment. All the winds of the world visit the city: it is said that they come to prostrate before God in Jerusalem before pursuing their course. Blessed be He Who knows the truth!

Today, I am living beneath the house of my illustrious teacher in Jerusalem. Twice this month, I delivered a homily at the synagogue. I spoke in the sacred language [Hebrew], which most understand. I am to them "like a song of love sung by someone endowed with a pleasant voice and who plays a musical instrument in a pleasing manner". When

I deliver my homily, they praise me and congratulate me,
understanding my points – " but not practicing them ".

O. de Bartenura, *A letter*

By now, the city of Jerusalem must have already shown
its sordid and unhealthy side that would shock so many
travelers during the 18th century and the first half of the 19th
century: An inextricable tangle of lanes, most unnamed, with
broken paving stones; animal traffic jams, especially camels;
hairless dogs that show their fangs to avert the shower of
blows; the religious, who are posted at the entrance of the
mosques, watching for blasphemers in order to deal severely
with heresy; gutters that drain all sorts of refuse, the remains
of cats, animal droppings, vegetable parings. Some travelers
even relate that the Ottoman authorities, the successors of
the Mamluks, have to open the city gates on a regular basis
to the hyenas to come and clean the refuse, fearing that the
Bedouin tribes will take advantage of this to enter with them.
Like wading birds, the lack of security, heightened by the
darkness, snatches up the ruins of a deserted and defiled
city, which, moreover, is inhabited by dignitaries exiled in
disgrace, retired soldiers and women of ill repute. Although
it does not date back to this period, Gustave Flaubert's
account of his visit in 1850 reconstructs its desolation:

The dump yard

Jerusalem is a yard surrounded by walls; the first peculiar
thing that we found here was the butcher shop. In a type
of square space, covered with mounds of refuse, there was
a large hole; in the hole, congealed blood, intestines, dung,
black and brown bowels, almost charred by the sun, all
around. The stench was very strong, as pleasant as filth
can get. This is what a man would say, making ingenious
comparisons and subtle allusions: "In the holy city, the first
thing we saw there was blood."

Everything is vaulted in Jerusalem: from time to time, we
pass under a half or a quarter of an arch in the street; houses
are set up in the ancient buildings and everywhere there are
vaults over our heads. Except for the vicinity of the Armenian
Quarter that is well swept, everything is dirty; it is almost

impossible for the horses to pass over the pavement and on the street of our hotel, a yellow dog can remain quietly in the middle without anyone thinking of pushing him away; the dung along the walls of the street is appalling and vile! But, nevertheless, there are less remains of watermelons than on Jaffa Street.

Ruins everywhere, it smells of death and desolation; God's curse seems to hover over the city, the holy city of three religions, which is dying of boredom, stagnation and neglect.

G. Flaubert, *A Voyage to the East*

This image will not improve before the decade of the sixties during the 19th century...

THE OTTOMANS

In 1517, the Turkish Ottomans, under the leadership of Salim I, seize the city without encountering any major difficulties. One century later, a leading citizen will recount:

The masters of the mosques

When the Circassians-Mamluks entered Jerusalem to seize it, all the scholars and pious men went to welcome [the new master] Salim Shahen in 922. They handed him the keys of the Mosque of Al-Aksa as well as those of the Dome of the Rock of God. Salim bowed and exclaimed: "Thank God! I am, henceforth, the proprietor of the sanctuary of the first Qible."

Three years later, Suleiman the Magnificent (1520 – 1566) succeeds Salim. He immediately undertakes the building of the walls. The work stirs up enthusiastic reactions among the Jews in the city. A man named Joseph ha-Cohen who writes chronicles expresses his gratitude in this manner:

The raising of the walls

In the year 1540, God was with Suleiman, the king of Greece and Persia, who undertook building the walls of Jerusalem, the holy city in Judea. He sent delegates on a mission to rebuild the walls and to open its gates as during ancient times, as well as to rebuild the towers as in the past. His popularity quickly spread throughout the region for having accomplished such a great achievement... May God bless him.

THE WAILING WALL

Suleiman the Magnificent is politically liberal and encourages religious minorities to populate the large cities, including Jerusalem, in order to discourage the Arabs from putting up any resistance. Jews expelled from Spain who had temporarily settled in Turkey, arrive in the holy city. Among other things, they build a complex of four synagogues – the Yohanan ben Zakkai synagogues[1]. The Sephardic section of the Jewish Quarter will develop around this complex. They also obtain permission to pray at the foot of the western wall of the Temple – that the pilgrims and Christian visitors name the Wailing Wall – which had survived the destruction of the city by the Romans and the erosion of the centuries. Suleiman even entrusts an architect named Sinan to arrange an area in which to pray at the foot of the heavy wall: an area of twenty-two meters by three meters is cleared in the Maghrebian Quarter that was inhabited by Muslims originally from Andalusia and Morocco. This area is nothing more than a passageway paved with stone between the Wailing Wall on one side and one of the supporting walls of the Maghrebian Quarter on the other side. You enter it from the north through a narrow path that leads to a small gate; the Wailing Wall remains hidden from the visitors until they enter the stone paved area.

This wall gives rise to many legends and gradually becomes a highlight of the pilgrimage. The presence of God permanently hovers over these places and the stones cry out and shed tears, disturbed by the impure stone that Jeroboam ben Nevat had slipped in there to induce Israel to sin and that David Reubeni, a fanatic or a visionary, attempted to repair in vain in 1523 to hasten redemption by removing it. The people only venture into the vicinity of the wall barefoot, bound by the rabbinical interdiction that declares: "One should not gain access to the Temple Mount holding his staff or wearing shoes or carrying his purse" (Berachot 9: 1).[2] They mumble prayers and ritual formulas of the type: "There is nothing other than the House of the Lord and that is where the gate to heaven is." Then the people begin to slip their vows and wishes in the interstices in expectation of the

1. The four synagogues are: the synagogue that bears the name of Yohanan ben Zakkai, a Pharisee teacher during the 1st century who fled from Jerusalem when it was besieged by the Romans and settled in Yavne with his disciples (see p.78); built upon Crusader ruins, it has two cabinets for the Scrolls of the Law; the "Istambuli" Synagogue whose architecture is that of Turkish buildings has four columns that support a cupola; the synagogue bearing the name of the prophet Elijah that preserves a chair that he had used; the "Kahal Zion" Synagogue – the Community of Zion. Destroyed by the Jordanians in 1948, they were restored in 1967.

marvelous properties of its stones. When the stones crumble, the fragments are religiously collected and buried with old Scrolls of the Law whose letters are tarnished, accompanied by a great procession. A strange symbol of downfall and of resistance in the collective memory of a nation that linked its vocation and its destiny to an unknown God who cannot be represented by any image made this supporting wall represents the gates that are favorable to prayer, permanently open and sensitive to the most secret vibrations of the Jewish soul. The sacred finds its final retreat in this vestige, guarded by beggars who, moreover, were the true builders – if one is to believe the rabbinic legend that dates back to the 7th or 8th century:

The wall of the poor

When we wanted to build the wall surrounding the Temple, the work was divided among the population's different social classes. The construction of the western wall was allotted to the poor who worked hard to build it for they were unable to hire workers to do the work for them. In fact, when the enemy destroyed the Temple, the angels descended from heaven and spreading their wings over the wall, they declared: "This wall, the labor of the poor, will not be destroyed."

There is another legend surrounding the extraordinary survival of the wall:

The remnant wall

When Vespasian conquered Jerusalem, he assigned each of the four walls of the enclosure to four of his commanding officers; Pengar received the western wall... It was decreed in heaven that it would not be destroyed. Why? Because the Divine Presence resides in the west... Seeing that the other commanding officers destroyed their walls and that Pengar spared his, Vespasian sent for him and asked him: "Why haven't you destroyed your segment?" He replied: "I swear! I spared it for the glory of the empire, for had I demolished it no one would have been able to measure the size of the monument that you have destroyed. Now, the people will see these ruins and will exclaim: "Consider the power of

2. The custom of removing one's shoes disappeared during the 19th century, persisting here and there until the first decades of the 20th century. Commenting on this change, Agnon, an Israeli writer and winner of the Nobel Prize in Literature, wrote: "Our ancestors were still close to the destruction of the Temple and conducted themselves as people in mourning during the seven days that follow a death, compelled to walk barefoot. While we, who are closer to the redemption, we act like people in mourning who, after the seven days have past, may wear their shoes."

Vespasian! What a powerful city he destroyed!" Vespasian declared: "I swear! You have spoken well, but since you did not obey my orders, you will climb to the summit [of the wall] and you will throw yourself off. If you survive, good! If you die, too bad!" Pengar climbed up on the wall, jumped and died...

Lamentations Rabba I, 31

The testimonies of pilgrims and visitors slowly evolve. It is not until the 18th century that the wall begins to stir up that uneasy excitation in which all sorts of often contradictory feelings mix in an inextricable tangle. Zionism awakens a new patriotic enthusiasm that is expressed in various ways. The following two reactions sum up the relations of the Jews to this solid vestige of the Temple. Mordechai ben Hillel ha-Cohen, who visits Palestine at the end of the 19th century, will become one of the leaders of the Zionist Movement:

The vestige of a legend

As soon as I arrived, I began to make all the arrangements necessary to make the most of my stay in Jerusalem, but I very quickly realized that I could not resist the desire – or should I say, the pressing need! – to rush to the Western Wall. I do not remember which path I took, allowing my legs to carry me, moving forward like a blind animal that follows his shepherd, with my eyes constantly looking upwards, watching for the first appearance of the wall: "Here is the Western Wall", murmured my guide with a sacred sigh... I do not remember how my shoes came off my feet, or how I flung myself full length on the ground, kissing the paving stones and shedding such copious tears that they seemed to flow in torrents. I was overwhelmed with emotion; my heart was all a flutter. I did not try to control myself or to stop the flow of childlike tears, lacking words and lacking meaning. My guide gently chided me and tried to calm me, handing me a book of Psalms and indicating which verses to recite. What a fool! Didn't he realize that at that moment I did not need verses or a prayer book or any other liturgical act!?

I left the wall, broken hearted, in the same frame of mind as when I had walked away from the Homel cemetery where I had buried my only child the previous summer. I left the wall as I had departed from the cemetery, leaving behind a part of my life – a part of my heart. I do not wish this on any one, for such moments in one's life can brutally destroy a man or at least drive him to insanity. When I recall this experience, it still overwhelms me! Everything all around me seemed so terrible!

It was not what I saw, the desolation of the wall, which overwhelmed me; for there is nothing in its appearance that can shake a man to such an extent and provoke such a storm in his heart. One cannot even speak of the sense of disaster in the case of this site. The stones had surely burned, but the wall remained intact. Its rows of stones did not acquire any sensation of death and the terrible destruction that Jerusalem had suffered merited a more appropriate memorial. That said, I must admit that this wall exerts an impressive effect. The sacred excitement that seizes the Jews in its presence is such that everyone should make a pilgrimage to Jerusalem if only to see it. The cities in Judea and the streets in Jerusalem are full of ruins, thousands of them that are dear to the Jews, and with every step one takes, one perceives the echoes of pleasant memories and sees the monuments that convey a sense of our glorious past. But even if these monuments did not exist or were hidden and only the wall remained, it would still be worthwhile for every Jew to spare nothing in the world in order to come and see it with his own eyes. Some researchers challenge the legends that have been associated with it – they are heartless and totally lack discernment! They do not understand that legends can reveal the truth, that a wall can withstand two thousand years, and that there truly exists somewhere in the world a vestige of the "house of universal prayer" that has survived the trials and the vicissitudes that this extraordinary country has unceasingly known from the day that Yehudah was exiled and that strangers had taken possession of it. Let the researchers be surprised – nothing surprises us! We know ourselves to be a legendary people. Perhaps even the Jewish people as a whole is a great legend! But a legend from which a source of life, animated by an exalted power, would flow, a legend that would allow itself to laugh at the small occurrences of real life! Why do I need to know which of its stones date back to the Temple Period and which are later additions? I know that no other nation and no other people prostrates and pours out its prayers in front of this wall besides our coreligionists who come from all the countries of exile to confess their sins before these sacred stones. Only Israel – out of all the families of humanity – cry in this place! ... This wall belongs to us – we will not allow anyone to touch it!

M. H. ha-Cohen, *Testimony*

Another leading figure of the Zionist Movement, A. S. Hirschberg, the author of *Eretz Hemda* – the Land of Grace – visits the wall in 1901:

The wall's endurance

The day after my arrival, I went with my young friends to the Western Wall, the first place that the Jews rush to on their visit to Jerusalem. It was a clear and hot day, which reminded me of the first days of summer in my native country even though it was the month of Kislev – in winter! We made our way to the vegetable market where we entered narrow and winding lanes, some sloping upwards and some descending, and went through alleys, some open and some enclosed by walls of stones [...] until we found ourselves in a narrow passageway. The Western Wall was on one side and the solid wall of a hovel in the Maghrebrian Quarter was on the other.

When we arrived, there were two men praying there and some Sephardic paupers begging, some were standing and others were seated on the ground or on boxes that they had brought with them. The Sephardic beadle headed towards me, tore a piece of my coat and handed me a small prayer book, prompting me to recite the obligatory blessing for a first visit to the Temple. I began to murmur the words and suddenly I broke into tears as never before, unable to control myself.

I was overwhelmed. The walk through the sordid lanes and dirty alleys in the midst of the Arabs, surrounded by filthy children dressed in rags and barefoot, had so depressed me that nothing else made an impression. When I came to the wall, I certainly felt that I was standing in a sacred place, but my senses were blunt and my heart was heavy. And then I pronounced that prayer that awakened in me, like a hereditary illness, a deep-seated pain, and the dam gave way! My personal distress mixed with the misfortune of the nation formed a torrent: there I was, standing before the wall, that silent witness to the past glory of Israel and at the same moment, I thought about all the places throughout the world and all the times throughout the centuries when we suffered persecution and torture! The times that our wretched nation endured being pursued and subjected to pogroms passed before me – and throughout all the time that our martyrdom lasted, these stones had not moved... Blinded by my tears, the letters in the book danced before my eyes; with tense nerves, I was so overcome that I felt that I was about to faint. I wanted to flee, to leave that wall like a fugitive without even completing the blessing that I had begun, but the beadle held me back and replaced for me the wick of the tiny oil lamp, which was placed at the end of the wall. It was as if he was giving me a memorial candle to light for the soul of our people that was dying in exile.

A. S. Hirschberg, *The Land of Grace*

The Christians' view of this wall has not always been merciful. Pilgrims and travelers would often see it as a symbol of the downfall of a people guilty of deicide. In 1838, Edward Robinson, the father of the geographer and archeologist who would lead research projects in Jerusalem, takes note of the protective narrowness of the place: "It is the place that is closest to their ancient Temple", he writes, "where they can venture. Fortunately for them, it is hidden from view by the narrowness of the passageway enclosed by the dead walls. There, rolling in the dust, they can at least mourn the lost glory of their race without disturbance, moistening with their tears this ground that thousand of their ancestors had long ago bathed with their blood." In 1864, the Scottish pastor, Norman Macleod, who considers the wall to be "one of the most remarkable sites in the world", does not allow himself to be deceived by the mispronounced accents of the faithful: "What light", he writes, "in this darkness, what darkness in this light, what immortal hopes for the future, what a passionate attachment to the past! What touching superstition, what credulity, what incredulity! Some sheets of paper bearing prayers distinctly written in Hebrew were inserted between the stones of the old wall." The French visitors, in general, appear to be less sensitive to the touching poetry of the downfall and of the endurance engraved on the stones of this wall and on the features of its caretakers than their Anglo-Saxon contemporaries. Melchior de Vogue (1829 – 1916), an ambassador, archeologist and anti-Semite in the tradition of the Second Empire, writes:

The concert of lamentations

There they are, hundreds of them, clasping the stones with their grasping hands, rocking their heads and their bodies with the rhythmic undulations of eastern prayer, chanting in high-pitched scales the lamentations of the prophets or some litanies in flat German. At times, the singing and the rocking of the heads subside, and then, at the cry of a leader, the long row of fur-lined skullcaps, turbans and European hats again begins to rise and fall with the movement of raging waves. Many actually weep upon the sacred and cruel wall that hides their view of Mount Moriah and of Solomon's parvis. The Muslim, who is on his way to pray in the mosque, curses the disgraceful pariahs; the tourists, who came on a pleasurable outing, laugh heartily at the grotesque details of the scene. Indifferent to the scorn and the insult, they furtively glance at the infidels with a hate-filled look and continue their mournful commemoration without allowing themselves to be distracted.

M. De Vogue, *Jerusalem, Yesterday and Today*

The most primitive anti-Semitism that resorts to the most worn-out stereotypes, is surprisingly found in the writings of Pierre Loti (1894), indisputably one of the most gifted French travelers during the end of the 19th century:

The enclosure of tears

It is Friday evening, the traditional time when every week, in a special site granted by the Turks, the Jews go to weep over the ruins of Solomon's Temple, which "will never be rebuilt". And we want to pass by that place of Lamentations before nightfall. After passing empty plots of land, we now reach some narrow lanes, scattered with refuse and finally a kind of enclosure, filled with the movement of a strange crowd of people who wail together in a low and rhythmic voice. A dim twilight has already begun. The back of this place, which is surrounded by dark walls, is closed, dwarfed by a tremendous building constructed by Solomon, a fragment of the surrounding wall of the Temple, made entirely of huge and similar blocks. We can see the backs of some men in long velvet robes, who, in general, are bustling about, waddling like bears in cages, facing the gigantic debris, knocking their foreheads against the wall and murmuring a kind of quivering chant...

The robes are magnificent: some black velvet, some blue velvet, some violet or crimson, lined with precious fur skins. The skullcaps are all made of black velvet – trimmed with longhaired fur that cast a shadow over their noses, which are shaped like knife blades, and they look at us with disapproval. The faces, half turning to examine us, are almost all particularly ugly, so ugly that they make you shudder: so thin, so tapered, so sly, with small cunning, watering eyes under drooping dead eyelids! ... Unhealthy complexions like white and pink wax and above every ear, corkscrew curly hair that hangs like the "British" in 1830, complete their disturbing resemblance to old bearded ladies.

There are mostly old people with base expressions, sly and ignoble. But there are also some very young, some very small Jews, fresh as sugar coated candy, already wearing the curled locks like the adults, and waddling and even weeping with a Bible in hand. This evening, moreover, they are almost all "Sephardim", that is, the Jews who returned from Poland [Loti confused the Sephardim with the Ashkenazim], made pale and white by centuries of bartering and usury under the skies in the North; very different from the "Ashkenazim", their brothers who returned from Spain and Morocco, where we see dark complexions and the wonderful faces of prophets.

Upon penetrating the heart of Jewry, my impression is, above all, one of surprise, of discomfort and almost fear. Nowhere have I ever seen such an exaggerated type of old merchants of garments, rags and rabbit skins; nowhere have I ever seen such pointed, long, pale noses. There is always a small commotion of surprise and disgust each time one of those old backs bent over under the velvet and the fur partially turns back and a new pair of eyes looks furtively at me from the side, under hanging eyelids beneath eye glasses. Truly, having crucified Jesus leaves an indelible stigma; perhaps it is necessary to come here to convince oneself of this, but it is indisputable that there is a characteristic mark inscribed on their foreheads, a stamp of opprobrium marking this whole race...

In itself, this is unique, touching and sublime: after so much unparalleled misfortune, after so many centuries of exile and dispersion, the unshakeable attachment of this people to a lost homeland! It would take very little to cry with them – if it weren't for that fact that they were Jews and if our hearts did not feel chilled by all their contemptible faces.

But before this Wall of Tears, the mystery of the prophecies appears all the more inexplicable and startling. Collecting my thoughts, my mind is confused by the fortunes of Israel, unprecedented, unparalleled in the history of men, impossible to foresee, nevertheless, foretold with disturbing, detailed precision even during the period of the glory of Zion.

P. Loti, *Jerusalem*

In the 19th century, philanthropists and Jewish organizations attempt to acquire the plots of land bordering the Wall. In 1897, Baron Edmond de Rothschild proposes moving the hovels belonging to the Maghrebians and building houses for them in another quarter of the city, but his proposal comes up against the rejection of the Muslim authorities that refuse to part with the real estate consecrated to Islam. At the end of World War I, the Anglo-Palestinian Bank submits a similar proposal to the Turks. It is only after the Six Day War (1967) that the Israelis, who control the Old City, can arrange the esplanade of the Wall as they please...

THE VALLEY OF JEHOSHAPHAT

The Valley of Jehoshaphat also bears the names, the Kidron Valley and the Valley of the Kings. It stretches east of the Old City between Mount Moriah, or the Temple Mount, on one side and Mount Scopus, the Mount of Olives and the Mount of Bad Counsel on the other side. The City of David, on the site of the Jebusean city, rises in tiers on its western slope. The Arabs divide this same valley in three parts: *wadi sit-Marian* – the Valley of Saint Mary – designating the upper section, *wadi Tantourat Paroun* – the Valley of Pharaoh's Pointed Hat – in middle section, and *wadi Silwan* – the Silwan Valley – that designates the lower section. According to this division, the Valley of Jehoshaphat occupies only the first part.

For three thousand years, the valley has continually been the burial site for the city's dead. During the First Temple Period, it houses its catacombs[3]; during the Second Temple Period, it is the site of numerous funerary monuments. Thus, it becomes the site of the most extraordinary legends that man has ever known: that of the Final Judgment when the nations will be summoned, and of the Resurrection when the day comes that the dead will set out on their way to this place through underground galleries. The prophets, Zachariah and Joel, greatly contribute to the embellishment of this legend surrounding the city:

3. The catacombs of the First Temple Period, see p.152.

The place of judgment

Behold, in those days and in that time, when I will bring back the captivity of Yehudah and Jerusalem, I will also gather all nations and will bring them down into the valley of Jehoshaphat and will enter into judgment with them for my people and for my heritage, Israel, whom they have scattered among the nations and have divided my land. [...] Proclaim this among the nations: Prepare for war, rouse the mighty men, let all the men of war draw near; let them come up; beat your ploughshares into swords and your pruning hooks into spears; let the weak say, I am strong. Hasten and come, all you nations, and gather yourselves together all around;

cause the mighty ones to come down there, oh Eternal! Let the nations be stirred up and come up to the Valley of Jehoshaphat for there I will sit to judge all the nations round about. Put in the sickle for the harvest is ripe; come tread down for the press is full, the vats overflow, for their wickedness is great. Multitudes, multitudes in the Valley of Judgment! For the day of the Eternal is near in the Valley of Judgment. The sun and the moon are dark and the stars have withdrawn their shining light. And the Eternal roars out of Zion and utters His voice from Jerusalem and the earth trembles. But the Eternal will be a shelter for His people and a stronghold for the children of Israel.

Joel 4: 1 - 16

The monuments, some of which are hewn in the rock, give this valley the appearance of a mortuary. The *Kings' Tomb* – for a long time was considered to be that of the kings of Yehudah and of the monarchs of the Hasmonean Dynasty – was instead that of Queen Helena d'Adiabene from Northern Mesopotamia who converted to Judaism and was buried with her own relatives in Jerusalem around the year 50 A.D. A staircase of twenty-three steps, 9 meters wide, led to a court embedded in the rock. Drainage channels on each side of the staircase fed rainwater into two cisterns reserved for ritual ablutions. A vestibule, flanked by two columns, led to the gate of the hypogeum, obstructed by a heavy stone that can still be seen at the site, which has a mysterious mechanism that automatically moves it. A second vestibule led to four funeral chambers. A staircase led to a chamber facing the entrance of the underground hall where the sarcophagi were placed. Josephus Flavius recounts a story about Queen Helena and her son, Izate:

Queen Helena

Seeing that King Izate, her son was enjoying profound peace, thank God, and that both foreigners and his subjects were in admiration of his happiness, Queen Helena decided to go and worship the Omnipotent and to offer sacrifices in the most renowned of all temples built in his honor in Jerusalem. Her son joyously granted her permission and even accompanied her part of the way. This is how she arrived in Jerusalem in a magnificent carriage, bringing a large amount of money with her. It inhabitants enormously benefited from her arrival for the famine there was great, and people were dying of hunger. Wishing to alleviate it, the queen sent envoys to purchase a supply of wheat in Alexandria and dry figs on the island of Cyprus to distribute to the poor, earning her the reputation among the Jews of goodness and generosity that such great charity merits. The king, her son, also earned this reputation; upon learning of the famine that prevailed in the country, he sent the leaders of Jerusalem large sums of money to relieve the poor.

J. Flavius, *Jewish Antiquities, XX, 1*

Josephus Flavius also reports that when Helena and Izate died, the latter's successor sent their remains "to Jerusalem to be placed under the three pyramids that the princess had built at a site three stadiums from the city". The excavations conducted during the mid-19th century stirred up the first protests among the Jews who are incapable of understanding how anyone can disturb the dead for the sake of the macabre curiosity of clearing the stones, and who cry out against this as sacrilegious. The queen's sarcophagus, nevertheless, was transported to the Louvre.

A Jewish legend considers this same tomb to be the burial vault of Kalba Sabua, the wealthy father-in-law of the distinguished master of the 2nd century, Rabbi Akiba, who would welcome guests with raisins and dates – the fruits that are the motifs appearing on the front of the tomb – allowing them to leave only after they had been satiated.

Zechariah's Pyramid, set on an Ionic base, is supposed to shelter the tomb of this prophet who announced the Redemption:

Judgment Day

Behold, the day of the Eternal comes when your spoil will be divided in your midst. For I will gather all the nations against Jerusalem to battle; and the city will be taken, the houses pillaged and the women ravished. Half of the city will

*go into exile and the other half will not be cut off from the city.
Then the Eternal will go out and fight against those nations
as in the old days when He fought on the day of battle. On
that day, His feet will stand on the Mount of Olives, which is
before Jerusalem on the east, and the Mount of Olives will
be split down the middle, forming a great valley from east to
west; half of the mountain will be moved towards the north
and half of it towards the south.*

Zechariah 14: 1 - 4

Jewish tradition, however, considers it to be the tomb of the
priest, Zechariah ben Yehoyada:

The assassination of Zechariah

*The spirit of God came upon Zechariah, the son of Yehoyada,
the priest, and he stood above the people and said to them:
"Thus says God: 'Why do you transgress the commandments
of the Eternal, although you cannot succeed? Because you
have forsaken the Eternal, He will forsake you. And they
conspired against him and stoned him to death upon the
orders of the king in the parvis of the Temple of the Eternal.*

II Chronicles 24: 20 - 21

Archeological ruins mark the site of the erection of the
pyramid in the middle of 1st century. Built in one piece in the
rock, it has no internal cavity and no opening. Only a hole,
perhaps the beginning of a gallery, leads us to believe that
the work undertaken to hollow out a burial vault under the
pyramid was abruptly suspended. Perhaps during the Great
Revolt against the Romans…

Hezir's Tomb was the necropolis of a clan of priests named
Hezir: a cave with Doric columns constitutes a vestibule that
opens on to some funeral chambers. For a long time, a Jewish
legend identified it as the tomb of King Ozias. According to
a Christian tradition, it was the tomb of Saint James, the
Lesser. Another Christian tradition considers it to be the
place where Jesus fell, hurled down by the Jews from the top
of the Temple Mount. An inscription in Hebrew, discovered
in the middle of the 19th century, declares: "This is the tomb

and the spirit of Eleazar, Hania, Yoezar, Yehuda, Shimon, Yohanan, the son of Yosef, the son of Oved and Eleazar, the son of Hania, the priests of the house of Hezir."

Avshalom's Tomb, shaped like a flattened cone on a cylindrical drum, dates back to the 1st century. The Arabs call it *Tanturat Paroun* – the Pharaoh's Pointed Hat. There is a small room with funeral beds mounted by an arch in the lower section. The legends that have spread throughout the valley are based on a passage in the Second Book of Samuel, which attributes the construction of the tomb to Avshalom, King David's rebellious son:

Avshalom's Tomb

Now during his lifetime, Avshalom had taken and raised a monument in the King's Valley, saying: "I have no son to perpetuate my name"; and he called the monument after his own name as it is called today.

II Samuel 18: 18

A first minor legend tells that the Muslims had the custom of hurling rocks through the opening in the top of the cone to give free reign to their anger against David's rebellious son. Another minor legend recounts that the Jews had the custom of dragging their unruly children to this place to show them what awaited them, throwing rocks into it to support their threats...

For a long time, another tomb, that of Simon, the Just, the last judge of the Great Assembly, would attract pilgrims on the thirty-third day of Omer – usually during the month of May – which commemorates the anniversary of the death of Rabbi Shimon bar Yohai, a 2nd century master to whom rabbinic tradition attributes the composition of the Zohar, and to give their young children their first tonsures. A gallery, hollowed out by King Ezekias to secure an escape route out of the city in case of siege also served as a sacred site ... of the Franks-Masons [4].

4. Two hundred fifty meters long and one hundred fifty meters wide, it served as a quarry, probably during the reign of King Herod. The stones of the wall that support the Temple Mount came from there. It is open to the public, leading to a small spring under the Muslim Quarter that is said to release "King Ezekias' tears".

The Jewish pilgrims looked upon this valley as a mortuary awaiting the resurrection. The following is a testimony by Rabbi Moses Basola (1480 –1560) who was in Jerusalem between 1520 and 1523.

A pastoral city

Jerusalem is perched on a mountain, separated from the Mount of Olives by the narrow Valley of Jehoshaphat. I descended this valley at the end of which there is an immense hole that would be the tomb of a king. It is said that this is where the entrance to Gehenna will open in the future when Gog arrives. Jewish tombs cover the slope of the Mount of Olives and part of the mountain on which Jerusalem is located. Half a mile below the city, the waters of Silwan flow, watering the beautiful gardens in the valley. They spring from the mountain without anyone knowing exactly from where they gush forth. They emerge among the ruins of a beautiful domed building, where, it is said, Solomon minted his money.

M. Basola, *Testimony*

David Reubeni, who claimed to be the prince of a Jewish kingdom in Arabia, ruled by his brother, visited the city in the summer of 1523. He also claimed to have located the Lost Tribes of Israel. Reubeni's plan was to visit the communities of the Diaspora to shake them out of the apathy of exile. His passage in Jerusalem is recorded in the following account:

The passage of a Messiah

I entered Jerusalem on the twenty-fifth of Adar (A.D. 1523), and that day I went into the house of the Holy of Holies [the Dome of the rock], and when I came to the sanctuary, all the Ishmaelite guardians came to bow before me and kiss my feet, and said to me, "Enter, Oh blessed of the Lord." And the two chief among them came and took me to the cavern which is under the Stone of Foundation, and said to me, "This is the place of Elijah the prophet and this is the place of King Solomon, and this the place of Abraham and Isaac, and this the place of Muhammad." I said to the guardians, "Now that I know these places, go you on your way, for I wish to pray and in the morning I will give you charity."

They went away, and I knew at once that their words were false and in vain. I prayed until all the Ishmaelites came to prayer. They left the Temple court after their prayer two hours after dark. I went below the Stone of Foundation. Then the guards extinguished all the lights in the court except four, and before they closed the gates they searched to see if any man were sleeping in the cavern, so as to turn him out. They found me and said, "Leave this place, for we are the guards and may allow no one to remain and sleep here. We have so sworn to the king, and if you will not go we shall ask the governor to remove you against your will." When I heard those words, I came out of the court, and they shut the court all night, and I fasted, and this was my fourth day.

In the morning, when the Ishmaelites came to pray in the court, I entered with them, and when they finished their prayer, I called out with a loud voice, "Where are the guards? Let them come to me." And I said to them, "I am your Lord, and the son of your Lord, the Prophet. I have come from a distant country to his Holy House and my soul desires to remain here to pray and not to sleep." After that, four of the guards came to expel me, and I said to them, "I am your Lord, the son of your Lord, if you wish peace, wish me well and I will bless you; but if not, I will be avenged on you and will write to the king of Turkey your evil deeds." They replied, "Forgive us this time, for we wish to serve you and be your slaves for as long as you remain in the Holy House, and will do your will." Then I gave them ten ducats for charity and stayed in the sanctuary and fasted in the Holy of Holies for five weeks....

The Ishmaelites have a sign on the top of the cupola of the court, and this sign is like a half moon turned westward; and on the first day of Pentecost of 5283, it turned eastward. When the Ishmaelites saw this they cried out in a loud voice, and I said, "Why do you cry?" And they replied, "For our sins this sign of the half moon is turned eastwards, and that is an evil sign for the Ishmaelites." The Ishmaelite workmen went on the Sunday to restore the sign to its place, and on Monday the sign again turned eastward while I was praying, and the Ishmaelites went crying and weeping, and they sought to turn it around and they could not.

Our elders had already told me, "When you see this sign, go to Rome," and I saw the Gates of Mercy and the Gates of Repentance and walked in the sanctuary. It is a big structure like the upper buildings, and I did that which the elders commanded beneath the sanctuary, out of men's reach, and the turning of the sign took place after I had done what the elders commanded beneath the sanctuary.

I went up to the Mount of Olives, and I saw two caves there and returned to Jerusalem and ascended Mount Zion. There are two places of worship there in the town; the upper place in the hands of the Christians, and the lower in that of the Ishmaelites. This the Ishmaelites opened for me and showed me a grave, and told me it was the grave of King David, on whom be peace, and I prayed there. Then I left and went to the upper place of worship, which the Christians opened for me. I entered and prayed there and returned to Jerusalem.... I left Jerusalem on the twenty-fourth of Sivan....

E. N. Adler, *Ed., Jewish Travelers: A Treasury of Travelogues from Nine Centuries*

Chateaubriand, in turn, would succumb to the sad magic of this valley that awaits the resurrection:

The cemetery of Jerusalem

The Valley of Jehoshaphat appears to have always served Jerusalem as a cemetery; there are monuments dating back to the remotest centuries as well as to the most modern times: the Jews come here from every corner of the world to die; at exorbitant prices, a foreigner sells them a patch of land to cover their bodies in the country of their ancestors. The cedar trees that Solomon planted in the valley, the shadow of the Temple that covers it, the torrent that crosses it, the canticles of mourning that David composed there, the lamentation of Jeremiah that were heard there would befit the sadness and the peacefulness of its tombs. By beginning his Passion in this solitary place, Jesus Christ will consecrate it to suffering once again: here, in order to wipe out our offenses, this innocent David will shed the tears that the guilty David poured out to expiate his own errors. There are few names that simultaneously awaken both the most touching and the most fearsome in one's imagination than that of the Valley of Jehoshaphat, a valley so full of mysteries that according to the prophet, Joel, all men must one day appear there before the formidable judge.

R. Chateaubriand, *An Itinerary from Paris to Jerusalem*

Pierre Loti, who came to the holy city on a pilgrimage in search of Christ, persists in pointing out the signs of desolation and destruction, which he considers definitive and irreparable. His narration sometimes takes on the throbbing accents of death, perhaps because his god is dead, perhaps because the city is haunted so that it is nothing more than a vast tomb for a god put to death by men. The Valley of Jehoshaphat is in some way the place that is most characteristic of his Jerusalem:

The eternal wait

They are waiting, the dead, by legions, under their countless stones – and the centuries pass and the millenniums pass, – and the sound of the trumpet of Judgment tarries, and terrible archangels of awakening cannot at all be heard flying in the air. But the bodies decay and then the bones disintegrate into dust, and in turn, the tombstones crumble; gradually everything melts into the same nothingness with unrelenting, slow tranquility. And the valley makes itself ever more forgotten, ever more silent...

P. Loti, *Jerusalem*

THE MOUNT OF OLIVES

The Mount of Olives rises 150 meters above Mount Moriah, or the Temple Mount. It is also known as the Mount of the Anointing – *har ha-Mishcha* – where altars stood during the reign of King David. Its eastern slope is covered with a vast Jewish necropolis that for centuries continually received the remains of the pious whose last wish was to rest at the threshold of that valley of the Judgment and of the Resurrection. Numerous commentaries and rabbinic legends nourish that disturbing wish:

The opening of the mount

At the time of the resurrection, the Mount of Olives will open and the dead of Israel will rise up from it, including the sages, who died in exile and made their way there through underground passages. Whereas the wicked, who died and were buried in Israel, will be ejected...

At that same moment, the people will wonder: "How does that nation merit having its members rise from the ground in such large numbers as on the day that they returned to the land from the desert and obtained its Master's favor as on the day that it stood at the foot of Mount Sinai to receive the Torah?!" At the same moment, Zion, the mother of Israel, will give birth to her sons; Jerusalem will receive the exiles.

Targum Song of Songs 8: 5

Christian tradition considers that mountain that stands halfway between Jerusalem and Bethany to be the future setting of the second coming of Christ, the battle between Christ and the anti-Christ, and the Final Judgment. The Mount of Olives was, above all, the main witness to Christ's teaching, to his arrest, to his death and to his ascension. Many anchorites retire to the caves, including the famous and beautiful Pelagie, one of Antiochus actresses during the 5th century, following her conversion. The Jews consider a cave located on the grounds of the Ascension to be the tomb of the prophetess Hulda, while the Christians present it as one of their own. The mount is gradually covered with monuments intended to perpetuate the events in the life of Jesus. According to Theodosius, there were no less than twenty-four sanctuaries and convents in the 6th century.

Bethany is the actual village of El-Azariah, whose name is derived from the Byzantine Christian locality of Lazarion, which is 2 kilometers from the Mount of Olives on the road to Jericho, draws its name from the contraction of Beth Hanania, the village where the house of Martha, Mary and their brother, Lazarus, was located, and where Jesus had resided. When Lazarus becomes ill, his sisters send for Jesus to heal him. It is too late when he arrives in Bethany:

The resurrection of Lazarus

Upon his arrival, Jesus found that he had already lain in his grave for four days. Now Bethany was about fifteen furloughs from Jerusalem: And many of the Jews came to comfort Martha and Mary concerning their brother. As soon as she heard that Jesus was coming, Martha went out to meet him, but Mary stayed in the house. Then Martha said to Jesus: "Lord, if you had been here, my brother would not have died. But I know that even now, whatever you ask of God, God will grant it to you." Jesus said to her: "Your brother will rise again." "I know that he will rise again in the resurrection on the last day", she said. Jesus said to her: "I am the resurrection and the life, he who believes in me, although he was dead, will yet live. And whoever lives and believes in me will never die. Do you believe that?" She replied: "Yes, Lord, I believe that you are the Christ, the Son of God, who comes to the world." And having said so, she went to call her sister, Mary...

When Mary came to the place where Jesus was, she fell down at his feet and said to him: "Lord, if you had been here, my brother would not have died." When Jesus saw her weeping and the Jews who accompanied her also weeping, he moaned in spirit and was troubled. He said: "Where have you laid him?" They replied: "Lord, come and see." Jesus wept and the Jews said: "See how he loved him!" Some of them said: "Couldn't this man who opened the eyes of the blind have prevented the death of Lazarus?"

Jesus again moaned within himself and came to the grave. It was a cave and a stone lay upon it. Jesus said: "Remove the stone." Martha, the sister of the deceased, said to him: "By now there is a stench for he has been dead for four days." Jesus said to her: "Didn't I say to you that if you believe, you will see the glory of God?" They then removed the stone and Jesus raised his eyes and said: "Father, I thank you for you have heard me and I knew that you always hear me, but I said it because of the crowd standing here so that they may believe that you have sent me." And having said this, he cried out in a loud voice: "Lazarus, come forth!" And the one that had been dead came forth, bound hand and foot in a shroud and his face was bound with a napkin. And Jesus said: "Unbind him and let him go."

John 11: 17 - 44

The resurrection of Lazarus is considered one of the most prominent of Jesus' miracles – it, moreover, completely alienates him from the priests in Jerusalem. A staircase with twenty-four steps that dates to the 17th century leads to *Lazarus' Tomb*, which is hollowed out in the rock. A first church, built towards the end of the 4th century, is destroyed in an earthquake. It is rebuilt during the 5th and 6th centuries. Under the Byzantines, a procession would leave the church on Palm Sunday to enter Jerusalem and arrive at the Church of the Holy Sepulcher – a tradition that continues to this day; it was interrupted under the Mamluks. The Crusaders restore that first church and build a sanctuary above the tomb as well as a convent. The Muslims, who also venerate Lazarus, convert this second church into a mosque in the 16th century.

The present day church, built in 1954 by the Franciscans on the ruins of the first chapels, is in the form of a Greek cross. It lacks windows and openings in order to create the atmosphere of a tomb. Furthermore, most of the altars have the shape of sarcophagi. The light that comes through the stain glass windows in the cupola, which is engraved with doves rising towards the sky, nevertheless, represents the resurrection of Lazarus. Some mosaics reconstruct the accounts of Jesus' stay in Bethany. One of them, on the western wall, depicts the scene of the anointing in the house of Simon, the Leper:

The anointing in Bethany

Now when Jesus was in Bethany in the house of Simon, the Leper, a woman bearing an alabaster box containing a very precious ointment came to him and poured it on his head as he sat at the table. But when his disciples saw this, they were indignant and said: "What is the purpose of this waste? This ointment could have been sold for a high price and the money could have been given to the poor." When Jesus became aware of this, he said to them: "Why do you trouble this woman? She has done me a good deed. The poor will always be with you, but I will not always be with you. By pouring the ointment on my body, she has prepared it for my burial. Verily, I say to you: wherever this gospel is preached throughout the world, what she has done will also be told as a memorial to her."

Matthew 26: 6 - 13

A Medieval tower, the vestige of a Benedictine monastery erected by Queen Melisande in the 12th century overlooks the neighborhood where the tomb is located. This is the place that popular tradition identifies as the site of Martha's house.

Since the 16th century, the domain of Dominus Flevit is considered to be the place where Jesus cried as he prepared to enter the city:

The Lord's weeping

And when he was near the city, he saw the city and wept over it, saying: "If you had even known at least on this day, how to find peace... but now is hidden from your eyes! For the days will come upon you when your enemies will besiege you, encircling you and pressing you from all sides. They will crush you and your children within you; and they will not leave one stone upon another because you did not recognize the time of visitation."

Luke 19: 41 - 44

In 1955, the architect, Barluzzin, builds the church, which is located in the area that served as a Jewish necropolis – perhaps also Judeo-Christian – upon the ruins of a Byzantine chapel. Its cupola is in the shape of a tear and its altar faces Jerusalem. It overlooks the Russian Church of Saint Mary Magdalene and is maintained by the Franciscans.

The **Enclosure of Eleona** – from the Latin *mons Elaeon,* the Mount of Olives – shelters a basilica – *Eleoiva* or Olive Grove – erected in the 4th century by Saint Helena, the mother of Constantine the Great. This basilica is the most important sanctuary on the Mount of Olives. Destroyed by the Persians, it was rebuilt by the Crusaders before being destroyed again by the Muslims. Excavations led by Father Vincent in 1910 draw the enclosure out of it desolation and in

1920, the corner stone of the Sacred Heart Basilica is laid. Its design, conceived in France during World War I, is intended to symbolize world peace. It shelters the cave where Jesus initiated his disciples to the mysteries of creation, teaching them, in particular, Christian love, and where he revealed the teachings of the Scriptures before his ascension:

The initiation of the disciples

As he sat on the Mount of Olives, the disciples came to him privately saying: "Tell us, when will these things happen and what will be the sign of your coming and of the end of the world?" Jesus replied: "Beware that no man deceive you for many will come in my name... You will hear about wars and rumors of wars...all of these are the beginning of the pains of childbirth..."

Matthew 24: 3 - 8

The Pater Noster Cloister, which houses the remains of the Italian princess, a relative of Napoleon III, who had repurchased the grounds in 1868, commemorates the place where upon returning to Bethany, Jesus taught his disciples the prayer, Our Father:

Pater Noster

Therefore, pray in this manner:
Our Father, who art in heaven,
hallowed be your name.
Your kingdom come,
your will be done,
on earth as it is in heaven.
Give us this day our daily bread
and forgive us our trespasses as we forgive those
who trespass against us.
Lead us not into temptation
and deliver us from evil.

Matthew 6: 9 - 13

The Garden of Gethsemane – from the Hebrew, *gat shemen*, or oil press – is the place where Jesus pronounced the prayer on the night of his agony, which profoundly impacted Christian theology:

The prayer at Gethsemane

And he came out and went, as he was wont, to the Mount of Olives and his disciples followed him. And when he arrived at the place, he said to them: "Pray that you do not enter into temptation." And he withdrew from them about a stone throw away, kneeled down and prayed, saying: "Father, if it is your will, remove this cup from me; nevertheless, not my will, but your will be done." And an angel from heaven appeared to him, strengthening him. In agony, he prayed more earnestly and his sweat was like great drops of blood falling to the ground. When he arose from prayer and came to his disciples, he found them sleeping from sorrow. He said to them: "Why are you sleeping? Rise and pray lest you fall into temptation!" And while he was still speaking, a crowd arrived and he who was called Judas, one of the twelve, led the crowd; he approached Jesus and kissed him. Jesus said to him: "Judas, are you betraying the Son of man with a kiss."

Luke 22: 39 - 48

The Basilica of All Nations, one of the most beautiful in Jerusalem, is built between 1919 and 1924 by the architect, Antonio Barluzzi, on the emplacement of the Basilica of the Agony that dates back to the 4th century. It is destroyed by the Persians and rebuilt by the Crusaders under the name of the Holy Savior Church. Its present day name comes from the many nations that collaborated to restore it, and whose emblems appear on the cupolas and the apses of the sanctuary. The architecture, the lighting and the decoration are intended to recreate Christ's feelings of sadness and despondency. The rock that Jesus was near when he pronounced the prayer, which was hewn all over, occupies a prominent place in the central apse. It is surrounded by iron bars designed like a crown of thorns mixed with olive branches. Some birds are arranged around the cup symbolizing men partaking of the cup of the death of Christ. Some doves caught in the iron bars offer their necks as victims. The mosaic on the front of the church depicts Christ as the mediator between God and humanity, who was sacrificed to obtain their salvation for them. The letters, alpha and omega, symbolize the divinity in Christianity. Both dignitaries and sages acknowledge their own vanity and ignorance. Two harts that flank the cross on the roof symbolize the believers in accordance with the passage, Psalms 42: 2: "As the hart pants after the water of brooks, so my soul pants after You, oh God."

The eight olive trees that stand in the area of Gethsemane date back to the period of Christ. The Franciscans surround this area with a fence and bury the roots of the trees under rocks to prevent the sacred vandalism of pulling out the roots and the bark to make into relics. The oil from the olives is used to light the lamps of the Holy Sepulcher and their pits, to make rosaries. A stone bench is identified as the one on which the disciples fell asleep. Arranged as a chapel, it has three altars consecrated to Jesus praying among the disciples, to the assumption of the Virgin and to Judas' kiss. For a long time, the pilgrims would consider the cave to be the site of the Passion of Christ.

The Greek Orthodox, the Franciscans' traditional rivals, allow themselves their own garden of Gethsemane not far from it. There is a church there that was built in 1888 by the Czar, Alexander III in memory of his mother, the Czarina Maria Alexandrova. In 1920, it receives the remains of the grand duchess assassinated during the Bolshevik Revolution. In 1934, a monastery is established on these grounds.

The ascension of Christ that took place on the Mount of Olives forty days after his resurrection is commemorated in the architecture of many sanctuaries throughout the ages, including the Church of the Ascension, which is now a mosque, the Russian Church, the Greek enclosure named Viri Galilaei, etc.:

The ascension of Christ

And as they spoke, Jesus himself stood in their midst and said to them: "Peace be with you." But they were terrified and filled with fear, thinking they had seen a spirit. And he said to them: "Why are you troubled and why do such thoughts rise in your hearts? Behold my hands and my feet: it is I, myself. Touch me, for a spirit has neither flesh nor bones as I have. And when he had said this, he showed them his hands and his feet. And although they were overjoyed, they still were incredulous and surprised and so he said to them: "Do you have any meat?" They offered him some grilled fish. He took it and ate it in front of them.

He then said to them: "These are the words I said to you when I was still with you: all the things that were written about me in the Law of Moses and in the Prophets and in the Psalms must be fulfilled." He then opened their understanding so that they might understand the Scriptures and he said to them: "Thus it is written: Christ will suffer and will rise from the dead on the third day, and repentance and the remission of sins will be preached in his name among all nations beginning in Jerusalem. You are the witnesses of these things. Behold, I send the promise of my Father upon you, but remain in the city of Jerusalem until you are endowed with power from on high."

He then led them as far as Bethany and he lifted his hands and blessed them. And it came to pass that as he blessed them, he parted from them and was carried up to heaven. And they worshipped him and returned to Jerusalem filled with joy, and were continually in the Temple praising and blessing God.

Luke 24: 36 - 53

A first, circular sanctuary is built in the 4th century by a wealthy Roman named Poemenia to perpetuate the ascension. An immense cross that can be seen from a distance is prominently placed on the monument. A column supports a cupola that is opened on the top. In the center, a detached kiosk preserves the Savior's footprints. The Crusaders restore the site and entrust its care to the Saint Augustine College for canons. Soon after Saladin's victory in 1198, the sanctuary is converted into a mosque. Today, the Christians venerate only the stone bearing the imprint of the Savior's left foot; the stone bearing the imprint of the right foot can be found in Westminster, in Rome... or in the Mosque of Al-

Aksa. A procession marks the celebrations of the Ascension that during the Middle Ages, began at the Holy Sepulcher and ended at the Church of the Ascension.

THE WALLS OF JERUSALEM

The wall surrounding the Old City is built more or less along the line of the wall that surrounded Jerusalem during the period of the Second Temple. It measures 4 kilometers in length and its height varies from 8 to 14 meters. The work that begins in 1537 continues until 1541 according to the inscriptions engraved on the walls. Most of its eleven gates date back to that period. Four have been condemned for centuries. Six have the form of an L and turn at a right angle under the porch to provide access to the Old City, while the Damascus Gate requires turning a first time to the right and a second time to the left. These indirect entrances permit the gates to be better defended.

The **Jaffa Gate** – *Shaar Yaffo* in Hebrew – in the western wall of the city is the most renown. The Arabs call it *Bab el-Khalil* or the Hebron Gate. The roads leading to Jaffa and to Hebron set out from this gate that provided access to the historic road that crossed the city from west to east along the present day David St. and its extension, Chain St., to the Temple mount. In 1898, the Turkish sultan Abdul-Hamid fills the ravine that separated the Jaffa Gate from the Citadel or the Tower of David in order to permit Kaiser Wilhelm II to enter by car – he is one of the first visitors to do away with the custom of entering the city by foot.[6] A small courtyard near the gate houses two tombs – those of the architects of the walls who, according to a legend, were decapitated by Suleiman for having excluded Mount Zion.

6. The visit of Wilhelm II, see p.190.

The **Zion Gate** – *Shaar Zion* in Hebrew – in the southern wall is known among the Arabs as David's Gate due to its proximity to the presumed tomb of this king.[7] During the Middle Ages, it was called *Bab Karat El-Yahud* or the Gate of the Jewish Quarter. Some stairs lead to the guardroom.

7. The tomb of David, see p.21.

The gate preserves the marks of bullets exchanged between the Israelis and the Jordanians in June 1967 during the battles for control of the Old City.

The **Dung Gate** – *Shaar ha-Ashpot* in Hebrew – is located on the site where the city's refuse was dumped in the Kidron. The Arabs call it the Gate of the Maghebrians because of its proximity to the ex-quarter of the Muslim Maghebrians who are moved by the Israeli in 1967 in order to arrange the prayer area in front of the Western Wall. The Jordanian administration had enlarged this gate, the lowest in the city, to allow vehicles to enter the Old City through it. Today, this entrance is the closest one to the Western Wall, as well as the busiest.

The **Simple Gate,** the **Double Gate** and the **Triple Gate,** all walled up, are located further to the east in the southern wall. The last two, which provided the main access to Herod's Temple, are known in the Talmud as Hulda's Gates. The Simple Gate and the Triple Gate lead to vast subterranean caverns measuring 400 square meters supported by eighty-eight columns, vestiges of the Temple, which the Templars used as stables.[8] Under Herod, the Double Gate provided access to a subterranean gallery that opened on to the Temple esplanade. Today, some steps still lead from the Mosque of El-Aksa to this gate, which is only partly visible from the outside.

8. The Stables of King Solomon, see p.99.

The **Gate of Mercy** – S*haar ha-Rahamim* in Hebrew – on the site of Solomon's portico, was replaced with the Herodian gate of Shushan. The Gate of Mercy, which the Arabs call the Eternal Gate and the Christians call the Golden Gate, is a condemned gate in the eastern wall. It provided direct access to the parvis of Solomon's Temple and then to that of Herod. Suleiman the Magnificent restores this Byzantine construction, which evidently dates back to the second half of the 7th century. It is laden with many legends throughout the centuries. Christian tradition compares it with the Beautiful Gate where John healed the paralytic:

The Beautiful Gate

Now Peter and John went up together to the Temple for the three o'clock afternoon prayers. A certain man who was lame from birth was carried and laid at the gate of the Temple, which is called the Beautiful Gate, to ask for alms from those entering the Temple. When he saw Peter and John entering the Temple, he asked them for alms. Then Peter and John fixed their eyes on him and said: "Look at us." And he heeded them, expecting to receive something. Then Peter said: "I have no silver or gold, but I will give you what I have. In the name of Jesus of Nazareth, rise and walk!" He took him by the right hand and lifted him up and the bones of his feet and ankles were immediately strengthened. He leaped up, stood, walked and entered the Temple with them, walking and leaping and praising God. All the people saw him walking and praising God. They recognized him as the one who had sat begging for alms at the Beautiful Gate of the Temple...

Acts 3: 1 - 10

Christian tradition identifies this gate as the site of Jesus' triumphal entrance on Palm Sunday where Joachim and Anne, the Virgin's parents, met him as well as the site of the return of the emperor Heraclius with the holy Cross that had been recovered from the Persians. For a long time, this same gate served as the gathering place for the Jews who came to implore divine mercy at the foot of the destroyed Temple, even claiming that it would receive the true Messiah[9] at the end of days. The Muslims, furthermore, condemned it in the 9th century only to prevent his entry and even established a cemetery there to prohibit his passage. The Jews immediately discovered this obstruction to the realization of one of Ezekiel's prophecies that declares:

9. The Gate of Mercy, see p.167.

The shut gate

Then he brought me back by way of the outer gate that faces the east and it was shut. And the Eternal said to me: This gate will be shut, it will not be opened and no man will enter through it because the Eternal, the God of Israel, has entered through it and, therefore, it will be shut. As for the prince,

being a prince, he will sit there and eat before the Eternal;
he will enter by way of the porch of that gate and he will go
out the same way.

Ezekiel 44: 1 - 3

The **Lions Gate** – *Shaar ha-Arayot* in Hebrew – was called
the Saint Mary Gate by the Arabs due to its proximity to
the site that is traditionally identified as Mary's birthplace.
Convinced that Saint Stephen was martyred in the Kidron
Valley, the Christians name it the Saint Stephen Gate. Its
name in Hebrew comes from the four lions sculpted on its
façade. Legend has it that these lions perpetuate the dream in
which Suleiman saw himself handed over to the animals if
he would not rebuild the walls of the city. Another tradition
considers it to be the Gate of the Purifying Pool owing to its
proximity to the Bethseda Pool or the Purifying Pool (where
the animals to be sacrificed were purified) – a vast Herodian
reservoir divided into two basins that could reach a depth of
13 meters.[10] This pool continues to be known as the site of
the healing of the paralytic by Christ:

10. The Purifying Pools, see p.88, 108.

The Gate of the Purifying Pool

Thereafter, there was a Jewish feast and Jesus went up to
Jerusalem. Now there is a pool by the sheep market, which is
called Bethseda in Hebrew. It has five porches where a great
multitude of impotent, blind, limp and ill lay waiting… There
was a certain man who had been infirmed for thirty-eight
years. Jesus saw him lying there and, knowing that he had
been in that condition for a long time, he said to him: "Do
you want to be made whole?" The invalid replied: "Sir, I have
no one to put me into the pool when the water moves and
before I can get in, someone steps in before me." Jesus said
to him: "Rise, pick up your bed and walk." And the man was
immediately made whole and picked up his bed and walked.

John 5: 1 - 9

Herod's Gate – *Shaar Hordous* in Hebrew – is also called
the Flowers Gate and the Gate of the Small Plain – *Bab el*
Sharireh – by the Arabs. The pilgrims gave it its first name

thinking that it provided access to King Herod's palace. The Rockefeller Museum[11], built in the 1930s, stands on one the campgrounds of the Crusaders.

11. The Rockefeller Museum or the Archeological Museum of Palestine, established in 1927 thanks to the donation from an American industrialist, houses remarkable collections of archeological pieces.

The **Damascus Gate** – *Shaar Dameseq* in Hebrew, or the Shechem Gate – is called the Gate of the Column, *Bab el-Amud* – by the Arabs. The latter comes from the Roman column that stands in the middle of the square to which the gate provides access. This gate, evidently built like an arch of triumph, overlooked the road that crossed the Roman city and then the Byzantine city, from north to south along the Cardo[12] to the Zion Gate. Excavations have uncovered some vestiges of more ancient gates dating back to the Herodian, the Roman and the Byzantine periods.

12. The Cardo, see p.87, 92.

The quarries of King Solomon stretch out under the hill of Bethseda, which today is occupied by the Muslim Quarter. Since the reign of King Solomon, they would supply the stones needed for the construction of the buildings and palaces in the city. The insurgents would use their galleries during the revolts that shook this troubled city. A legend identifies the entrance to one of the quarries as the site of the birth of the Order of the Franks-Masons[13]...

13. Ezekiel's tunnel, see p.39.

The **New Gate** – *ha-Shaar ha-Hadash* in Hebrew – or the Sultan's Gate that opens on to the Christian Quarter, is opened under the reign of the sultan, Abdul-Hamid II (1876 – 1909).

[•]

Suleiman undertakes construction projects on the Temple Mount. He sets up four fountains within the city and another outside of the city near the Sultan's pools in the Hinnom Valley that are restored under his administration. On her part, his wife, Roxelane, becomes involved with the circles of Muslim theologians and mystics in the city, establishing many institutions that are subsidized by the taxes levied on the villages throughout the country. The Turkish governor and his escort of janissaries establish themselves in David's Citadel. But this period of development is followed by a period of decline since the city is the center of a province that is relatively less important than those of Safed, Nablus or Gaza. Its governor is subordinate to the governor of Saida and then to the one of Akko, and the management of municipal affairs is entrusted to the *cadi*, the Muslim judge, who even has authority over the non-Muslims. The absence of Turkish nationals, who no longer settle in Jerusalem or elsewhere in the country, nevertheless, encourages the rise of an Arab aristocracy that combines wealth with power. Neither Daher-el-Omar, who takes possession of the country in 1773, nor Napoleon, who is only interested in the coastal villages during his disastrous passage through the country, wants the city.

The liberalism of the Turks does indeed raise the hopes for the restoration of Jerusalem among the Jews, yet for a long time there are still be no more than 1,500 members in the community in Jerusalem that is dispersed throughout the present day Jewish quarter. The development of the community will have to wait until the decline of Safed. In the 17th century, Jerusalem includes many congregations: the Sepharadi, the Ashkenazi, and the Italian, as well as a Maghrebian congregation and a few descendents of the Karaite sect. The community continues to live on the subsidies from the Diaspora, dispatching emissaries on a regular basis to collect donations. Shabbetai Tzvi is one of them. When he arrives in Jerusalem for the first time in 1662, his influence is so great that he is immediately entrusted by the Rabbis to collect funds in Egypt. The money is used to orchestrate one of the most stinging Messianic campaigns in the history of the Jews. Backed by a visionary in Gaza, Shabbetai Tzvi in turn presents himself as the Messiah, rousing the support of the communities in the Diaspora. The rabbis in Jerusalem very quickly excommunicate him, provoking a backlash in the city and alienating the partisans of the false messiah throughout the world until his spectacular conversion to Islam. Gershom Scholem, the historian of the Kabbalah, devotes a monumental study to this striking individual. He retraces his first stay in Jerusalem as follows:

A false messiah in the city

*In the beginning, Shabbetai would frequent the Talmudic
academies on a daily basis where he would study with the
others after the morning prayers. After a few months, he
purchased the house of a Sephardic Jew (where he had
a house built)... In this house, Shabbetai set aside a room
for a specific purpose; he would lock himself in or cloister
himself there, fasting from one Shabbath to another... He
also would observe other pious rules, such as personally
making all the purchases required to prepare Shabbath,
exerting himself to such an extent that his clothing would
become "soaked with perspiration". Reserving a "room for
solitude" was an established practice that the handbooks to
asceticism and ethics of the period recommended. Every now
and then, Shabbetai would leave his house and would spend
many days in deep solitude in the mountains and caves in the
Judean Desert... In short, he led an ascetic life of a hermit,
seeking nothing but the presence of God...*

G. Scholem, *Shabbetai Tzvi*

[•]

In 1700, Rabbi Juda the Pious visits Jerusalem. Upon
returning to Poland, he encourages his disciples to immigrate
to Palestine. His death does not hinder them from settling in
Jerusalem. They are determined to defy the interdiction by
the Turkish authorities and to build a new synagogue and
we suspect that they are partisans of the false messiah. They
purchase a complex of houses that opened on to an inner
courtyard – the *Hourva* – and they settle down to the task
of building their synagogue. But they get into so much debt,
compelled to pour out bribes to the authorities, that they are
not able to fulfill their commitments, and their creditors
unceasingly demand more money, threatening to prohibit
the continuation of the work. They are finally discouraged,
even to the point of despair, as confirmed by the testimony
of a certain Gedalia:

The misfortunes of the Ashkenazim

Let us speak now of the serious difficulties that the construction of the new building is causing. Our debts weigh down on us like a yoke upon our necks. We live under the constant threat of being arrested; as soon as we have worked out an agreement with one of our creditors, another initiates new proceedings against us. Furthermore, we only rarely venture out into the streets where, on top of everything else, the tax authorities are on the lookout for us like lions watching out for wolves, ready to devour us. When we decided to come to settle in Jerusalem with our teacher [Rabbi Judah], we traveled throughout all of Germany where we had been promised assistance. At the time, we thought we would be able to live in a dignified manner. But we are riddled with debts and in addition, we must turn over large sums of money to the Turks to assure our safety and to avoid ending up in prison – the worst of all.

It is particularly difficult for us, the Ashkenazi Jews, who do not speak the language of the country, to venture into the market. The Sephardi Jews speak Ladino, the Arabs speak Aramaic [evidently Arabic] and the Ottomans speak Turkish, however, no one speaks German. What, moreover, could we sell? It is true that there is no lack of wine in the land of Israel, but neither the Turks nor the Arabs drink. Should a Jew risk selling any, even just a small quantity, to a Muslim and should the latter be caught drunk, the unfortunate merchant would immediately be arrested, beaten and charged with a heavy fine...

The Arabs often attack the Jews in public. Only the most distinguished among them permit themselves to ignore us when we cross their paths. On the other hand, meeting a common man often proves to be unpleasant. We cannot raise a hand against the Turks or the Arabs who are of the same religion. When one of them attacks a Jew, the latter can only run and hide, keeping his mouth shut in order not to receive any more blows.

At least that is how the Sephardim are accustomed to behaving at this stage of events. The Ashkenazim, who have not yet accepted the idea of receiving blows without reacting, revile their aggressors if they speak Arabic or jump on them in fury, receiving even more blows. Nevertheless, when a respectable Turk arrives unexpectedly, he scolds the Arab aggressor, chases him away and even waits for the Jew to move on before continuing on his own path. The Christians are also subjected to similar humiliation. When a Jew provokes the anger of a Turk, he is shamefully and severely beaten with a shoe and no one can come to the poor man's rescue. It is no different for the Christians who are subject to the same oppressive regime although, because they do not lack money, they can allow themselves to bribe the Turks and keep them at a distance. Unfortunately, the Jews do not have access to as much money and their situation continues to deteriorate.

Gedalia, *Testimony*

Finally, Gedalia's fears are confirmed. On November 8th, 1720, the synagogue is destroyed and pillaged. The new congregation falls apart, leaving behind a debt that the authorities demand be reimbursed by… all the Ashkenazim who, furthermore, have to flee:

The flight of the Ashkenazim

I had to escape from Jerusalem during the night because life in that city had become practically impossible. The persecution and the extortion increased day by day. The debt of the Ashkenazim rose to over 50,000 reichsmarks and that of the Sephardim to almost 200,000 guldens. How could we possibly reimburse such amounts? A day does not go by without someone being thrown in prison, sometimes a leader, sometimes a scholar, who is beaten until he agrees to repay the sum demanded of him… Also, I was only able to arrange to leave the city at night on a camel heading to Hebron…

I am living free of charge here in the home of a scholar, Rabbi Isaac Caregal's brother-in-law. I had searched at length for someone who would agree to offer me their hospitality for six or seven months, the time it would take to receive assistance from abroad. Everyone said that they did not have enough money to meet their own needs. Indeed, life in Hebron is very expensive and it is very difficult to earn a living there. The debt of the people is as high as almost 50,000 guldens – there are only twenty to thirty families.

Having moved to different places, I was able to see for myself how much the people of the country despise us, the Ashkenazim. We are, after all, lunatics! ... I can tell you that in fifty years, there will not be any Ashkenazim in this country. If God had not sent me signs and performed wonders to sustain me, I would have been dead long ago.

More than two hundred families have left cities like Jerusalem this year. Life is no less difficult in Hebron, Safed and Tiberias. The political situation is particularly difficult and is continually deteriorating as a result of our grave sins, the persecution to which we are subjected and the denunciations against us, etc.

Gedalia, Testimony

The Ashkenazim who are prohibited from staying in the city, do not appear on the streets unless they are dressed up like the Sephardim. Rabbi Abraham Gershon from Kutow, the brother-in-law of the Baal Shem Tov, the father of Hassidism, is the first among them to openly do so. The waves of immigration do not prevent the new decline of the city and of its community. The Jewish population decreases from 10,000 people in the middle of the 18th century to 5,000 at the end of the century due to famine, epidemics and natural catastrophes. The difficult living conditions in the city are the source of this warning that Rabbi Abraham Kalisher delivers to those who envisioned immigrating to Palestine:

A warning

Many, many unpleasant surprises and troubles, vexations and misfortunes await those who are preparing to venture into that country before they adapt, finding joy in their prayers and loving its dust, and before the ruins of the land of Israel become dearer to them than the places abroad and before their dry bread becomes sweeter to them than the good things that there are elsewhere. But this will not occur in one day or in two, neither in one month nor in a year. Many years are required for their initiation – an initiation to the true life.

A. Kalisher

The situation is so terrible that even Christian pilgrims are rare. Volney ushers in the tradition of the great travelers during his visit to the region in 1784 –1785. He describes the Turkish government in the country and their domination as follows:

The arbitrariness of the Turks

By virtue of the sultan's image, the pasha is his government's Chief of Police; criminal justice falls within the authority assumed under this title. He has the most absolute power over life and death, which he exercises without guidelines and without the possibility to appeal his judgment. Wherever he comes across a misdemeanor, he has the guilty arrested and the executioners accompanying him strangle the offender or decapitate him at once; sometimes he does not disdain carrying out their duties. Three days before my arrival in Tyre, Djezzar had disemboweled a mason with the blow of an ax. The pasha often prowls in disguise and woe to whomever is caught by surprise! Since he cannot carry out this task in all places, he entrusts an officer, called the ouali, to fill in for him; this ouali fulfills the duties of our watch guards. Like them, he prowls night and day, watching out for revolts, arresting thieves; like the pasha, he judges and condemns without the possibility of appeal. The guilty lowers his neck, the executioner strikes, the head falls and the body is taken away in a leather bag. This officer has a multitude of spies, who are almost all rogues, to keep him informed of everything that is going on...

The duties of the ouali do not at all accomplish the useful and pleasant ends that are a credit to the police among us. They do not look after the cleanliness or the sanitation of the cities, which are not paved, swept or watered down, in Syria as in Egypt; the streets are narrow, winding and almost always obstructed with rubbish. It is especially shocking to see a throng of hideous dogs that do not belong to anyone there. They form a kind of independent republic that lives off of public alms. They are confined to families and to neighborhoods and if one of them leaves its borders, fights will ensue, disturbing the passers-by. The Turks who so easily spill the blood of men, never kill the dogs; they simply avoid touching them like filth. They claim that they make the night safe in the cities; but the ouali and the gates that lock every street do a better job. They add that they eat carrion with the help of the jackals that hide in the gardens and among the rubbish in the gardens.

Volney, *A Voyage to Egypt and Syria*

The French writer, Chateaubriand, the author of *The Genius of Christianity* leaves us his account of the four days he spent in Jerusalem in October 1806:

A city of deicide

You enter the city. The appearance of sadness will provide nothing to console you: you loose your way in the small, unpaved streets that rise and descend on uneven ground. You walk through waves of dust or upon rolling rocks. Cloth thrown from one house to another adds to the darkness of the labyrinth; vaulted, foul smelling bazaars completely eliminate the light of the desolate city. Some wretched boutiques display nothing but poverty, and they are often even closed out of fear that the cadi will pass by. The streets are empty and there is no one at the gates of the city. Sometimes there is a lone peasant sliding in the shadows, hiding the fruits of his labor underneath his clothing, fearing that a soldier will rob him. In an isolated corner, an Arab butcher slaughters an animal hung by his legs on a dilapidated wall; the haggard and fierce look of the man with his bloody arms makes you think that he has just killed his fellow man instead of a lamb. Amidst all the noise in the city of deicide, the gallop of the mare from the desert is heard: it is the janissary who brings the head of a Bedouin or who is on his way to attack the fellah.

R. Chateaubriand, *An Itinerary from Paris to Jerusalem*

Thirty years later, Lamartine wanders around a quarantined city that had been severely struck by the plague. On November 3rd, 1832, he writes:

The infected city

Ravaged by the plague, the city of Jerusalem was flooded with the rays of a dazzling sun that were reflected on its thousands of domes, its white marble, all its towers of golden stone and its walls that had been polished by the centuries and by the salty winds of Lake Asphaltite. Not a single sound rose from its enclosure, mute and dead like the bed of a dying man; its large gates were opened and every now and then, we caught sight of the white turban and red coat of the Arab soldier, the unnecessary guard of its abandoned gates. Nothing would come in and nothing would leave. Only the morning air would raise the undulating dust of the roads, creating for a moment the illusion of a caravan; but when the gust of air would pass, when it would come to die, whistling through the crenellations of Pisans' Tower or through the three palm trees at the home of the Caliph, the dust would settle, the desert would again appear and not a single step of any camel or any mule would resound on the paved road. Every fifteen minutes, the mounted double doors of the gates of Jerusalem would open and we would see the dead that the plague had finished off, carried on stretchers by two nude slaves, passing through to the tombs scattered all around us. A long procession of Turks, Arabs, Armenians and Jews would sometimes accompany the dead, singing as they walked between the trunks of the olive trees and then returned slowly and silently to the city.

Lamartine, *A Voyage to the East*

There will not be a change in the status of the Ashkenazi Jews until the conclusion of the agreements between Turkey and the European powers. Then, the Ashkenazim will even be exempted from certain taxes that were imposed on their Sephardic coreligionists. The following is a testimony, dated 1834, by Joseph Shwartz from Bavaria:

The return of the Ashkenazim

We, the others, the Germans as well as the other immigrants from Europe who are not the subjects of the Turkish sultan – referred to as the Franks in the language of this country – are completely exempt from the taxes mentioned above and, more generally, from all the heavy burdens that the pasha imposes on his subjects. Thank God, we now have the benefit of the special protection of our respective European consuls, and the oppressive laws that govern the country do not affect us in any way when just a few years ago, the Jews dressed in European clothing were subject to humiliation and harassment by the crowd. This explains why I had to exchange my European clothing for a Turkish outfit. But now, the European Jews are pleasantly and respectfully received. As for me, I wear German clothing when I appear in the courts of justice and as a European, I am treated with respect.

J. Schwartz, *Testimony*

In 1856, the philanthropist, Moses Montefiore, obtains a document authorizing the resumption of the work on the synagogue in the enclosure of the *Hurva*. The work is completed in 1864 thanks to the funds collected throughout Europe and to the support of the King of Prussia. The Ashkenazi synagogue – *Beit Yaacov,* that bears the first name of the Baron de Rothschild – remains, for a long time, the largest and the most impressive synagogue in Jerusalem and the center of the Ashkenazi community until its destruction by the Jordanians in 1948. Its restoration is confined to the rebuilding of one of the arches of its cupola.

BEYOND THE WALLS

Throughout this period, the Europeans take little interest in the city, intervening only to guarantee the safety of the pilgrims and the safekeeping of the holy Christians sites. The French are the most enterprising – they are the first to conclude treaties of surrender with the Turkish authorities in 1735, which entrust them with the responsibility of maintaining the holy sites. Europe does not truly rediscover the Holy City until the beginning of the 19th century.

The Egyptians' brief reign (1831 – 1839), under the leadership of Mehemet-Ali and his representative in Palestine, Ibrahim

Pasha, marks a turning point in the government, the management and the development of Jerusalem. They tear it away from the arbitrary power of the *cadi*, limiting the prerogatives and privileges of the Muslims, to endow it with institutions that provide it with a certain degree of municipal autonomy. Second to Damascus, it becomes an important political center that is open to Europe and to its changes. The salaries accorded to the judges, officers and other civil servants protect the non-Muslims from the venality of the authorities, who until then were reduced to extorting the religious minorities, ransoming their sanctuaries and their projects to become wealthy as quickly as possible. Furthermore, the Egyptians authorize free access to the holy sites of the Christians, the building of new churches and the restoration of the ancients ones. Among other things, they take political measures to assure the safety of the cities and the roads, looking out, in particular, for the well-being of the pilgrims, who are no longer required to pay tolls to the Bedouin tribes, and to the people in the villages that border the road to Jerusalem, such as Abu Gosh. But these and other measures provoke the displeasure of the Islamic authorities and of the fellahs, who are compelled to hide in the mountains to escape the general mobilization decreed in the country. The latter openly revolt against the authorities in 1834 – "the fellahs' revolt". Jerusalem, subsequently, is occupied by thousands of insurgents who attack the religious minorities. Ibrahim Pasha, in turn, marches into Jerusalem leading many thousands of men. He recaptures the city, is forced to retreat and recaptures it once again.

Finally, the European powers ally themselves with the Turks to demand the withdrawal of the Egyptians from Palestine. The Ottomans evidently negotiate their return to power by committing themselves to pursue the liberalization policies of the Egyptians. On November 11th, 1840, a municipal council, which, in truth, is more advisory than executive, is formed, composed of representatives of the different religious communities. The agreement signed in Paris on May 30th, 1856 at the end of the Crimean War (1853 – 1856) specifies the status of the non-Muslim communities and their spiritual leaders within the Ottoman Empire. Henceforth, the pasha in Jerusalem is directly subject to the Turkish governmental authorities. The influence of the foreign powers, more specifically of their consular representatives, proves to be greater than the mandate, which will not be in effect for more than one year.

Jerusalem receives numerous delegations and representative that undertake a wide range of missionary, educational and medical activities. The rivalries that arise between them, in general, benefit the development of the city – for example, as soon as the Austrians open a postal service, the French, Prussians and Italians imitate them. The European powers even begin to compete... to guarantee the protection of the Ashkenazi Jews. In the middle of the 18th century, Jerusalem has a population of 18,000 inhabitants; 8,000 are Jewish. For the first time since the destruction of the city by the Romans, they become the largest group in the population.

[•]

In 1838, Great Britain opens a consular office, followed by the establishment of the representation of the Protestant Church directed, in turn, by an English bishop and a Prussian bishop. The bishop immediately begins missionary activities – the first prelate assigned to Jerusalem is, moreover, a converted Jew from Dublin, Michael Solomon Alexander. At first, he devotes all his efforts to the most dispossessed members of the Jewish community since the authorities had forbidden converting the Muslims. The British, moreover, establish their own religious institutions to compete with those of the Catholics and of the Orthodox sponsored by the other European powers, especially the French and the Russians. Under the sponsorship of the Society of London for the Propagation of Christianity among Jews, the masons, who came from Malta and from England (1841 – 1848), openly build the Protestant Church of the Savior[1]. Gustave Flaubert, evidently one of its first visitors, does not like its austerity:

1. The Church of the Savior or the Church of Christ is located near the Citadel of David.

A waiting room

Upon returning, we entered over the threshold of the Protestant Church: gentlemen in black were seated on benches on each side; another gentleman wearing a clerical band sat in a chair on the left, reading the Gospel. The walls were completely bare; it looked like an elementary school or like a railway station waiting room. I prefer the Armenians, the Greeks, the Copts, the Catholics, the Turks, Vichnou, a fetish, anything! Goodbye! Good evening! Enough! Let's get out of here! We weren't there for even a quarter of a minute and I had enough time to get truly and profoundly bored.

G. Flaubert, *A Voyage to the Orient*

In 1855, the British build the first house located outside the walls of the Old City in the Talbieh neighborhood. Following the construction of the summer residence of the British consul, the first Protestant school, a teacher-training seminary, is built on the southeast side of Mount Zion. In 1862, a sanatorium is established outside the walls, followed by the establishment of an ophthalmology clinic in 1882. In 1897, a hospital is set-up on the grounds of the sanatorium, which the rabbis boycott, denouncing its missionary ruses and encouraging the Jews to establish their own medical services.

In 1833, a British general, rather a mystic, named Charles Gordon, identifies a knoll in the shape of a skull outside the walls of the city as the site of the tomb of Christ. In 1867, tombs evidently dating back to the First Temple Period are discovered there as well as in other places in the cemetery of the Greek convent of Saint Stephen, which served as an "asnerie" to the Hospitalars and a reception center to the pilgrims. In 1894, the Protestants buy the plot of land; henceforth, one of its tombs is considered to be the true sepulcher of Christ.

In 1886, the Anglicans and the Lutherans separate. The former establish a new mission that gradually directs its efforts towards the Muslims, opening scholastic and medical institutions. One complex bordering the road to Shechem – that consolidates lodgings for pilgrims, the bishop's residence and a library designed according to the model of the New College in Oxford – is inaugurated in 1891 under the name of the College of Saint George. However, the tower bearing the name of King Edward VII is not completed until 1912. Mark Twain (1835 – 1910), American writer and traveler, made the journey to Jerusalem with a group of Pilgrims:

The illustrious city

At last, away in the middle of the day, ancient bits of wall and crumbling arches began to line the way – we toiled up one more hill, and every pilgrim and every sinner swung his hat on high! Jerusalem!

Perched on its eternal hills, white and domed and solid, massed together and hooped with high gray walls, the venerable city gleamed in the sun. So small! Why, it was no larger than an American village of four thousand inhabitants, and no larger than an ordinary Syrian city of thirty thousand. Jerusalem numbers only fourteen thousand people.

We dismounted and looked, without speaking a dozen sentences, across the wide intervening valley for an hour or more; and noted those prominent features of the city that pictures make familiar to all men from their school days till their death. We could recognize the Tower of Hippicus, the Mosque of Omar, the Damascus Gate, the Mount of Olives, the Valley of Jehosaphat, the Tower of David, and the Garden of Gethsemane – and dating from these landmarks could tell very nearly the localities of many others we were not able to distinguish.

I record it here as a notable but not discreditable fact that not even our pilgrims wept. I think there was no individual in the party whose brain was not teeming with thoughts and images and memories invoked by the grand history of the venerable city that lay before us, but still among them all was no "voice of them that wept".

There was no call for tears. Tears would have been out of place. The thoughts Jerusalem suggests are full of poetry, sublimity, and, more than all, dignity. Such thoughts do not find their appropriate expression in the emotions of the nursery.

Just after noon we entered these narrow, crooked streets, by the ancient and famous Damascus Gate, and now for several hours I have been trying to comprehend that I am actually in the illustrious old city where Solomon dwelt, where Abraham held converse with the Deity, and where walls still stand that witnessed the spectacle of the Crucifixion.

M. Twain, *The Innocents Abroad*

The tombs of the principal architects of Protestant penetration into the Holy Land are in the old Protestant cemetery on Mount Zion. Four other Protestant cemeteries cover this Mount of Dormition: An Armenian cemetery, with a section reserved for the patriarchs; a Latin (Franciscan) cemetery where monks and pilgrims are buried; a Greek Orthodox cemetery, in which, contrary to all expectations, the Ottoman authorities, who are all Muslims, chose to be laid to rest; and the cemetery of the American mission. These cemeteries require a guide to reveal the legends sealed underneath all these slabs of stone – the tragedy of the burial of the Jews who converted to Protestantism and who returned *in extremis* to Judaism was that their remains were claimed at the same time by both the pastors and the rabbis, and were sometimes transferred from one place of dormition to another place of resurrection, or would end up in neutral places, under the orders of the Muslim authorities...

[•]

The Russians, in turn, open a consular office. They immediately settle down to the task of building a vast and ambitious complex (1860 – 1864) on a plot of land that they had acquired outside of the walls. It includes hostels, a hospital, a residence reserved for the religious authorities, the residence of the Russian Consul, large reservoirs of water and the Russian Orthodox Cathedral with its green domes and gold cross; surrounded by a wall, the compound could accommodate almost one thousand pilgrims. The cathedral is the first church in Jerusalem to be equipped with a bell – one of the two bells brought from Russia in 1864 in circular cases that 150 Russian pilgrims rolled from Jaffa to Jerusalem; the second and larger of the two bells went to the Church of the Holy Sepulcher to the great disappointment of the other Christian communities. The cathedral is inaugurated in 1872 in the presence of Prince Nicholas and numerous members of the Russian court. Once the work is completed, the Russians name the compound Nova Jerusalem. From then on, the bells, which had been prohibited for a long time in Jerusalem, could be sounded, mixing their chiming with the chanting of the muezzins and the litanies of the rabbis. Today, the Israeli Police Department, the jailhouse, the Hall of Heroism[2] as well as a series of other institutions occupy the premises of the Russian Compound – *Migrash ha-Russim*. Some Russian religious authorities continue to manage the monastery and the basilica. A 12-meter stone column placed at the entrance of the church is presented as one of the pieces destined for Herod's Temple or as the finger of the giant Og, the king of Bashan, and the victor over the Hebrews during the time of Moses...

2. The Hall of Heroism is set up in the prison where the British detained members of the Jewish resistance movements.

The activities of the Russians continue until the beginning of the revolution. They devote themselves to archeological excavations and continue to build churches, such as that of Gethsemane or the Russian Church of Saint Maria Magdalena with its five golden bells[3] (1885 – 1888) on the slopes of the Mount of Olives.

3. The Russian Church of Saint-Maria Magdalena, see p.110.

[•]

In 1843 – 1844, the French open their consulate, setting themselves up as the protectors of the Roman Catholic community and its holy sites – a role that the Berlin Conference ratifies, moreover, in 1878. They even succeed in convincing the Pope to appoint a Latin patriarch in Jerusalem to counter the prelates of the other Christian communities, the Greek Orthodox and especially the Protestants. Its consuls play an important role in the development of the city. Flaubert, however, harshly judges one of the most eminent among them, Paul-Emile Botta (1848 – 1855) that Lamartine named: "The man in ruins, the man of ruins, in the city of ruin; he denies everything and he seems to hate everything but the dead; he is nostalgic for the Middle Ages, and admires M. de Maistre. He is now learning to play the piano and admits that he is a dilettante. It is a phase in the life of this man: tired of trying things out (a physician, a taxidermist, an archeologist, a consul – his life is a weave of experiments), he has tried all this and he wants nothing more; he's had enough." The priest, Marie Alphonse Ratisbonne, is another artisan of this Latin disparagement of the Holy City in which the French indulge. An Alsatian Jew who converted to Catholicism, he arrives in Palestine at the beginning of the 1870's. In 1874, he opens an orphanage – Saint Peter of Zion – within the walls of the Convent of the Sisters of Zion in the Old City. Together with the Sisters of Zion, he builds a monastery in the village of Ein Kerem. But his dream is to establish a school that can accept more than two hundred students. In 1876, he buys a plot of land located outside the walls of the city where he begins a construction project. When he dies in 1884, only one wing of the convent bearing his name is completed.[4]

4. A statue of Saint Peter stands in he courtyard of the Saint Peter of Ratisbonne Convent, which was completed in 1897. Located on Shmuel ha-Nagid St., it hosts meetings and seminars. Ratisbonne is buried at the Sisters of Zion's Saint John of Montana Convent in the village of Ein Kerem. See p.253.

In 1856, the sultan bestows the Saint Anne Church to Napoleon III, consecrating the dominant role of France in the region. The church is located on the site of the conception and the birth of Mary as determined by the proto-evangelist, James – according to a tradition that is more common in the East then in the West – in the house of Joachim near the Purifying Pools or Pools of Bethesda. Built in the 7th century, it is restored by the Crusaders when Arda, the wife of Baudouin I, the king of Jerusalem, as well as Judith, the daughter of Baudouin II and the sister of Melisande, visit its convent. In 1192, Saladin converts the church into a Muslim institution – *el-Salahiyyeh* – as certified by the Arabic inscription above the large door. In 1842, the Muslims begin some restoration projects that are not completed; the site appears to them to be haunted. In 1878, the French entrust it to the White Fathers. Its restoration, undertaken at the beginning of 1856 under the direction of a French architect, preserves the bare and austere form of the original basilica. The church has a central nave and two aisles. The evangelists, Saint Matthew and Saint Luke, are respectively represented by the head of a man and the head of a bull. Two generous French consuls in Jerusalem, Charles de Ledoul

(1844 – 1899) and Rene de Neuville (1899 – 1952) are buried at the foot of commemorative plaques. A staircase descends to a crypt in which a Baroque altar is prominently placed. The crypt is considered the house of Anne and Joachim, Mary's parents, and her birthplace.

The French indisputably prove to be the most industrious of the Europeans. Four religious institutions are built during the course of ten years. The members of an order that was founded in Nazareth by an Arab Christian priest, a native of Ein Kerem, build the Convent of the Sisters of the Holy Rosary – located on Agron St. The Saint Louis Hospital, originally built in 1851 within the walls of the Saint Salvador convent in the Old City, relocates in 1891 to its new premises outside the walls in cooperation with the Sisters of Saint Joseph and the support of Countess Marie Amadee de Piellet and her son. The order of the Fathers of Augustine of the Assumption (1884 – 1904) builds the Notre Dame of France Hospice facing the Shechem Gate to receive French pilgrims. Finally, the enclosure of the Dominicans houses the Saint Stephen's Basilica where the Biblical School is established in 1890. Its basilica, consecrated in 1900, rises on the foundations of the church that the patriarch, Juvenal, and the empress, Eudocia, built in the 5th century on the site of the stoning of Saint Stephen, a deacon and the first martyr (out of between 31 to 36), accused by the members of the Sanhedrin of having made blasphemous remarks:

Stephen's death

"...You stiff necked and uncircumcised of heart and ears, you always resist the Holy Ghost as your fathers did. Which of the prophets have your fathers not persecuted? You have slain those who announced in advance the coming of the Just One whom you have betrayed and murdered. You received the Law that the angels disposed and have not kept it."

When they heard these things, they were cut to the heart and they gnashed their teeth against Stephen. But being full of the Holy Ghost, he looked up steadfastly into heaven and saw the glory of God and Jesus standing on the right hand of God. He said: "Behold, I see the heavens opened and the Son of Man standing on the right hand of God." They cried

*out with a loud voice and covered their ears. Then, together
they seized him and cast him out of the city and stoned him...
As they stoned him, Stephen called upon God, saying: "Lord
Jesus, receive my spirit." Then he kneeled down and cried
out with a loud voice: "Lord, do not charge them with this
sin." And after he said this, he died.*

Acts 7: 51 - 60

Destroyed by the Persians in 614, this first basilica is replaced
at the end of the 7th century by a chapel, which the Crusaders
restore. Saladin, in turn, destroys the latter in 1187.

A second tradition situates the site of the stoning of Stephen
in the Kidron Valley near the Lions Gate or Saint Stephen's
Gate. The museum of the Biblical College displays a
collection of ceramics, of stone slabs, of inscriptions and of
coins, etc.

Furthermore, the French complete the railway linking
Jerusalem to Jaffa (1892).

[•]

5. The site of the
Schneller has
since housed the
largest barracks in
Jerusalem.

At the beginning, the German missionaries work in concert
with the British. Johan Ludwig Schneller is one of the most
enterprising. On October 11th, 1855, he buys a plot of land
in the region of the Arab village of Lifta, three kilometers
northeast of the Jaffa Gate, where he builds a house, one of
the first buildings outside the walls. But he has to wait for
the Turks to install watchtowers and to monitor the length
of Jaffa Road in order to be able to move in with his family,
no longer in fear of being attacked by the villagers. In 1860,
he receives the first boarders of an institution that becomes
the largest orphanage in the country. His motto is *Gottes
Wort und Arbeit*, the word of God and work. The institution
continues to grow, receiving orphans from all parts of the
country and then later, also the blind. In 1910, a fire destroys a
large part of the premises, which are immediately restored.[5]

A second educational institution, this one for girls, that will
admit more than 150 students, is built in 1866 – 1868. It
is called *Talitha Qoumi*[6], a name taken from the passage in

Mark that is devoted to the miracles that Jesus performed on the shores of Lake Tiberias:

Talitha Qoumi

As he was speaking, certain people came from the house of the head of the synagogue, saying: "Your daughter is dead; why do you continue to bother the Master?" When Jesus heard the words that were spoken, he said to the head of the synagogue: "Do not be afraid, just believe." And he did not allow any man to follow him except Peter, James and John, James' brother. He came to the house of the head of the synagogue and saw the tumult, the people weeping and wailing greatly. And when he entered he said to them: "Why are you so agitated and weeping? The maiden is not dead, but sleeping." And they laughed at him with scorn. But he made them go out and he took the father and the mother of the maiden and those who had accompanied him and entered the room where the maiden was lying. He took the maiden by the hand and said to her: "Talitha qoumi", which is interpreted as: "Maiden, I say to you, rise!" And the maiden immediately rose and began to walk.

Mark 5: 35 - 42

6. Today, only the school's portico remains, mounted by a clock and the words: "Talitha Qoumi".

In 1866, the Germans open a first shelter at the foot of Mount Zion for the lepers who would frequent the streets of the city and would die in wretched shanties. The Brothers of Bohemia even build a hospital in Talbiyeh (1885 – 1887) – *Jesus Hilfe* – known today as the Hansen hospital.

In 1873, the Templars, a Protestant sect from Germany led by Christopher Hoffman (1815 – 1885), build their own neighborhood – *ha-Moshava ha-Germanit*. They draw their name from the Temple – "that building that is not built of either wood or iron that will, nonetheless, be with God, the sanctuary of God." Persecuted because of their religious practices in Germany, they arrive in Palestine where they intend to found a kingdom of priests. They establish the first neighborhoods in Haifa and Jaffa. In 1878, they install their headquarters in Jerusalem, also moving their educational institutions, especially their high school whose students come from Russia, Germany and America… On the eve of the World War II, they must leave the country. In the Eighties of the 20th century, their neighborhood becomes one of the most high-class neighborhoods in the city. Their cemetery, located in the neighborhood, provides an account of their necrology.

In the autumn of 1889, the city welcomes the German emperor, Wilhelm II, his wife and an entourage of four hundred people. The distinguished visitor arrives in the Old City as a modern day Crusader, almost conquering it. The Arabs, in their caustic manner, caricature his pretensions and his poses, calling him "Cook's Crusader" (the name of a German pilgrimage agency). The Turks, moreover, are compelled to make an opening in the wall near the Jaffa Gate in order to allow him to enter the city on a horse and because he was prohibited from entering the city through the gate itself, which was reserved for Muslim dignitaries only. His visit provides the occasion for many work projects: repair of the pipes, laying out new roads, the extension of lighting in the city… In addition, the Turks offer him a plot of land on Mount Zion where the German Catholics build the Abbey of the Dormition (1900 – 1906) in Roman style on the vestiges of a medieval sanctuary. It stands on the site where the disciples of Jesus met and where the Virgin Mary is said to have slept for the last time. In the crypt consecrated to her, there is an image of her turning towards the cupola where her son, surrounded by Eve, Miriam, Yael, Ruth, Judith and Esther, summon her to him upon pronouncing this verse in the Song of Songs: "Rise, my beloved, my beauty, and come…" Twelve columns symbolize the apostles. There are six altars all around that are dedicated to the six nations that venerate the holy Virgin. A mosaic mural in the central nave depicts Mary as well as Jesus holding a book on which these words are written: "I am the light of the world" (John 8:12). A verse of the prophet, Isaiah, appears below: "Behold, the young woman is with child and she will bear a son and will call his name Immanuel" (Isaiah 7: 14). The prophets who announce the coming of the Savior are depicted between the windows. Under the rotunda, there is a mosaic with three concentric circles and the word "holy", written in Greek three times; the three inner circles symbolize the Trinity.

The outer circles symbolize the phases of divine revelation: the first represents light; the second lists the names of four major prophets, Daniel, Isaiah, Jeremy and Ezekiel; and the third comprises the names of the minor prophets. The following circle represents the four animals that appear in one of the prophecies of Ezekiel. The twelve apostles symbolize Christianity. They are surrounded by the signs of the zodiac and some verses: "Before the mountains were settled, before the hills, I was brought forth, before God had made the earth and its fields or the highest part of the dust of the world" (Proverbs 8: 25 - 26). Six chapels are respectively consecrated to Saint Boniface, John the Baptist, Joseph, Mary's husband, Saint Benedict, the founder of the Benedictine Order that is responsible for these sites, the first British pilgrim to have visited Jerusalem in 724, and the Three Wise Men. The church[7] is inaugurated with great pomp and ceremony in 1910 at the same time as the Augusta Victoria Inn on the Mount of Olives. The latter is built in response to the wish of the emperor and the empress who wanted to create a center for meetings and rest. In the "war of the bells" in which the European powers engage, the imperial couple also want the chiming of the bells in the tower overlooking the inn to drown out that of the other bells in the city. Their statues – in the clothing of the Middle Ages – occupy a prominent place in the Crusader style building. Today, it houses a hospital and a nursing school.

7. The Basilica of the Dormition often hosts liturgical and classical music concerts.

On their part, the German Catholics build a number of charitable institutions including the Saint Charles Old Age Home and the Saint Paul Inn, located in a square in front of the Shechem Gate. In 1900, Father Schmidt, the promoter of the inn, writes: "I would like to name our square Saint Paul's Square because this is the place where for the first time, Paul received Saint Stephen's blessing. Also, he will pass through there once again on his way to Damascus. And finally, so that there will be a square here similar to the one in Rome – a Saint Paul Square outside the walls." The building, inaugurated in 1910, simultaneously or successively houses a school, a seminary, a science museum, and a research institute...During World War I, the Germans establish their headquarters there, and during World War II, it serves as the headquarters of the British Air Force. Today, it has recovered its humanitarian vocation, in particular, by housing a school for young Arab girls.

[•]

In 1873, the ship carrying Anna Spafford and her four daughters, from Chicago to France, for the vacations sinks in the open seas. Only Anna survives. When she regains consciousness, she vows to devote herself together with her husband to the service of God and man. A few years later, their son who was born after the sinking, dies of an illness. Feeling increasingly unhappy in their Presbyterian community, dependent on the hospitality of the other members, they decide to settle in Jerusalem where they arrive in September 1881, leading a group of ten adults and as many children. They attempt to integrate themselves into the life of the city, but their convictions and their religious practices alienate the pastors there who accuse them of heresy. In 1888, Spafford dies and his wife assumes the leadership of the miniscule community. In 1896, eighty people, including twenty-five children, mostly Swedes who had moved to the United States, join them. They are soon joined by forty of their relatives and friends who come directly from Sweden. Contrary to all expectations, the community manages to find a residence large enough to accommodate all its members. Selma Lagerlöf, winner of the Nobel Prize for Literature, recalls life in the Colony where she resided in 1900, emphasizing the role of the Swedes, in a novel entitled *Jerusalem*:

The American Colony

The colonists were very happy to be able to rent the brand new, beautiful and immense residence located outside the Damascus Gate. It was so large that it could accommodate almost everyone; only one or two families had to rent rooms elsewhere. Furthermore, it was wonderfully arranged with covered terraces and open colonnades – that provided precious shelter in the heat of the summer. They could not help but think that it was a special, divine favor that such a house was available at the very moment that they needed it. They, moreover, often acknowledged that they would not have known how to assure the comfort and unity of the community if they had not found this house and had to live dispersed throughout the city.

This came about in the following manner: The house belonged to Baram Pasha, the governor of Jerusalem at the time. He had it built three years before for his wife whom he loved more than anything in the world. He knew that it would greatly please her to build a house large enough to accommodate her large family, their sons and wives, their daughters and their husbands as well as their children and their servants.

But when the house was ready and Baram Pasha had moved in with all his family, a great misfortune fell upon him and his family. During the first week, one of his daughters died; the following week, another daughter died; during the third week, his beloved wife died. Crushed by grief, Baram Pasha immediately left his new palace, closed it and swore that he would never again step foot in it.

Since then, the house remained empty until the colony... proposed renting the house from Baram Pasha. We were very surprised that he agreed because we thought that he would not allow any human being to pass through the doors of the residence.

S. Lagerlöf, *Jerusalem*

The American-Swedish community organizes itself around this residence. The Swedish plant vineyards and olive trees, cultivate grains, go about the work of weaving and sewing and open a bakery and a first photography studio; the Americans dedicate themselves, above all, to teaching English in the Jewish and Arab schools. They contribute greatly to the introduction of new techniques in the city more than the other colonists.

The expansion of Jerusalem mobilizes other nations. The Ethiopian monarchs choose a mountain outside the walls, *Dabret Gaunet* or the Mountain of Paradise – a knoll located in the center of the western part of the city along Ethiopia Street – where they consecrate a church to Mary in 1893. It has the same circular shape of the churches in Ethiopia, enclosing the Holy of Holies, which is designed as a separate building in the center of the two concentric aisles. Four inscriptions, in Ethiopian, Italian, Arabic and French, mention that the building is the work of the kings, John IV (1872 – 1889) and Menelik II (1889 – 1913). During the first decades of the 20th century, the buildings, which are constructed thanks to donations from the dignitaries of the court primarily for the monks, are built all around.

The Austrians also contribute their share to the development of the city. In 1847, they open a consulate, setting themselves up as the protectors of the Jews, providing their assistance in a number of real estate deals. In 1856, the city welcomes Archduke Maximilian, the brother of the Emperor. A few months later, he sends a bronze statue of Queen Helena, as a gift to Church of the Holy Sepulcher that is being restored. In 1867, the emperor, Franz Joseph, himself, arrives, accompanied by the crown prince of Prussia, Frederick Wilhelm III. His visit compels the Turks to lay a road from Jaffa to Jerusalem to allow him to arrive by coach.

Built and maintained by the villagers who are mobilized especially to carry out this forced labor, this road will more or less serve the first stagecoaches driven by German coachman. It is said that the first Jewish coachman – Haim Shabbazi – would politely invite his passengers to get off the vehicle at the base of a slope "out of pity for the animals", at the summit of a slope "to reduce the dangerous risks", and on flat ground to enjoy a walk". A trip with him took one day longer than by donkey…

The road traversed the new Jewish neighborhoods up to the Jaffa Gate, which had become the commercial center of Jerusalem. The Jaffa Gate, the first gate to remain open all night, allowed the old city to extend into the new city, which would bottleneck at the entrance of the old city. It was a busy gate, frequented by all the homeless who lived, worked and prayed on the street upon whose threshold all kinds of people thronged: Bedouins coming to barter their animals or their produce, laborers waiting for the manager of some monastery to offer them work picking olives or bringing water, money changers following the pilgrims, guides on the lookout for travelers, barbers proposing their services, and butchers chasing away the flies over their meat stands. A modern city, still in disorder and muddled, promises to save the Old City, where the sacred had obviously been allowed to be overtaken by the filth. During a visit in 1898, Theodore Herzl, the visionary of the Jewish state does not hide his disappointment in the face of the desolate condition of the Old City:

Lourdes-in-Jerusalem

In the days that follow, it will not be with great pleasure that I will remember you, Jerusalem, moldy pile of two thousand years of neglect and obscurantism, and that filth in your streets with its nasty odors... If one day, Jerusalem belongs to us and if I can still do something, my first act will be to purify it. I will give the order to clear it of all that is not sacred. I will build lodgings for the laborers outside the walls. I will empty and break the nests of garbage, the ruins that are not sacred; I will burn them and will move the boutiques. Then while preserving as much as possible the ancient styles of the houses, I will create a new city, spacious, open to the air and equipped with drainage pipes, around the sacred sites...I wholeheartedly believe that it is possible to establish a new and wonderful Jerusalem outside the walls of the Old City that will simultaneously remain both a Lourdes of sorts, a Mecca and "Jerusalem, the Holy City".

T. Herzl, *Memoirs*

[•]

On their part, some important European, Jewish individuals intervene to attempt to improve the living conditions of their coreligionists. In 1840, they succeed in obtaining a document from the Turkish government extending the rights guaranteed to the sultan's subjects throughout the Ottoman Empire to the Jews. The authorities undertake assuring the preservation of the Holy sites and the protection of the places of worship. The restrictions concerning the establishment of new synagogues and institutions are lifted. The first educational institutions are established. First, a school for girls is opened to supplement the work of the rabbinical institutions; then some vocational schools that combines the teaching of general subjects, such as mathematics and languages, with that of traditional, sacred subjects. The opening of these establishments as well as of some medical institutions, like Rothschild Hospital in 1854 and Bikur Holim Hospital in 1857, moreover, aim at warding off the missionary influences of the European powers, especially of England and France. The Chief Rabbi of Palestine – the *hacham bashi* – will, henceforth, maintain his office in Jerusalem.

The development of international relations, the measures taken by the Ottoman authorities to consolidate their power, and the extension of roads encourage a new influx of immigrants and pilgrims. In 1837, the ancient printing house of Safed moves to Jerusalem. The first books immediately are published, followed by the first tracts and the first newspapers.

MOSES MONTEFIORE

The most industrious and the most renowned philanthropist of this period is Moses Montefiore (1784 – 1885). Born in Italy, he grows up in England where he becomes a wealthy businessman and marries Judith Cohen, whose family is one of the wealthiest in the country. At the age of 40, he retires from business in order to exclusively devote himself to philanthropic activities. He visits the most remote communities, intercedes on behalf of his coreligionists wherever they are threatened with danger, and distributes donations wherever there is a need. His photograph has a prominent place in many Jewish homes where he is admired as a prince. Furthermore, in 1837, Queen Victoria, who does not hide her approval of his political intervention on behalf of his coreligionists, bestows him with the rank of nobility. However, his great passion will continue to be Palestine and the Holy City, which he visits no less than seven times, launching a new enterprise each time.

In 1855, he launches a vast campaign to collect funds to relieve the inhabitants of Jerusalem who live in intolerable, over-crowded conditions that allowed no privacy. Using his connections, he manages to have the municipal slaughterhouses that infest the atmosphere of the Jewish Quarters moved. He, moreover, has a mill built outside the walls in 1857 that is operated at first by millers from Canterbury and then by Jewish millers.[8] In 1858, through the intermediary of the Austrian Consul, he buys a lot in the Old City near Mount Zion where the first shelters for the poor are built – the Battei Mahasseh (the Houses of Refuge). Their construction is made possible thanks to donations collected in the Diaspora. During his visit in 1869, the emperor, Franz Joseph, contributes his share by financing the building of the portico bearing his name. The most impressive building, which bears the name Rothschild is completed in 1871. The construction of Mishkenot Shaananim (Residences of Tranquility) outside the walls on the western slope of the Hinnom Valley follow that of the Battei Mahasseh. Thanks to the annulment by the Turks of the restriction preventing the authorization of strangers to buy land, the plot is purchased with funds from the inheritance of a wealthy Jew from New Orleans. The houses are built in a row with meter-thick walls, and doors and windows with checkered bars opening towards the walls of the Old City. The first houses are comprised of two rooms and a small courtyard. Numbering twenty-two, half are allocated to Ashkenazim and half to Sephardim, who are among the poorest in the community. At the beginning, Montefiore's representatives do not want to allocate them for more than a three-year period so as to guarantee a rotation of tenants and permit as many people as possible to enjoy their comforts. But they very quickly become disenchanted, unable to find many people who are ready to settle outside of the protective walls of the Old City. As a last resort, they pay an annual premium to the volunteers to compensate them for the risks they take, and also supply them with grains and utensils. The most anxious, moreover, are content to spend the day in their new houses, and to return to the Old City as soon

8. This mill is a tourist spot in Jerusalem. It houses a museum dedicated to Moses Montefiore's work as well as the carriage that the dignified elderly man used during his final days. See p.196.

9. The *Mishkenot Shaananim* residences are used to house distinguished guests of the Jerusalem Municipality.

as night falls.[9] The tenants are compelled to observe strict hygienic and ritual rules such as: "Every day, after the study of a chapter of the Mishna, one of the faithful pronounces the kaddish ordained by our teachers for the repose of the soul of the deceased donor, Rabbi Judah Touro, blessed be his memory." In addition, two synagogues are built, one for the Ashkenazim and the other for the Sephardim, as well as a ritual bath, an oven and some cisterns. The extension of Mishkenot Shaananim constitutes the neighborhood of Yemin Moshe (the Right Hand of Moshe).

In 1874, Montefiore resigns from the presidency of the Council of the Representatives of British Jews and founds the Sir Moses Montefiore Testimonial Committee, which collects a sum of 12,000 Sterling Pounds earmarked for the construction of some new neighborhoods, *Ohel Moshe* (Moshe's Tent) and *Mazkeret Moshe* (Commemoration of Moshe). At the time of his seventh and final voyage in July 1875, at the age of 91, almost fifty years after his first trip, Montefiore is enthusiastic about the expansion of the city and the enterprising spirit of his coreligionists:

The reward of a benefactor

As we were approaching Jerusalem, my eyes were unceasingly drawn to the new houses on the right and on the left, sometimes immense buildings located along our path. Their inhabitants came out and I had the pleasure of seeing hundreds of our brothers at the entrance of their homes.

Upon advancing further, a new synagogue was pointed out to me. I was told that some fifty families inhabited the houses surrounding it. Someone drew my attention to a lot belonging to a person who intended to build sixty houses. Near the Gihon Spring, not far from the mill that I had built in Kerem Moshe ve Yehudit eighteen years before, I noticed two other recently built mills that I was told brought in large sums to their Greek owners.

How great was my joy when I realized that only a few years had elapsed since the time when not a single Jewish family lived outside the gates of Jerusalem where you could not see a single house. Now before my eyes, there was a new Jerusalem with buildings as beautiful as in Europe.

M. Montefiore, *Memoirs*

After this last voyage, Montefiore writes a document entitled *An Account of a Forty-day Sojourn in the Holy Land* in which he expresses his admiration for the settlers in Palestine and in which he calls upon his coreligionists all over the world to come to their aid:

New neighborhoods

The Jews in Jerusalem, as well as throughout the Holy Land, work. They are more industrious than many people in Europe and must work in order to subsist. Unfortunately, the work does not earn them enough for there is a lack of markets where products are sold, and famine, cholera and other calamities strike its inhabitants on a regular basis. We, the Israelites, to whom God revealed Himself at Sinai, must, more than any other nation, come to their aid and rescue them from their difficulties. If you ask me: "We would like to contribute to a fund aimed at providing them the necessary assistance; we are ready to agree to all the sacrifices according to our means; what do you propose that we do to realize the specified objective?" I would reply: "simply do what they suggest. Begin by building houses in Jerusalem. Buy plots of land outside the city and build some European standard houses in a square or in a crescent. At the center of the square or the crescent, put a synagogue and a public bath and leave a patch of land in front of every house large enough to some plant olive trees and a vineyard and to cultivate the required vegetables so as to develop a taste for agriculture in the inhabitants."

M. Montefiore, *Memoirs*

[•]

The cholera epidemic that breaks out in the city in 1866 spares the inhabitants of *Yemin Moshe*. The inadequate, crowded and filthy living conditions finally induce the people to leave the Old City. In 1868, *Mahaneh Israel* (the Camp of Israel) is built for the Jews of the Maghrebian community. It is soon followed by the *Nahalat Shiva* neighborhood (Restablished since September 1869), built at the initiative of Yossef Rivlin, who establishes the Association of the Builders of Jerusalem in 1857, which unceasingly establishes new neighborhoods. Rivlin, moreover, will be entered in the history of Jerusalem as one of the most industrious architects of the city's expansion outside the walls:

Nahalat Shiva

In those days there was still no semblance of a settlement outside of the walls of Jerusalem.... There was the "Russian Compound" where a large cathedral had recently been erected, and houses which served as hostels for the numerous Russian tourists who came for their holidays every year. And there were the Montefiore houses near the railway station.

Then, in 1869, seven men from Jerusalem were inspired. We bought a plot of land on the crossroad opposite the "Russian Compound" with the intention of building a new neighborhood and we called it Nahalat Shiva, named after the seven pioneer investors...

We then came to the administrators of the halukah communities and said to them: "Our fathers failed the yishuv by not purchasing houses in the city at cheap prices at a time when the Christians were acquiring complete blocks with many houses... In any case, they sinned and may God forgive them. But now a settlement is developing outside the wall... and many Christians have already begun to buy plots of land around the "Russian Compound" on which they will surely build houses, and thus the settlement will expand and grow. Therefore, do not miss this opportunity while the land is cheap. At least, use some percentage of the Halukah income, purchase and build houses for the poor and in the course of years they will repay the sums which they are now paying annually to the Gentiles in the form of rent. Besides, the rent payments are rising from year to year."

To our regret, those who were in charge shut their ears and paid no attention to our words, saying: "The immediate is more important than the future." Disheartened and dispirited, we left them.

The first members to build were Reb Michal Hacohen and Reb Yosef Rivlin.

A. Yaari, *Zichronot Eretz Israel*

The neighborhood of *Mea Shearim* (1874 – 1882) receives its first inhabitants the week that the passage in the Torah read in the synagogues declares: "Isaac sowed in that land and received in the same year a hundredfold [*mea shearim*], for the Lord blessed him" (Genesis 26: 12). From the beginning, this neighborhood wants to be a ghetto, reserved only for the pious. It has to make concessions, attracting people of all orientations, of every sect and wearing all kinds of dress: the *Neturei Karta* – the Guardians of the Wall – anti-Zionists, who pose as the strict guardians of Judaism, awaiting the supernatural Messiah who will liberate them of the State of Israel that they do not recognize; the Habad *Hassidim*, the followers of the Rabbi of Lubavitch who resided in Brooklyn, are strong supporters of Israel; also the *Hassidim* of Bratslav, the followers of Rav Nachman, who preach joy at all times and meditation in the forests and who, after two centuries, continue to mourn the death of their irreplaceable teacher. A whole gamut of sects, one more interesting and more astonishing than the other, makes up this ghetto that is maintained in the center of the Holy City among all the others. The memory of their former ghettos is perpetuated by the men and women dressed in the kind of clothing worn in exile – perhaps the dignitaries of God, in perpetual prayer. Dark boutiques offer you their sacred books, hardcover with black bookbinding, having passed the censure of heaven as well as that of majestic rabbis infused with knowledge. Venerable artisans of the Scriptures religiously copy the Law Scrolls, meticulously tracing its letters with a trembling pen in their ateliers. In the schools and rabbinic academies, heads framed with ringlets, lean over old, dry texts, chanting immemorial sacred letters, reconstructing disturbing controversies between the sages, extricating the divine plans, made memorable in writing. Placards, directed at visitors, calls for propriety. Bulletin boards, reserved for the initiates, announce the death of a Genius of Knowledge, denounce archeological sacrilege, and call for mobilization against the moral corruption of the sons and daughters of Israel who have been led astray from the path of our ancestors. A particular brightness penetrates the shadowy light.

In 1883, the Jews resume the expansion of the city outside the walls, building *Eben Shmuel* (the Rock of Samuel) and

Mishkenot Israel (the Dwelling of Israel), also at Rivlin's initiative. A donor from Anvers takes the initiative to build the *Battei Ungarine* (the houses of Hungary that are reserved for integrationists from Hungary, as opposed to *Mea Shearim);* then some *Batei Varsha (the Houses of Warsaw)* are erected on a plot of land purchased thanks to the inheritance of a rich rabbi who came to die in Palestine. In 1885, the Yemenites appropriate their neighborhood – *Mishkenot ha-Temanim* (the Residence of the Yemenites); they will also settle in the village of Silwan in 1888, evacuating it in 1938 at the recommendation of the British authorities. The construction of *Beit Israel* (the House of Israel) is begun in 1886 on a plot of land near *Mea Shearim*; its name comes from a verse in Ezekiel that declares: "I will multiply your population, of all the house of Israel, the cities will be repopulated and the ruins rebuilt." Around 1887, *Mahaneh Yehudah* (the Encampment of Yehuda) is built by the representatives of a banker; today it is the site of the most blustering, the most abundant and the liveliest market in the city. In the Nineties, the Jews of Turkistan acquire for themselves a neighborhood, "the eternal property of the community" that "cannot be sold or rented until the coming of the Savior." The neighborhood – *Shehunat ha-Buharim* – is established northeast of *Mea Shearim*, not far from *Sanhedriyya*, the site of the catacombs that date back to the Hasmonean and the Herodian Periods and, perhaps, also the tombs of the judges of the Sanhedrin – from the Greek word, *synedrion*, seated together – the supreme council of 71 supreme legal experts.

The expansion of the Jewish city does not come about without controversies and rivalries. The Ashkenazim from the ghettos in Central and Western Europe bring their quarrels between the *Hassidim* – pious people who are more concerned with the intentions motivating the religious acts than with the knowledge that feeds them, and who generally form a group around a teacher whom they consider to be a mediator between the community and the Divinity – and the *prushim* or *mitnagdim* – who, in general, are scholars who consider the study of the sacred texts, especially the Talmud, as the most important religious act. Furthermore, the Ashkenazim and the Sephardim engage in a dispute over the partition of the subsidies from the Diaspora. They maintain separate slaughterhouse as well as separate cemeteries. There are other clashes between the opposing traditionalists who strictly adhere to rabbinic Law and the liberals or the emancipated – the *maskilim* – who are more open to foreign cultures. History repeating itself, with the same disputes, the same controversies, the same threats, perhaps...

The expansion of the Jewish neighborhoods that preceded by many years the establishment of the first settlements throughout the country is, above all, the work of pious men concerned with improving their living conditions. The establishment of medical and academic institutions that accompany it agitates the rabbinic circles. In 1888, the first Jewish hospital – the Rothschild Hospital – outside the walls, is inaugurated, replacing the hospital bearing the same name in the Old City. Likewise, *Bikur Holim* (Visiting the Sick) extends its services and begins the construction of a new building in the new city in 1910. A third hospital, *Shaare Tzedek* (the Gates of Justice), established at the entrance of the city is so far from the new city that for a long time, the sick object to being treated by the German doctor there. The *Alliance Israélite Universelle*, a philanthropic organization working to propagate French culture in the Jewish communities in North Africa and the Levant opens a school in the Sixties. Ten years later, it must close its doors, but in 1882, it opens a new school in memory of Adolphe Cremieux, a Jewish political figure. The adoption of Hebrew as the language of instruction raises a general outcry among the religious circles that claim that Hebrew should only be taught in rabbinic institutions under the supervision of rabbis. They, moreover, threaten to deprive the parents, who send their children to the Alliance, of their subsidies. The majority of students are Sephardim, who, in general, are more open to general culture.

In spite of the perpetual threats of excommunication by the orthodox milieu, the expansion of the city, nonetheless, will stir up the enthusiasm of the visitors and the first secular scholars with nationalist motivations living in the city. In 1881, Eliezer Ben Yehuda, the supporter and architect of the renaissance of Hebrew as a spoken language, founds an association – *Tehiyyat Israel* (the Renaissance of Israel)

– together with Y. M. Pines with the intention of "bringing the land of Israel back to life, of raising it from its downfall, of strengthening its spirit and of restoring its past glory" by developing agriculture, industry and the crafts, and by encouraging the renaissance of the Hebrew language. He creates a newspaper that will become the mouthpiece of the secular circles, and he establishes an association, the "Spoken Language", which aims at "eradicating the various jargons and putting the Hebrew language in the mouths of all the Jews inhabiting our land". In 1894, he writes:

Some Jewish houses

When a Jew, who comes from afar, arrives in Jerusalem, he discovers a first house to his right at the foot of the mountain where the city is perched; it is a beautiful building with the mark of wealth. Upon asking the coachman to whom it belongs, he hears the reply: "It belongs to a Jew." Traveling a little further, our guest discovers about thirty houses, two-story stone buildings, together in one neighborhood. He again asks: "To whom do these houses belong?" The coachman likewise says: "These houses are also Jewish; it is the Beit Yaacov neighborhood that a Jewish community built during the last few years." As the stagecoach continues on its way, our visitor will not cease to discover new houses, large and beautiful, surrounded by gardens, and others grouped in neighborhoods. Everywhere, he inquires about their owners and in every place, he receives the same reply. He will then realize: "Would this be the devastated Jerusalem that they claim is utterly desolate? Here I discover beautiful houses and beautiful gardens that all belong to Jews. This city is beginning to shake off its dust and it is the Jews who are building it."

E. Ben Yehuda, *Mevasseret Zion*

The Muslims also participate in the development of the city. In the middle of the 19th century, the tomb of a saint – *nabi* Mussa – becomes a highlight of the Muslim pilgrimage. The wealthy and important families are the first to leave the Old City. The mufti builds himself a residence outside the walls, *Ksar al-Mufti*; the neighborhood of Sheikh Jarrah – named after the holy Muslim buried there - develops around it. In the Seventies, Rabah al-Husseini builds the palace that houses the American Colony. The Arabs move into the Templars' neighborhood, into that of Musrara and into a number of other neighborhoods, which they will have to evacuate in 1948. During the 1870s, they build the neighborhood of Abu Tor, overlooking the Mount of Bad Council, which Christian tradition identifies as the location of the summer residence of the high priest, Caiphe, and the site where Judas lost his way.

[•]

In 1900, the city's population is estimated to number almost 52,000: 35,000 of the inhabitants are Jewish, 15,000 in the Old City and 20,000 outside the walls, 8,000 Christians and 8,000 Muslims. On December 11th, 1917, the British General Allenby enters the city escorted by a French and an Italian representative. He receives the keys from the hands of the Turkish pasha in the courtyard of *Shaare Tzedek* Hospital. The British mandate begins…

THE BRITISH MANDATE

As soon as they arrive, the British set up a rationing system to ward off the terrible shortage threatening the city with famine. On July 1st, 1920, the military administration is replaced by a civil administration headed by a high commissioner whose office is in Jerusalem. At first, he sets up his office on the premises of the Augusta Victoria Inn, which had been severely damaged by an earthquake in 1927. From 1931, he occupies a new residence built on the Mount of Bad Council – *Armon ha-Natziv*. The British appoint a municipal council composed of two Muslims – one of them assumes the position of mayor –, two Christians and two Jews. In 1924, municipal elections are held for the first time in the history of the city. Henceforth, the municipal council is made up of twelve members, six Jews and six Arabs, including four Christian and two Muslim Arabs. Nevertheless, the British authorities continue to appoint the mayor, persisting in naming a Muslim although the majority of the inhabitants are Jewish.

The expansion of the western section of the city is resumed immediately after the war. New neighborhoods are built outside the walls, such as the Jewish neighborhoods of Beit ha-Kerem and Talpiot, the Arab neighborhoods of Talbiyeh, initiated by the Greek Orthodox who build a mill there, and Baka and Katamon, where the Greek Orthodox establish one of their monasteries. More and more Jews leave the Old City. In 1931, there are no more than 5,600 Jews in the Old City; and in 1947, on the eve of the War of Independence, there are only 2,000. The consulates and the public buildings also move into the new city. In addition to businesses, public institutions, such as the Police Headquarters, the Main Post Office, the radio station, etc., move to *Yafo* Street.

The Jewish community continues to endow itself with educational institutions. Following the opening of Bezalel, the School of Fine Arts founded in 1906 by Boris Schatz, a member of the Bulgarian Academy of the Arts. The first secular high school – *ha-Gimnasia ha-Ivrit* – is opened in 1909. On April 1st, 1925, Lord Balfour officially inaugurates the Hebrew University. All the political and cultural personalities of the Jewish population in Palestine – the *Yishuv* – gather together for the ceremony. Marvin Lowenthal, the writer, journalist and historian, attends the inauguration ceremony. In a text dedicated to Chaim Weizmann, a scientist of international renown and the leader of the Zionist Movement who becomes the first president of the State of Israel, Lowenthal describes the excitement and the enthusiasm that reigns on that day on Mount Scopus:

Hebrew University

The inauguration of Hebrew University in Jerusalem on the eve of Passover in 1925 was more than the opening of a unique institution of learning. It was more than a Zionist triumph – more than another foundation stone laid in the rebuilding of the nation. It was, in fact, the first time since the Roman legions destroyed Jerusalem, the first time in seemingly endless centuries… that the Jewish people, thousands of them… gathered together… When the throngs on Mount Scopus shouted: "Yehi Balfour!" *and* "Hedad Weizmann!", *they were not merely acclaiming two statesmen or the much vaunted Jewish love of learning or a university that could hardly be said to exist; they were also acclaiming their own joy of being together after two millenniums of separation. They were proclaiming a reversal of history. It would not be surprising if Chaim Weizmann felt that the 1st of April in the year 1925 was the proudest day of his life…*

The inauguration ceremony took place at the site of the university, at the top of Mount Scopus that rises northeast of the walls of the city. This mountain neighbors the Mount of Olives and was mentioned only once in history when Titus concentrated his legions there to launch the final assault against Jerusalem. Now, totally new legions reinstated Mount Scopus in the Jewish annals. The number of participants, who were as much legions of peace, exceeded all expectations: "Like a swarm of grasshoppers, to refer to the statistical conditions of this country, countless, like the sands of the sea." *Throughout the whole morning and all the afternoon, they ascended the mountain, on horseback, on the back of a donkey, in carts, in buses, in trucks, in cars and on bicycles, not to mention the multitude that came by foot...*

All around me, a vast amphitheater carved in the mountain and lined with stone benches was thronged with the most motley Jewish nation. Below us, an abyss opened that descended on ten miles of white rubble and gray sand up to the ribbon of the Jordan River and blue mirror of the Dead Sea – a drop of four thousand feet for a rock that would begin to tumble down the slope. On the other side, like a backdrop for the speakers' podium, thirty miles away, the purple and bronze mountains of Moav scintillate.

The mortals bustling in this divine theater were doing their best. There were oriental carpets everywhere. There was a vast gamut of costumes, the odd uniforms of the of the High Commissioner's guards, the finery of the Arab sheikhs and the robes of the academicians; the flashing of the blue and white shirts and skirts of the neatly dressed, young pioneers. A Psalm in Hebrew for the opening – "the heavens celebrate the glory of God" – flooding the amphitheater, sending its echoes to die against the mountains of Moav...

Wearing the brown robe of the doctors of science like the cloak of a prophet in a Renaissance painting, Weizmann welcomed the assembly – rather, he was welcoming one of his most cherished dreams that was coming true before his eyes. Many years later, when oratory would become dispensable, he would speak freely about his vision in simple terms: "In the early stages of our movement, we had a dream about a university. It was a great dream. Dreams are always more beautiful than reality, and it was not difficult to dream of the most magnificent Temple of Learning. I had that dream."

But now, on the threshold of its realization, he spoke more solemnly: "Today, we are inaugurating a Hebrew University", he said. "Hebrew will be the language of its schools and its colleges. But a university is nothing if it is not universal. It should not only dedicate itself to the pursuit of every form of knowledge, but also for the commonwealth of learning freely, open to all men and all women of every creed and race." This pledge, it should be noted, was not given to reassure the world of the Jewish nation's intention to stand for the freedom to teach and to learn, but to remind the world by contrary example that only in very few countries was the commonwealth of learning open to Jews. "Within these schools", Weizmann continued, "all creeds and all races will, I hope, be united in the great task of searching for truth, in restoring to Palestine the thriving civilization that it once enjoyed, and in giving it a place of its own in the world for thought. Conceived in this spirit and animated by these ideals, the University has before it, if all our hopes are realized, a future with possibilities not only for the Jews or for Palestine, but also for the awakening of all the East and for the whole of humanity..." With these words, the prophet's mantle became the cloak of Hillel, the robe of Rashi and the caftan of the Gaon of Vilna...

Bialik [the national poet], crowned with unseen laurels, voiced in Hebrew the confidence that gleamed in every eye when he proclaimed: "The inauguration today on this spot is not an empty dream; today is a great and holy day to God and to our people." His last words, the final words of the ceremony, were directed to the youth, to the courageous pioneers who came from their toil in the valley and now fluttered in blue and white – to the strength of the promises of the future: "They plow among the rocks, drain the swamps and lay out roads, singing and dancing. These young people have learned to exalt simple, rough labor, to the sacredness of a religion. We must light this holy fire within the walls of the institution that has now been inaugurated on Mount Scopus. Let some build the physical Jerusalem with fire and others, the spiritual Jerusalem – for You, Oh Lord, have burnt her with fire and with fire, You will rebuild her."

The most impressive moment of the inauguration came after the closing. Without quotation marks, I will describe the scene as witnessed by the young man that I was then. Descending from the mountaintop, the participants wound down a twisting road to the Valley of Jehoshaphat and then went up a circuitous road to the walls of Jerusalem. By the thousands, a black multitude of people coiled around the Old City. Twilight fell on the long moving columns and with their faces turned towards the glow of the sunset, a song rose and passed like a wave through the lines of moving men. "And there will be a highway... and the ransomed of the Eternal will return and enter Zion in song."

This was not the time to remember that the University had been inaugurated as an idea and a plan rather than as a completed reality. First inaugurate, then create – that is the prophetic way.

M. W. Weisgal, *Chaim Weizmann*

The speech by Chaim Nachman Bialik (1873 – 1934), "the poet of national renaissance", stressed the importance of a rebirth of Hebrew culture that would not be cut off from Jewish tradition:

Bialik's speech at the inauguration

. . . [A] people that aspires to a dignified existence must create a culture; it is not enough merely to make use of a culture – a people must create its own, with its own hands and its own implements and materials, and impress it with its own seal. Of course our people in its "diasporas" is creating culture; I doubt whether any place in the world where culture is being produced is entirely devoid of Jews. But as whatever the Jew creates in the Diaspora is always absorbed in the culture of others, it loses its identity and is never accounted to the credit of the Jew. Our cultural account in the Diaspora is consequently all debit and no credit. The Jewish people is therefore in a painfully false position: Whereas its true function culturally is that of a proletariat – i.e., it produces with the materials and implements of others for others – it is regarded by others, and at times even by itself, as a cultural parasite, possessing nothing of its own. A self-respecting people will never become reconciled to such a lot; it is bound to arise one day and resolve: no more. Better a little that is undisputedly my own than much that is not definitely either mine or somebody else's. Better a dry crust in my own home and on my own table than a stall-fed ox in the home of others and on the table of others. Better one little university but entirely my own, entirely my handiwork from foundations to coping stones, than thousands of temples of learning from which I derive benefit but in which I have no recognized share. Let my food be little and bitter as the olive, if I may but taste in it the delicious flavor of a gift from myself.

It was in this frame of mind that we took refuge in this land. We are not come here to seek wealth, or dominion, or greatness. How much of these can this poor little country give us? We wish to find here only a domain of our own for our physical and intellectual labor. We have not yet achieved great things here. We have not had time to wash the dust of long wanderings from our feet and to change our patched garments. Undoubtedly many years have yet to pass until we have healed this desolate land of the leprosy of its rocks and the rot of its swamps. For the present there is only a small beginning of up-building; yet already the need has been felt for erecting a home of the intellectual work of the nation. Such has ever been the nature of our people: it cannot live for three consecutive days without Torah. Already at this early hour we experience cultural needs that cannot be postponed and must be satisfied at once. Besides, we are burdened with heavy cares of the cultural fate of our people in the Diaspora. Nations born only yesterday foolishly imagine that through intellectual parching, by means of a numerous clauses, they can do to death an old nation with a past of four thousand years of Torah. We must therefore hasten to light here the first lamp of learning and science and of every sort of intellectual activity in Israel, ere the last lamp grows dark for us in foreign lands. And this we propose to do in the house whose doors have been opened this day upon Mount Scopus.

There is an ancient tradition that in the time of the Redemption the synagogues and houses of study of the Diaspora will be transported, along with their foundations, to Palestine. Naturally this legend cannot come true literally; the house of knowledge and learning that has been erected on Mount Scopus will differ greatly, not only in the materials of which it is made but in its nature and purpose, from the old bet-midrash. But, Ladies and Gentlemen, amid the ruins of those hallowed structures there are many sound and beautiful stones that can and ought to be foundation stones of our new edifice. Let not the builders reject these stones. At this hallowed moment I feel impelled to pray: May those stones not be forgotten! May we succeed in raising the science and learning that will issue from this house to the moral level to which our people raised its Torah! We *should not be worthy of this festive day if we proposed to content ourselves with a poor imitation of other peoples. We know well that true wisdom is that which learns from all; the windows of this house will therefore be open on every side, that the fairest fruit produced by man's creative spirit in every land and every age may enter. But we ourselves are not newcomers to the Kingdom of the Spirit and while learning from everybody we also have something to teach. I feel sure that a time will come when the moral principles upon which our Houses of Torah were founded, such as those enumerated in the wonderful short baraitha knows as "The Chapter on the Acquisition of Torah," will become the heritage of humanity at large.*

H. N. Bialik

The university develops rapidly under the presidency of Juda L. Magnes who succeeds in attracting many donors and very talented people. Furthermore, offices of the Zionist Executive are set up in Jerusalem, establishing it as the capital of the *Yishuv*. Some new neighborhoods receive successive waves of immigrants, bringing the architectural styles of their countries of origin. The King David, the first hotel of international standing, is opened in 1930, the YMCA complex beginning in 1928 and Hadassah Hospital on Mount Scopus in 1938.

However, the political tensions between the Jews and the Arabs become increasingly severe, engendering riots for the first time in 1920, and a second time in 1929. The Muslim inhabitants are incited by their religious leaders, including the mufti of Jerusalem, Amine al-Husseini, who leads a campaign of defamation against the Zionist Movement, not in the least bit reluctant to provoke and denounce the Jews, accusing them of preparing to seize the Temple Mount. In the summer of 1929, he orders his men to mark a passage along the Western Wall to impede access to the narrow esplanade where the Jews gather to pray. Seeing that the British remain deaf to the protests made by prominent Jews, the Jewish youth movement, Betar, decides to march the length of the wall, waving flags and sounding the horn. The mufti couldn't have waited for a better opportunity. On August

23rd, the preachers incite the thousands of Muslims gathered in their mosques to occupy the Jewish neighborhoods. During a tour of Palestine, Albert Londres, (1884 – 1932), a poet and journalist, recounts:

The riots of hate

On August 23rd, the feast day of Saint Bartholomew, dawn sees crowds of Arabs invading Jerusalem. Marching in groups, each man holds a stick or an unsheathed dagger. Upon entering the Holy City, they are singing:

The religion of Mohammed
defends its right with the sword,
with the sword, we will defend it
the Prophet Mohammed.

The big day has arrived. The tracts uttered by the charming young man [the mufti] did not miss their mark. Those holding daggers and drum majors holding bludgeons descended towards the Damascus Gate. They pass directly in front of the French, religious establishments, in front of the hospital, in front of Our Lady of France:

The religion of Mohammed
defends its rights with the sword.

Today, children of Christ, do not be afraid: this is directed towards the Jews... a large fortress style building rises in front of the Damascus Gate; it houses the offices of the British High Commissioner. Six young Jews are grouped together there, outside. It would be best for them to clear the way for this fanatic wave. They remain, all six of them, representing the revolt of the new Jewish spirit. They have had enough of hearing that the Jew can only bow down in submission. A sense of pride that was contained for too long makes them forget that heroism does not always go hand in hand with reason. One of the six, an Austrian journalist, Dr. Von Veisel, refuses to yield a meter of ground to the advancing column. A Muslim marches towards Veisel. The two men take hold of each other. Veisel has the upper hand.

Well! He cries out to the four British soldiers and to the police who are there in front of the offices, armed and ready, a man is attacking me, I'm holding him, come and arrest him!

The authorities' agents do not move. Two Arabs come forward and stab Veisel.

The representatives of the law contemplate the scene; they don't even frown. Why then should they restrain themselves? Every one passing by "passes".

The more they kill the Jews, the more immobilized the police remain. As for the British High Commissioner's Office, he went out to get some air, like a Zeppelin! At least that is what one may assume, because for three weeks, no one has heard anything about him!

–Death to the Jews!

–The government supports us!

With these cries on their lips, daggers in hand, the sons of the prophet roam through Jerusalem...

A. Londres, *The Wandering Jew Has Arrived*

The riots spread and result in 133 dead and more than 300 wounded, mostly in Hebron, Safed and Jerusalem. More disturbances break out in 1936, and again spread throughout the rest of the country. The Arab High Commission declares a general strike to compel the British authorities to halt Jewish immigration. Lord Peel, presiding over a commission charged with finding a solution to the war between the two communities, recommends the partition of Palestine in two States and the continuation of the British Mandate over Jerusalem and Bethlehem.

The redoubling of the Arab attacks against Jewish institutions, nevertheless, compels the authorities to take measures against the agitators. The Arab High Commission is dissolved, the mufti must seek refuge in Lebanon, and the Muslim mayor of the city is deported to the Seychelles. Concerned with appeasing the Arabs, nonetheless, the British publish the White Paper that limits Jewish immigration in 1939. This document arouses the indignation of the *Yishuv*. The protests and the demonstrations continue until the declaration of war between the European powers, and are resumed immediately after the war, backed by attacks against British institutions. In July 1946, the struggle against the British culminates in the bombing of the King David Hotel, which housed the

British headquarters, by members of the Irgun, one of the three Jewish resistance movements. The chief commander of this organization, Menachem Begin, who later becomes the Prime Minister of Israel from 1977 to 1983, recounts in his autobiography:

The blowing-up of the King David

During World War II, the southern wing of the King David Hotel in Jerusalem housed the central institutions of the British Mandate: the military QG, the secretariat and the civil government. When the revolt against the British presence had spread, the large hotel became a genuine fortress in the heart of the city. The British Military Police and the famous Special Investigation Bureau established their quarters in an adjoining building. A powerful military unit was camping in the open space between the two buildings. Nests of machine-guns were dispersed all around. Soldiers, policemen and agents maintained tight and constant surveillance over the building that sheltered the most important members of the British government in the land of Israel...

The unit that was to launch the attack on the hotel under the command of Gideon (dressed in the uniform of the hotel's employees) led the attack with great bravery and fulfilled its instructions with rigorous precision. Its men brought in the milk cans as close to the hotel as possible. Then they divided up into two groups, one to enter the hotel and one responsible for providing cover. The first took the milk cans to the basement passing through the Regency. Its members subdued the employees and locked them in a room. The fifteen Arabs did not spring any surprises on our men. The neutralization of the cooks and the waiters – the only people present at the café at that moment – went according to our plans, without a hitch. On the other hand, our men were surprised by the sudden appearance of two British soldiers who became suspicious and fired their revolvers. The inevitable confrontation caused casualties on both sides. During this time, the second group had encountered some British military patrols. The nature of the operation prevented our men from carrying submachine guns and they had to make do with Stens and their revolvers. However, the first group had achieved its goal. The commander of the operation set the delay mechanism to thirty minutes and posted warning signs. Then the Arab employees were released and ordered to run as fast as they could to save their lives. The last of our men to get out was Gideon who shouted: "Get out, the hotel is going to blow-up!" At that moment, a smoke bomb exploded and our men were able to withdraw. The explosion and the unexpected shots chased the passers-by off the streets.

At ten minutes past noon, Gideon was at the spot where our switchboard operator had been waiting for him. She immediately phoned the King David to warn its occupants that explosives had been placed under the hotel and that they should evacuate the premises with minimal delay: "Leave the building!" she lashed out. Then she phoned the office of the Palestine Post to announce – as its receptionist would later confirm – that "some bombs had been placed at the King David Hotel and that we had requested that the building be evacuated as quickly as possible." The third and final warning was communicated to the French Consulate along with the recommendation that they open the windows wide in order to avoid the effects of the blast. Incidentally, they opened the windows and the building did not suffer any damage.

It was now a quarter past noon. Gideon was counting the minutes. Up to that point, everything was going according to plans, with the exception of the losses suffered during the unexpected exchange of fire. The milk cans had been placed under the governmental wing of the building. All the warnings had been transmitted. The British had undoubtedly begun the evacuation of the hotel, and if everything went on as in the past in similar circumstances, they would soon be finished. Only one question plagued him. Will the explosion take place or not? Did an error slip by during the set-up of the mechanism? Will the building really blow-up? Will the documents be destroyed?

Each minute seemed like an eternity. Twenty-one minutes past noon, twenty-two. Zero hour was approaching. Gideon was getting nervous. The half hour had almost passed. Twelve thirty-seven... Suddenly the whole city seemed to shudder. Not a single error had been made. Yitshak Sadeh of the Haganah had doubted that it could hit the third or even the second floor. Gidy, on his part, continued to declare that although only 500 pounds of explosives – a mix of T.N.T. and some gelatin – had been placed in the milk cans, the confined space of the basement would augment the escape of the gases and the explosion would reach the roof. It reached the entire building, from the basement to the roof, six floors of stone, concrete and steel. As the BBC would later announce, it looked as if the whole wing of the immense building had been cut off with the blade of a knife.

M. Begin, The Revolt

The British do not take the Irgun's warnings seriously and the bombing of the hotel results in many victims.

A new partition plan, submitted in November 1947, recommends the internationalization of Jerusalem. The skirmishes between the Jews and the Arabs become war. The entire Old City, including the Jewish Quarter, is cut off from the western sector of the city. On their part, the British protect themselves from attacks by the most extremist resistance movements, the Lehi and the Etzel, by partitioning themselves off with barbed wire. The western sector is practically besieged by the Arabs who attack the convoys coming from the coastal plain. The Jewish inhabitants of the neighborhoods of Atarot and Neve Yaacov in the north are evacuated. Deir Yassine, a village from which the Arab attacks are launched, is occupied by the members of the Etzel and the Lehi who in retaliation execute more than 250 Arab civilians. A few days later, some gangs of armed Arabs attack and destroy a convoy of doctors, nurses and sanitation workers on their way to Hadassah Hospital on Mount Scopus, killing 78 people. Dominique Lapierre and Larry Collins give an account of this tragedy:

The Mount Scopus convoy

Since the Partition, Dr. Ben David's undertaking to supply provisions to the hospital and to the university was unceasingly problematic for the Jewish Agency. The only road that went up towards the hill passed through the

Arab neighborhood of Sheikh Jarrah. From the month of December, ambushes had compelled the Jewish Agency to organize weekly, armed convoys in order to continue to supply provisions to Mount Scopus. In the meanwhile, for a month, a truce of sorts had been established on this part of the road and the convoys had passed through without incident. Everything indicated that the passage of the convoy on the 13th of April would also be accomplished without any problems.

At the last outpost of the Haganah, at the end of Samuel ha-Navi St., Moshe Hillman, the Jewish security officer, halted the column while he phoned a British police inspector named Webb to enquire if the road was clear.

–Send the convoy, the Englishman replied. We are coming on patrol.

Hillman signaled to the column to begin its four-kilometer voyage. A light armored car led the way. Following behind it were a white ambulance displaying the Star of David – the Jewish Red Cross – then two buses, another ambulance, four trucks and a second light armored car that protected the rear of the convoy.

Benjamin Adin, the Haganah's most famous driver, was driving one of the trucks. The dangerous habit that he had of going out alone to supply provisions to the isolated settlements earned him the nickname of "Meshuga" – the Lunatic...

Crouching in the pit on the side of the road, the Arab mechanic, Mohammed Neggar, held his breath, calculating the exact moment that he would trigger the explosion, his fingers clenching the switch. Two days before, in a bar that he frequented, a British officer had revealed to the Arab the day and hour that the Jewish convoy would pass. The officer himself had even hinted that if the column would be attacked, the British would not intervene except if the Arabs fired at the patrols...

The hum of the motors became louder as the front armored car turned the corner. The Arab marksman did not take his eyes off of it. It looked like "a big, hideous cockroach". He clenched his fingers until the final click. An explosion shook the ground and the armored car disappeared in a cloud of smoke. When it had dissipated, the Arab was startled. He had pressed it one second too soon. Instead of destroying the vehicle, he had opened a huge crater in the asphalt. Having been unable to stop on time, the heavy machine had fallen into the hole.

The entire column was immobilized... Everyone was at an anxious loss about what to do, but they did not have to wait for the answer. At the signal of the mechanic, a hail of bullets struck the vehicle.

Drawn by the shooting and the explosions, waves of guerrilla fighters from the neighboring Arab neighborhoods and the ramparts of the Old City stormed the convoy. Already suffocating in their metal prisons, the passengers discerned a new sound that rose above the din. It was a guttural outcry, a furious cry of vengeance, the name of the peaceful village that the two wounded men in the ambulance had helped occupy three days before – Deir Yassine.

The authors give an account of the lone efforts that Colonel Jack Churchill made to come to the aid of the ambushed convoy that was being shot at by the Arabs posted on the roofs. The British, on their part, did not hasten to intervene. The members of the Palmach – sent to the rescue were, in turn, immobilized. Lapierre and Collins continue:

Half of Jerusalem witnessed the death of the besieged convoy from the roofs, the terraces, the balconies, the Mount of Olives, Mount Scopus, the Hill of Bad Counsel and even from the windows of the Government House where the general, Macmillan, tarried.

In spite of the tens of S.O.S sent to them, the British remained impassive. It was not until eleven thirty, two hours after being notified for the first time of the ambush, that the first two armored vehicles of the Lifeguards arrived at the scene of combat. The first vehicle had only fired one shell when its canon jammed. It was necessary to wait two hours for the arrival of other armored vehicles. Colonel Churchill did not receive permission to use his mortars until the afternoon. The order to use heavier arms never arrived. As for the Haganah, it had been warned that it would be forcibly prevented from intervening.

Inside Zvi Sinai's (the commander of the fifteen men sent by the Haganah to rescue the convoy) armored car, which was practically the only Jewish fortification against the hundreds of Arabs besieging the convoy, the situation was critical. Sinai and his company fired through all the openings, but the unprotected roof of their vehicle made them particularly vulnerable to the volley fired from the terraces. The crew's nurse was the first to be killed. A machine gun jammed. The wounded huddled together in confusion in the suffocating darkness. Through a shutter, Sinai saw a group of Arabs approaching the bus armed with Molotov cocktails. The heat was unbearable. The Jews emptied their last cartridges. Most of them were wounded or dead. The survivors jumped over the bodies from one side to the other to shoot. Sinai would remind himself: "If they would survive, it was because they were still alive then." In the back, a man whose hand had been partly torn off was using the only machine gun. It was not possible to dress any wounds. All we could do was support the dying who were loosing all their blood to the last drop...

It was three fifteen in the afternoon when Doctor Yassky opened the small shutter of the ambulance door. One hundred meters behind him, large tongues of fire were consuming the two buses filled with his friends and his colleagues. He turned towards his wife.

–Goodbye, my love, this is the end, he said to her.

He then toppled over and rolled on the ambulance floor. The director of Hadassah was dead. A bullet had entered through the half open shutter and had struck him the very moment that he was turning towards his wife.

A few moments later, the occupants of the ambulance heard frantic knocking on the door of their vehicle.

–Open the door quickly, the voice begged.

It was a survivor of one of the burning buses. The poor man jumped in among the passengers, crying:

–Save yourselves, you are all going to burn!

The Yemenite driver immediately slid out the door. Dr.

Yehudah Matot decided to follow him... Rolling into the pit, he had a strange thought. "Finally", he said, "I'll be able to smoke a cigarette." The sight of the driver lying with his arms extended like a cross brought him back to his senses...

It was a little after three thirty when the British High Commissioner ordered the military at the site to use force to intervene. Almost six hours had passed since the explosion of the mine set off by the Arab mechanic. While Churchill and his men provided cover, Captain Naylord Leyland personally led his armored vehicles towards the wrecked vehicles. When he was near, he requested firing a smoke bomb to hide his movements. To his fury, "there was an interminable discussion to determine what kind of smoke was required." In the end, he fired some smoking explosives. He then moved his vehicles forward and dispatched his men to search for survivors - half a dozen in all.

D. Lapierre & L. Collins, Oh Jerusalem

The Jordanian Legion joins some bands of armed Arabs while the Etzel, the Lehi and the Haganah mobilize their men and their resources. During the nights of May 14th and May 15th, 1948, the last British soldiers leave Jerusalem. The Jews immediately take control of the administrative buildings in the center of the city, the central post office, the police headquarters and the radio station. The Arab siege of the western part of the city continues for two more months and the Israelis have to lay a circuitous road – the Burma Road – in order to dispatch provisions and men and to lay down a new water pipe to guarantee its supply to the besieged.

Some Iraqi and Egyptian troops rally the Jordanian army in the nearby suburb of the city. Kibbutz Ramat Rachel repeatedly changes hands. The Legion, moreover, tightens its stranglehold on the Jewish Quarter of the Old City that falls on the 27th of May 1948, at the end of lengthy resistance. Some of its 2,000 inhabitants, for the most part, children and elderly, are evacuated to the western sector; the rest are taken prisoners. Dr. Abraham Laufer provides an account of the last days in the Jewish Quarter. He himself, two other doctors and four nurses choose to join the prisoners:

The fall of the Jewish Quarter

On May 15th, we began to hear the Arab rifle fire, the roar of the exploding grenades and then during the days that followed, the rattle of the machine guns and the explosions of the artillery shells. The bullets would whistle through the rooms of the patients that were located on the upper floor, the shells exploding under the roof. We brought the sick and the wounded to the bottom floor where we put them on mattresses and blankets… Within a few days, we had seventy patients lying on mattresses spread out on the floor with only a few centimeters between them. We were sometimes forced to put two of the wounded on one mattress. The synagogue, which we had first used as a diagnostic room, was now filled and busy. It was an immense room whose only window had been partly walled off to protect us from enemy bullets. Its walls had been covered with bookshelves and we had to remove the sacred books in order to arrange the medical supplies and some clothing. The benches against the wall… currently served as temporary beds for the wounded men who were waiting for an operation. They lay there quietly after having received an injection of morphine to relieve the pain and to help prevent shock. We would place the wounded who were brought to us on two tables in the center of the room, examine their wounds and decide upon the necessary treatment… Those requiring surgery were placed on the benches while those who were seriously wounded were taken to one of the other rooms. On the other hand, those who were slightly wounded and did not require hospitalization, under the prevailing conditions, would receive a cup of coffee and one or two hours of rest before being sent back to the front. More than once, I saw a seriously wounded man brought back to the hospital for the second time on the same day that a short time before, had been sent to the front with a slight wound.

I must admit that more than one wounded man, who under more normal combat conditions should have been hospitalized, was sent back to the front lines with a simple bandage. We couldn't do otherwise since we were so short of men to the point that children had to replace the wounded on the front lines. Some of the fighters had broken arms set in casts, others had lost fingers and others had infected and swollen limbs…

I will never forget that handsome young man of about twenty years of age who came to see us with a piece of shrapnel in his left eye. I invited him to lie down so that I could treat his eye with cocaine and remove the splinter. He wanted to know how long that would take: "Fifteen to twenty minutes."
– "No", he said, "that would take too long. The situation at our post is too serious for me to allow myself to be gone for so long." He asked me to pour a few drops of cocaine into his left eye and to bandage it and he promised to come back as soon as the attack had been repulsed. A short hour later, he was brought back. A shell had blown off his beautiful face. There was no need to worry about his eye anymore. He was dead.

There was a young Yemenite woman on my staff who had been sent to us by the Magen David [the Red Cross] and was of great assistance in administering first aid. When the situation on the front lines would take a turn for the worse, she would take off her white apron, take a Sten gun or rifle from one of the wounded and would run to the aid of the most threatened post. As soon as the attacks eased, she would return and resume her work as a nurse…

On the night of May 18th, during the final hours, the Palmach [the elite unit of the Haganah] stormed the Arab siege and forced its way into the Old City. On the 19th of May, at the first rays of dawn, the hospital's courtyard was full of men wearing helmets and carrying Sten guns slung over their shoulders. Our joy knew no bounds at the sight of the first properly armed Jewish soldiers who had come to our aid. They announced the declaration of the State of Israel and the establishment of our own army, which was resisting the enemy, holding on to their positions and inflicting serious losses. Furthermore, they informed us that almost all of Jerusalem was in our hands.

The long awaited shipment of medical supplies also arrived… We had breakfast in a good atmosphere. Calm reigned all around. It was almost ten o'clock and there was no sign of the imminent attack. According to the rumor that was circulating in the quarter, the Arabs had deserted Jerusalem and we thought we had control of the entire Old City.

But at eleven o'clock, the Arabs launched their harshest attack yet. The burst of the machine gun fire and the explosions of the shells made such a commotion that we couldn't hear each other. The wounded began to arrive in unprecedented numbers – the commander of the reinforcements was among them.

The heroic battle in which these young people (who were, in fact, children) would engage during the next ten days was incredible. Almost empty-handed, they defended their posts, attempting to advance and fortifying their positions during the night. They resisted until the moment when there were only thirty fighters left and almost no ammunition.

I remember many heroic scenes that took place during those days of desperate battle. The children, were the first to rush to the wounded to recover the unused bullets in their pockets to bring them to the posts... I recall the mothers who came to identify their slain sons. I can still see the courageous commander of the Haganah silently gazing at his dead parents for a long time without batting an eye, and who, upon leaving the hospital, returned to the front lines. He had no time to mourn.

The area under our control was shrinking, the stranglehold was tightening and the front was continually getting closer to the hospital. More than once, only fifteen meters separated us from our assailants. Barricades were quickly raised in front of the entrance in case we would have to make our final retreat. A liaison officer announced the arrival of reinforcements. One of our airplanes flew over the quarter, but to our great regret, the munitions that it dropped fell behind enemy lines. We would, nevertheless, preserve the hope of seeing reinforcements arrive... We had to hold out twenty-four more hours and we did. The following day, May 27th, brought many civilians casualties. The shells rained down on the houses, killing and wounding many.

Night fell and we were still waiting – in vain. The hours dragged slowly without anything unusual happening. In spite of being terribly exhausted, we were too tense to sleep. We thought it was our last night. Tomorrow would be the end. The ammunition had run out. There were one hundred and twenty wounded in the hospital. About seventy men had been killed and only about thirty were manning the posts, and they too were exhausted. Tomorrow, the Arabs would launch their final attack and we would probably be slaughtered.

The morning of May 29th was clear, bright and sunny; everything was quiet. The hour of battle was approaching with diabolical cruelty. Some of the inhabitants came to beg our commander not to miss this last opportunity to save the lives of the women, the children, the elderly and the wounded. They begged him to heed the Arabs' calls, which were proclaimed on a loud speaker every evening, summoning us to surrender. The commander saw no other alternative.

The Arabs were very surprised when they discovered the weakness of our forces! But since the representatives of the Red Cross were present, they could no longer go back on their word.

Everything was veiled in darkness. The inhabitants left the premises. The soldiers were taken prisoners. Suddenly, the sky blazed up in red – the houses of the Jewish Quarter were on fire. The flames were approaching us, creeping dangerously close. The houses in front of us were burning and behind them, some Arab rioters were coming towards us, plundering and thirsting for blood. The wounded and the members of the medical staff were seized with panic. For the first time, I felt my heart sinking. We had the choice of dying by either being consumed by fire or being slaughtered. I explained the danger we faced to the Arab officer. He himself was bewildered. I told him that it was his duty as the commander to prevent a tragedy that would forever sully his country's flag. He suddenly regained his composure, as if awakening from a dream, assembled his men and turned towards the rioters. He took out his revolver, fired it, threw two grenades and the mob immediately withdrew. We attended to one of his soldiers who had been lightly wounded.

The danger had passed, but the fire was continuing to creep forward. For the third time, we had to transfer the patients as rapidly as possible. Everyone who could stand on his feet, including those who had stomach, chest or head injuries, walked by themselves. Only those with serious foot injuries were carried on stretchers as, moreover, were the elderly invalids that the Arab Legionnaires or we carried.

Before leaving the premises, we brought the wounded soldiers together in one room. When they were transferred to the ambulances, they began to sing. The Arab Legionnaires were astonished by their reactions; they expected tears and sobbing at the moment of separation.

A. Laufer, *Testimony*

The Jewish Quarter is plundered; its synagogues are desecrated. A general ceasefire goes into effect on June 11th, 1948. It leaves the eastern section of Jerusalem in Arab hands, with, nevertheless, an Israeli enclave on Mount Scopus. The renewed confrontations that break out on the 7th of July allow the Israelis to recover the village of Ein Karem as well as Mount Zion. The armistice agreement with Jordan, signed on April 3rd, 1949, recommends the establishment of a bilateral commission entrusted with reaching an understanding regarding the terms to resume the activities of the Hebrew University and of Hadassah Hospital, and to provide free access to the Jews to the holy sites in the Old City and to the cemetery on the Mount of Olives. However, classes will not be resumed on Mount Scopus and the Israelis will no longer have access to the holy sites – they will not be authorized to cross over the barbed wire and the barricades that will divide the city for nineteen years. In 1948, Jerusalem has 165,000 inhabitants: 100,000 Jews, 40,000 Muslims and 25,000 Christians. It will be divided by a winding, mine-strewn border until the Six Day War. In 1962, the poet and writer Hayyim Guri wrote: "Occasionally you remember that the town is torn. Not always. You are far away; you are busy. Then, one day you find yourself standing opposite it as through trying to see it anew. You walk, walk and then stop. Before you are steps. A rusting garbage can, a piece of fifteen-year-old barbed wire. Stop! For your own good. If you carry on, at best you will be thought to be mad; at worst you will be shot. For here they shoot. Everything is as though dozing in the noon's sun. Stones and trees and domes and crosses…"

THE DIVIDED CITY

On December 10th, 1948, the United Nations passes a motion advocating the internationalization of the city and of its close surroundings. The Israeli government reacts by declaring Jerusalem "the eternal capital of Israel" and by announcing the transfer of its ministers from Tel Aviv to Jerusalem. During the nineteen years that the city is divided, the Jordanian sector develops, especially towards the east, spreading its residential neighborhoods through *Shuafat*, *Beth Hanina* and *Kalandiyya* up to the suburb of *El-Bireh*. Only a few institutions and luxurious buildings, in particular hotels such as the Intercontinental Hotel are built on the Mount of Olives. Tourists pass from one section to another through a gate in the wall of hate and of iron that divides the city. The bullets of Jordanian snipers disturb the calm on a regular basis, frequently degenerating to an exchange of brisk fire. Terrorist incursions from the Jordanian sector occur from time to time, leaving dead and wounded on both sides.

At the same time, the western section of the city welcomes waves of immigrants who at first move into the houses abandoned by the Arabs in neighborhoods such as Ein Karem and Katamon. The authorities then create new neighborhoods, undertaking the hasty and awkward construction of public housing. A new road that passes through Ramla connects Jerusalem to the coastal plain while other roads approach it via Ein Kerem.

MOUNT HERZL

The park that spreads over Mount Herzl today houses the tomb of Theodor Herzl (1860 – 1904), the father of political Zionism and the founder of the World Zionist Organization, as well as the tombs of many other leaders of the Zionist movement and of Israeli political personalities, including that of Prime Minister Yitzhak Rabin, who was assassinated in 1995. A small museum at the entrance of the park reconstructs Herzl's life and work.

He is born in Budapest on May 2nd, 1860 to a rather wealthy, liberal Jewish family where he receives an education that is open to the general socio-cultural environment. In 1878, he moves to Vienna with his parents where he studies law. He practices law for only one year, abandoning it to devote himself exclusively to literature, publishing a series of articles, philosophical tales and plays dealing, for the most part, with the social issues rocking the epoch. In 1889, Herzl marries Julia Naschauer and from this rather unhappy marriage, three children are born.

From October 1891 until July 1895, he is the correspondent in Paris of the *Neue Freie Presse*, an influential, liberal Viennese daily newspaper. To Herzl, the Jewish question is but one of numerous social problems sullying the bourgeois regimes. Its solution is supposedly a massive conversion of Jewish youth to Socialism and membership in the Socialist movement. But the passions unleashed by the Dreyfus trial, which he covers for his newspaper, cure him of his assimilationist inclinations. At the end of the trial and the public humiliation of the French captain, he reaches the conclusion that the solution to the Jewish question is the exodus of the Jews from the European countries hopelessly contaminated by anti-Semitism, and their gathering in a country where they would be able to freely decide their destiny.

Herzl does not cease to work for the realization of this idea. He first attempts to establish contacts with wealthy Jewish donors. Disappointed by their hesitant reactions, he prepares a pamphlet that he considers sending to the Rothschilds to interest them in his project. The text – *Der Judenstaat* – is completed in June 1895. He claims that the Rothschild's wealth would be nothing more than a sand castle that would be threatened with collapse at any moment without the guarantee of a Jewish State. Their own interests would compel them to invest a part of their capital in a vast project that would assure the transfer of their European coreligionists to an independent state. The first reactions to his text question his sanity. He, moreover, becomes discouraged and in a letter – the fourth! – to Baron Hirsch, who is, nevertheless, organizing and financing a broad program of Jewish colonization in Argentina, he writes:

"My letter requires a post-script. This is it: I'm dropping everything... For the moment, there is no salvation for the Jews. When someone decides to show them the Promised Land, they immediately mock him because they are totally disheartened. However, I know where that Land is: within us! It is in our assets, our work and precisely in the combination of the two. But undoubtedly, we must fall even lower, be even more humiliated, covered with spit, mocked, beaten, vilified and slaughtered to be ready for this idea... We are not yet desperate enough and any savior that would arrive today would be greeted with laughter."

Herzl recovers from his crisis, henceforth, refusing to be diverted from his mission by mockery or by obstacles. In July 1895, he is summoned to Vienna where he is named the Director of the Literary Section of the *Neue Freie Presse*. The disappointing reactions on the part of noted Jewish personalities induce him to rewrite his pamphlet for publication. It is published in February 1896, followed that year by its translation to Hebrew, English, French, Russian and Romanian. His article, which appears in the English Jewish Chronicle in January 1896, summarizes his principal points:

The Jewish State

The idea that I am proposing is not new, on the contrary, it is ancient. An idea that is as universal as it is old – which, moreover, would be to its great credit – that even during periods of the worst calamities, the people never ceased to cherish: the restoration of the Jewish State.

It is, nevertheless, remarkable that we, the Jews, had to cherish this regal dream throughout the night of our history. But from now on, day is breaking for us. All we have to do is chase away the sleep from our eyes, stretch our limbs and realize our dream. Although I am neither a prophet nor a visionary, I acknowledge nourishing the hope and

*sharing the conviction that one day the Jewish people will
be overcome with a splendid enthusiasm. In the meanwhile, I
would like to simply and calmly appeal to the common sense
of the people who are endowed with a practical sense of
judgment and nourished by modern culture. A second task
will consist of addressing the most disadvantaged among us
to instruct them and to inspire them. I cannot assume this
second task alone; I will settle down to it with my friends
and my worker comrades whom I will try to mobilize and
gather together around a common cause. I do not say "my
followers" so as to not run the risk of making this movement a
personal affair and, consequently, absurd and contemptible.
For it is a question of a national movement and it will be
a glorious movement if it preserves itself from the stain
of personal desires although these often take the form of
political ambition. Those of us who are among the first to
launch this movement will probably not witness its glorious
realization. Launching it will not be any less of a source
of joy in our lives. We will sow for our children, like our
ancestors who transmitted their traditions, and our lives will
be but a moment in the permanent existence of our people.
Now that moment has its responsibilities.*

*Because of their significance, two phenomena draw our
attention: on one hand, the high cultural level of our era;
on the other hand, its profound barbarism. I intentionally
formulated this phrase as a paradox. By high culture, I
mean the marvelous development of technical inventions
intended to harness the forces of nature to serve man and his
objectives. By profound barbarism, I mean anti-Semitism...*

The Jewish People. *We constitute a people – one people.
We have sincerely tried to actively be integrated into
our respective societies, preserving only the faith of our
ancestors. In vain. It is in vain that we are loyal patriots,
even pushing our loyalty to the extreme on certain occasions.
It is in vain that we agree to sacrifice our lives and our
property like our compatriots. It is in vain that we fight to do
our part for the glory of our countries in the fields of science
and art and for their economic prosperity. However, in these
countries where we have lived for centuries, we are still
considered strangers; and, often, by those whose ancestors*

did not even inhabit these countries at a time when the Jews had already had a long history of persecution behind them. In spite of this, we are loyal subjects, as loyal as the Huguenots, although we were forced to emigrate. If only they could have left us in peace...

We constitute a people – our enemies have made us an exceptional people in spite of ourselves, as this has often happened during the course of history. Distress binds us and united in this way, we suddenly discover our strength. Yes, we are strong enough to establish a State, a model State. We possess all the human and material resources necessary for this....

The Society of the Jews. *Everything should be undertaken within the framework of acquired rights and in absolute conformity with the law, freely, openly and in broad daylight, under the supervision of the authorities and the surveillance of public opinion...*

Our clergy, to whom I make a special appeal, will put its energy in the service of this ideal. However, its members should know that we have no intention of founding a theocracy now, but a secular, modern and tolerant State. We will, nevertheless, rebuild the Temple in Jerusalem to commemorate the glorious faith of our ancestors. Waving the new flag of Judaism – a banner with seven stars on a white background. The background symbolizes the purity of our new lives, the stars, the seven hours of light of a workday. For we must move forward to the Promised Land waving the flag of labor...

Likewise, we should zealously work to promote the Jewish political cause... This task should obviously not be limited to an individual for only a madman or an imposter would assume this gigantic task alone. It would, consequently, be necessary that the activity not be personalized in order to preserve the integrity of our ideal and to guarantee its vigorous realization. The agency in question should unite many people. I propose that it first of all be composed of recruits from among the energetic British Jews to whom I submitted my proposal in London. Furthermore, I propose that this agency be called the Society of Jews, to distinguish it from the Jewish Company that I previously mentioned. The Society of Jews will accomplish whatever the entire Jewish movement will decide to undertake. It will work in the field of science and that of politics because, in my opinion, the establishment of a Jewish State will require having recourse to scientific methods... In short, the Society of the Jews will constitute the first nucleus of our future public institutions...

***The Historic Homeland.** Should we choose the Republic of Argentina or Palestine? We will take what will be offered to us and what will gain the approval of Jewish public opinion. Argentina is one of the most fertile countries in the world; it extends over a vast surface and has a small population. It would greatly benefit from yielding a part of its territory. The actual settlement of the Jews would certainly stir up tension and it would be necessary to enlighten the Argentine leaders about the unusual nature of our movement.*

Palestine is nothing less than our memorable and eternal historic homeland. The name of Palestine itself would attract our people with extraordinary power. If His Majesty, the Sultan, grants us Palestine, in exchange, we would be able to commit ourselves to putting the finances of Turkey in order. We would form part of the wall of Europe in the face of Asia, an advanced post of civilization in its battle against barbarism. We would constitute a neutral State, maintaining close relations with Europe, which would guarantee our existence. The protection of the Christian Holy Sites would be assured by the bestowal of a status recognizing their extra-territoriality in accordance with the laws enforced among the nations. On our part, we will post an honor guard around these sites, assuming in this manner a duty that is inherent in our being. In my opinion, this honor guard would symbolize settling the Jewish question after almost nineteen centuries of persecution and suffering...

***The Promised Land.** I am well aware that by expressing an old idea in a new form that I am exposing myself to the risk of all kinds of attacks. Some noble minds will qualify my idea as utopian. However, what is the difference between a utopian project and one that can be realized? The first could present itself as an intelligently and well-designed mechanism that* *simply requires the impetus necessary to set it in motion...*

We will be unable to do anything without the enthusiasm of our people. The idea must make its way to the most remote hovels inhabited by our people. They will awaken from their sad sleep to a life full of new meaning. Let each one be concerned only with joining us and our movement will assume vast proportions! What glory awaits those who will dedicate themselves to our cause! A wonderful new generation of Jews will appear. The Maccabees will rise again.

This is how it will be: it will be precisely the poor and simple people who do not doubt the power that men exert over the forces of nature that will imbue this new message with firm faith. For they have not lost the hope for the Promised Land.

This is my message, Jewish comrades! It is neither a fable nor a fraud! Each one must examine the truth that he carries within himself and test it because each one preserves a portion of the Promised Land within himself – one in his head, another in his arms and still another in his wealth. Finally, we will live as free men on our land and we will die in peace in our own houses.

T. Herzl, *The Jewish State*

The assimilated Jews receive Herzl's book with derision, the liberals, with sarcasm. Only the Zionist organizations like the *Hovevei Zion* – at least the majority of its members – receive it with enthusiasm. Disappointed by the Jewish leaders, Herzl turns to non-Jewish, especially German and Turkish, political personalities. Nevertheless, the warm welcome that he receives from some communities compensates for his rebuffs. In July 1897, he launches a weekly paper, *Die Welt*, to diffuse the Zionist theses and convokes the First Congress of the Zionist Movement from the 29th to the 31st of August. Delegates from all over the world meet in Basle – it is the first Jewish assembly of a secular and national character –, to provide the Zionist Movement with a platform and to found the World Zionist Organization. Herzl immediately settles down to the task of consolidating this organization, which is entrusted with the mission of establishing "a national, Jewish home in Eretz Israel". The Second Congress in 1898 decides to found a bank entrusted to gather the funds required to carry out the Zionist Movement program. Established in 1899, it will become one of the leading banks in the country, *Bank Leumi*.

Herzl pursues his political course of action. On November 2nd, 1898, he meets with the German emperor in Jerusalem. Now again, the meeting falls short of his expectations. His contacts with Constantinople are not pursued – the Sultan receives him on May 17th, 1901, but without the backing of the Jewish bankers who continue to ignore him, he cannot make any commitments to the Turkish. He directs his efforts to Great Britain where the Fourth Zionist Congress is held. The deliberations deal, in particular, with the territorial solution of settling the Jews in another territory rather than in Palestine. The Foreign Office rejects the Cypriot solution; the Sinai solution runs up against the opposition of the Egyptian government; Herzl is tempted by the Ugandan solution. The pogroms in Kichinev in 1903 intensify the urgency of a solution and Herzl submits the Ugandan proposal to the Sixth Zionist Congress, which assembles in Basle from August 22nd to the 28th, 1903. The debates are stormy and the Russian delegates protest the betrayal of the Land of Israel. Herzl must use all his authority to pass a motion to authorize dispatching an investigative commission to Uganda.

Nevertheless, Herzl continues to promote the Palestinian solution, especially before the Russian authorities. In January 1904, he resubmits his proposals to the Turks. He then meets the Pope, the King of Italy and members of the Italian government. The Ugandan solution continues to stir up opposition. The Russian members of the Zionist Executive insist that Herzl totally renounce that solution. The controversy spreads to many Jewish communities. Finally, during a meeting held in April 1904, Herzl reiterates his support for the Palestinian solution and in this way, manages to reestablish unity within the Zionist Movement. On July 3rd, 1904, he dies after a series of cardiac ailments. The creed of his book: "If you will it, it is no dream" characterizes in some way the accomplishments of the Zionist Movement in Palestine...

In his will, Herzl requests being buried in Vienna next to his father who had persistently supported his efforts, placing all of his wealth at his disposition. In addition, he requests that his remains be transferred to the new Jewish State immediately after its creation. The following passages describe his burial in Vienna (*Die Welt*, July 8th, 1904) and his funeral in Jerusalem in 1949:

The funeral in Vienna

A Zionist flag covered the coffin, the same one that used to flutter over the Congress Building in Basle where the Congress took place during those happy days when Herzl alone directed it with a firm hand. Now, solemn people wept bitter tears upon the coffin while hundreds of delegates and representatives walked in procession. The funeral began at ten o'clock. The only people authorized to enter the room where his body lay were the members of the Executive Committee, close friends, representatives of the Viennese Jewish Community and members of the Press. Many thousands of people thronged together and hundreds of cars blocked the traffic in front of the building and in the neighboring streets. The long procession of more than 6,000 people walked in close ranks, flanked by students and workers, members of the Zionist Movement.

The funeral in Jerusalem

The coffin arrived in Tel Aviv on the 16th of August at 15:30. The Knesset members were the first to pay their respects; then the high-ranking government officials, who left the Knesset Building to go to the Knesset Square where the coffin lay in state, surrounded by an honor guard. During the evening and throughout the night, more than 200,000 people from Tel Aviv and the surrounding areas marched by the remains to pay their last tribute to their dead leader.

The following morning, on the 22nd of Av (August 17th) at 5 o'clock, Herzl's final journey began. The convoy escorted by representatives of the State and of the Zionist Organization passed Mikveh Israel, Ness Ziona, Rishon le-Zion and Rehovot, the places that Herzl had visited during one of his trips to Palestine in 1898. Wherever the funeral procession

237

passed, silent and reverent crowds had gathered to meet it. The coffin arrived in Jerusalem around 9 a.m. and was placed in the courtyard of the National Institutions Compound. M. Berl Locker, the president of the Zionist Executive, delivered the following address from the heights of the balcony of the Jewish Agency Building:

"Today we are privileged to bring our founder and leader, Benjamin Zeev Herzl, to his final rest in the eternal city. The first to behold the vision of our redemption, he inspired the best of our nation. He gathered together the seeds of revival dispersed throughout our numerous lands of exile and fashioned the Zionist Movement as well as the Zionist Organization. To the Zionist Movement, he entrusted the historic task of fulfilling the cherished wish of many generations of exiles and of establishing itself in the eyes of the entire world as Jewry's representative and as the guardian of its most vital interests. There was true prophecy in his remark that once he had established the Zionist Organization he had in essence already founded the Jewish State... By bringing his remains to the State of Israel, we mark in an unprecedented and symbolic manner, the dramatic change that has occurred in our history.

It is true that the dream that Herzl cherished – the independence of the State of Israel – has only been partially fulfilled. The liberation of Zion is inseparably tied to the return to Zion. The Zionist Movement, in collaboration with the State of Israel, will continue to invest with ever increasing energy in its historic task of accomplishing the Zionist mission that consists of the Ingathering of the Exiles. Let us imbue the masses of our nation and its youth with Herzl's ideas; let us echo his vision overseas. Let us gather on this land the dispersed of Israel, let us establish a new society based on the ideals of human justice and social equity in accordance with that dream and in order to be able to transmit the heritage of Herzl to future generations."

The inhabitants of Jerusalem filed past the coffin until 4 p.m. Then an honor guard consisting of all the members of the government, the members of the Knesset, the surviving delegates who had participated in the First Zionist Congress presided over by Herzl, and members of the Zionist Executive *and of the General Zionist Council escorted the coffin to the hill near the Bayit va-Gan neighborhood, henceforth known as Mount Herzl. The burial ceremony took place in the presence of thousands of people representing the Zionist Movement and the Yishuv. The chief rabbis of Israel, the president of the Knesset, the acting president of the State of Israel, the prime minister, the president of the Zionist Executive, the chairman of the Committee for the Transfer of Herzl's Remains and the representatives of the ground, sea and air military forces escorted the remains of their leader to their final resting place. The representatives of hundreds of villages and settlements throughout the country who had also been invited to participate brought small bags of sand from all parts of the land of Israel to sprinkle over the leader's remains in the grave. Rabbi Zeev Gold, a member of the Zionist Executive, then recited the kaddish and the ceremony ended with the memorial prayer El Malei Rahamim and the national anthem, Hatikva – the song of everlasting hope.*

S. U. Nahon, *Theodor Herzl*

[•]

The northern slope of Mount Herzl is the site of one of the many cemeteries scattered throughout the country where the soldiers who fell during the battles to defend Israel are buried. One of them, Lieutenant Colonel Yonathan or Yoni Netanyahu, left us some letters in which a particular portrait is revealed – perhaps that of an anti-hero – the model that the Israeli Army presents to its new recruits.

In June 1976, some terrorists hijack a French airplane during a regular flight between Tel Aviv and Paris. They head for the Entebbe Airport in Uganda where a dictator, Idi Amin Dada, gives them a heroes' welcome. The travelers are held hostage at the airport under the surveillance of the Ugandan soldiers. The terrorists threaten to execute all the Jewish passengers if their demands are not met. The Israelis then engage in an operation that will mark a turning point in the history of the fight against international terrorism. Some airplanes with elite army units on board cross the continent of Africa. The terrorists are killed and the hostages are freed. There is only one casualty among the combatants, the commander of the operation – Yoni Netanyahu, whose brother, Benjamin, will become Prime Minister in 1996. His letters are collected in a book dedicated to his memory. In one of them, addressed to his parents and to his younger brother, he portrays the Israeli army in the following terms:

An anti-army

May 3rd, 1970

Dear Father and Mother,
Dear Ido,

You asked me, Father, what my plans are. Well, in the long run, there is nothing definite in sight although some initial ideas are beginning to take shape in my mind.

I will serve in the army for another year, the time it will take to complete the tasks which I have assumed... After that, a huge cloud veils the future. Of course, it will depend on how the situation in the country evolves, which could improve (I am rather pessimistic about this at least for the upcoming year) just as it could become worse (as if it could possibly get worse). Today, it is difficult for me to say what I will decide when the times comes, although I think that my place is in the army. Completing my education is also very tempting, especially at Harvard, where I would like to return. When? In about eighteen months, at least that is my hope, but obviously nothing has been decided yet. In truth, the army offers many things that I would like to be able to find elsewhere – the kind of people that I like, who are energetic, who have initiative and are unconventional when they must be, refusing to adhere to the ideas handed to them, endlessly seeking new paths and new solutions. The army allows all the freedom to develop and to test new ideas. Furthermore, you do not have the carelessness, the hypocrisy (sometimes), the bureaucracy and the insensitivity that you find on the outside. Perhaps the word "outside" says it all. In this country, at this moment, to be in the army is to be on the inside – to act, to believe, to know that your work, in spite of everything, contributes to bringing about peace, at least by saving lives and warding off the threat of war at our gates.

J. Netanyahu, *Self-Portrait of a Hero*

Israel's unique destiny is revealed in the customs of Israeli society. Memorial Day precedes the celebration of Independence Day in accordance with Jewish tradition. Ceremonies are held in schools, public institutions and cemeteries. An entire people reflects on the memory of the men and women who died to guarantee its liberty while a siren reverberates from one end of the country to the other like a collective wail. This day of meditation and anguished protest against fate echoes in poetry as well:

God Full of Mercy

God full of mercy,
Were it not for the God full of mercy
There would be mercy in the world and not
Only in Him.
I, who picked flowers on the mountains
And looked into all the valleys,
I, who brought corpses from the hills,
Know to say that the world is devoid of mercy.
I, who was the king of salt by the sea,
Who stood without decision by my window,
Who counted the footsteps of angels,
Whose heart lifted weights of pain
In the awesome contests.

I, who use only a small portion
Of the words of the dictionary.
I, who must solve riddles against my will,
Know that were it not for the God full of mercy
There would be mercy in the world

And not only in Him.

Y. Amichai

YAD VASHEM

A Candelabra designed by Zehava Schatz welcomes the visitor. Its six branches symbolize the six million Jews who perished in the Shoah. The Law of the Memorial to the Martyrs and the Heroes that the Israeli Parliament passed in August 1953 specifies the vocation and the duties of Yad Vashem:

The Mount of Remembrance

1. *We hereby establish an organization of remembrance, Yad Vashem, in Jerusalem to commemorate:*

    1) *the memory of the six million members of the Jewish People who died as martyrs, exterminated by the Nazis and their accomplices;*

    2) *the memory of the Jewish families annihilated by the oppressor;*

    3) *the memory of the communities, the synagogues, the movements and the organizations, as well as the public, cultural, educational, religious and social institutions destroyed in a heinous attempt to forever obliterate the name and the culture of the people of Israel;*

    4) *the devotion of the Jews who sacrificed themselves for their people;*

    5) *the heroism of the Jewish soldiers and the members of the Resistance in the cities, the villages and the underground who risked their lives in the fight against the Nazi oppressor and his accomplices;*

    6) *the heroic resistance of the besieged populations in the ghettos and the fighters who ignited the torch of revolt to salvage the honor of their people;*

    7) *the constant and glorious struggle of the masses of the House of Israel that was carried out to the very end in order to guarantee their human dignity and their Jewish culture;*

   8) *the unceasing efforts exerted by the besieged to reach the land of Israel, in spite of all the obstacles, as well as to the self-sacrifice and the heroism demonstrated to rescue and liberate the survivors;*

   9) *the acts of the Righteous among the nations who risked their lives to save the Jews.*

2. *Yad Vashem's mission will be to collect on the soil of the regained homeland the documentation and the material related to all the members of the Jewish People who perished, fought and revolted against the Nazi enemy and his accomplices and to perpetuate their memory as well as that of the communities, the organizations and the institutions that were destroyed because they were Jewish; towards this end, Yad Vashem will be authorized to:*

   1) *establish commemorative projects at its own initiative and under its own management;*

   2) *collect, study and publish testimonies about the Shoah and about the heroic acts to which it gave rise and to draw lessons for the people;*

   3) *institute in Israel, among the people, a day designated by the Knesset as the Day of Remembrance of the Martyrs and the Heroes of the Shoah and to promote rites to commemorate the memory of the heroes and the victims;*

   4) *grant the nationality of the State of Israel to the members of the Jewish People who perished in the Shoah and in the Resistance in commemoration and as a testimony of their reunion with their people;*

   5) *approve and encourage activities aimed at perpetuating the memory of the victims and the heroes of the Shoah and participate in these activities;*

   6) *represent Israel in international projects aimed at perpetuating the memory of the victims of the Nazis and those who died in the fight against them;*

   7) *do all that is required to accomplish these tasks.*

The Avenue of the Righteous Gentiles among the Nations, where carob-trees are planted here and there, encircles the site. The women and men who helped, hid and saved the Jews during the turmoil of the war at the risk of their lives, or their descendents, planted the trees. A monument designed by S. Selinger is dedicated to the Nations' Unknown Righteous.

Of all the countries, Denmark was one of the few, if not the only, to demonstrate sympathy for the tragedy of the Jews. For two years after the Germans invaded it in 1940, its king, Christian X, courageously resisted pressure from the Nazis to impose discriminatory measures. "Gentlemen", he retorted to the German authorities that reproached him for neglecting the Jewish problem, "having never considered ourselves inferior to the Jews, we do not have that problem in Denmark". On another occasion, he declared: "If the Germans want to introduce the yellow star in Denmark, my family and I will wear it as a sign of high distinction."

In August 1943, when the Germans decided to deport the Jews, the Danish somehow managed to save almost 7,000, sending them to Sweden, which having declared itself neutral, was not occupied. A boat on the Avenue of the Righteous commemorates this resistance of a country against the political and racial terror of the Nazis. It was used to transport 600 Jews to the city of Gilleleje in fishing boats that waited for them out at sea to take them to Sweden.

The Wall of Remembrance: The Avenue of the Righteous opens on to an esplanade where a large commemorative ceremony takes place each year on the Day of Remembrance of the Martyrs and Heroes of the Shoah, the 27th of Nissan. The Wall of Remembrance, designed by Nathan Rapaport, represents the last march of the deportees as well as the revolt of the ghetto. The two words engraved on the wall – *bedamayih hayyi*, from your blood, live – were drawn from a passage in the book of the prophet Ezekiel.

The Crypt of Remembrance, situated at the bend of the Avenue of the Righteous, houses the ashes of victims collected from concentration camps, the name of which are engraved on plaques:

Memorial Prayer for the Martyrs

O God full of Mercy, dwelling on high, bring to perfect rest on the wings of Shechinah – among the exalted, the holy and pure, shining as the brightness of firmament – the souls of millions of Jews, men, women and children, killed, slaughtered, burned alive, who perished at the hands of the Nazi oppressors in the countries under their domination, for the sanctification of Thy divine name.

All of them holy and pure, and among them men of great learning and saintliness.

Please, O Lord of Compassion, shelter them forever under the cover of Thy wings, and let their souls be bound up in the bond of eternal life. The Lord is their inheritance; may they rest on peace. And let us say, Amen.

The Monument Dedicated to the Soldiers and Fighters of the Ghettos and of the Resistance, designed by Bernie Fink, extends over a vast esplanade in the form of a candelabra, which juts out over the Valley of the Destroyed Communities. It is composed of six oblong blocks of granite representing the six million dead, placed in such a way as to demarcate an inner space in the form of the Star of David that is crossed by the blade of a weapon, symbolizing the fight against the Nazis. The monument bears the following inscription: "To the glory of the Jewish soldiers and the members of the Resistance who fought against Nazi Germany."

One of the most heroic revolts was that of the Warsaw Ghetto, whose inhabitants were evacuated little by little by the Germans to be sent to the death camps. Its commander, Mordechai Anilewicz, a young man of twenty-nine, expresses his last wish in this passage:

The last choice

It is clear to me that all that has happened until now exceeded all my expectations. Through our resistance against the Germans, we accomplished far more than our paltry means permitted. Now our forces have been diminished. We are on the verge of exhaustion. We forced the Germans to withdraw on two occasions – they returned even stronger than before.

One of our groups has held out for forty minutes. Another has fought for almost six hours. The mine placed next to the brush factory exploded as planned. We then attacked the Germans who suffered heavy losses. Our losses are, in general, small, which is also an achievement. Z. was killed near his machine gun.

I feel that great events are taking place and that what we have dared to undertake is of considerable value.

We have no other choice than to apply the partisans' methods of attack as we did today. Tonight, six groups of fighters will leave the ghetto on two missions: to conduct a reconnaissance of the areas and to bring back arms. Remember: short-range weapons are useless to us. We rarely use them. On the other hand, we need rifles, grenades, machine guns and explosives.

I have no words to describe the current living conditions of the inhabitants in the ghetto. Only a few individuals will be able to survive so much suffering. The others will die sooner or later. Their fate is sealed even if thousands of them try to hide in burrows and mice holes. The lack of air makes it impossible to light candles.

I send my greetings to you who are on the outside. Perhaps a miracle will occur and we will see each other again. But it is unlikely.

I have realized the last wish of my life. Henceforth, the self-defense of the Jews is a fact. Jewish resistance and vengeance have become a reality. I am happy to have been among the first Jewish fighters of the ghetto.

From where will help come?

M. Anilewicz, *A letter*

The Valley of the Destroyed Communities spreads over 8000 square kilometers at a level below the site. Five thousand stones reconstitute the map of the communities destroyed in the Shoah. Mordechai Gebirtig, a carpenter in Krakow, was the composer of popular ballads. He was killed in the ghetto in his native city in 1942. This poem, written in 1938, would be repeated in the ghettos, in the concentration camps and by the survivors of the horrible massacre:

The fire in the city

Our city is burning, my brothers, it is burning,
our poor little city is burning.
Surly winds stir up
the leaping tongues of the flames and the fire
Evil winds howl!
Our entire city is going up in flames!

You are witnessing it, your arms folded,
shaking your head.
You are witnessing it, your arms folded
while the fire spreads!

Our city is burning, my brothers, it is burning,
our poor little city burns.
Surly winds stir up
the leaping tongues of the flames and the fire.
The fire is sweeping through our city,
entering through the roofs and the windows.
Everything is burning up all around us.

You are witnessing it, your arms folded,
shaking your head.
You are witnessing it, your arms folded
while the fire spreads!

Our city is burning, my brothers, it is burning.
At any moment, the fire threatens
to sweep through our whole city,
leaving only ashes, black and gray.

You are witnessing it, your arms folded,
shaking your head.
You are witnessing it, your arms folded
while the fire spreads!

Our city is burning, my brothers, it is burning.
Everything depends on you now.
The only help we can get depends on what you do.
You can still extinguish the fire
with your blood if that is what you want to do.

Stop watching it with your arms folded,
shaking your head.
Stop watching it with your arms folded
while the fire spreads!

M. Gebirtig

The Memorial to the Victims of the Death Camps, designed by Nandor Glid, northwest of the site, evokes the memory of the millions of Jews exterminated in the concentration camps.

The Historic Museum reconstructs the chain of events that led to World War II and to the unleashing of the hate that preceded the extermination of the Jews in Europe. A bas-relief by Naftali Bezem welcomes the visitor. Mixing numerous Jewish symbols, it presents four scenes from left to right: the extermination, the resistance, the immigration to Israel and the national renaissance. The exposition is divided into five parts. The first reconstructs the circumstances of Hitler's rise to power, his expansionist ambitions and his racist policies. It also presents the assault, the detention and the persecution of the Jews until the invasion of Russia. The second part presents the implementation of the Final Solution: the systematic extermination of the Jews throughout Europe. The third part is dedicated to the armed revolt of the Warsaw Ghetto; the tunnel that connects the two buildings of the museum symbolizes the sewer that the insurgents went through to move around within the ghetto and to pass to the other side of the walls in search of arms and munitions. The fourth part is dedicated to the partisans. The fifth part presents the liberation of the deportees and the efforts of many of them to arrive in Palestine in spite of the restrictions imposed by Britain.

The Hall of Names contains the names of the victims that have been collected on pages of testimonies, listed in alphabetical order. More than three and a half million testimonies have been gathered to date. The Hall of Names also houses some books of remembrance dedicated to the Jewish communities that were annihilated.

The deportees did not have names; they were nothing more than numbers. In Auschwitz, the most terrible death camp, the numbers were even tattooed on the arms of the deportees. Primo Levi (1919 – 1987), an Italian writer detained in Auschwitz, wrote:

The registration number

The operation was not painful and did not take more than a minute, but it was traumatizing. Its symbolic significance was obvious to everyone: it was an indelible sign that you would never leave; it was the mark imprinted on the slaves and the animals destined to be slaughtered and it was what you had become. You no longer had a name; this was your new name. The violence of the tattoo process is unwarranted, an end in itself, a pure outrage: weren't the three cloth numbers sewn on the pants, on the jacket and on the winter coat enough? No they were not: one more was necessary, a non-verbal message to make the innocent feel his condemnation written in his flesh. It was also a return to barbarous methods, which was all the more disturbing to the Orthodox Jews; indeed, and precisely in order to distinguish the Jews from the "barbarians", Mosaic Law forbids tattooing (Leviticus 19: 28).

After forty years, my tattoo has become a part of my body. It is neither a source of glory nor of shame; I do not exhibit it or hide it. I reluctantly show it to those who purely out of curiosity ask me to, promptly and not without being irritated by those who avow their disbelief. The young frequently ask me why I do not have it removed and that astonishes me: why should I do so? Those of us who bear this testimony are very few in number.

P. Levi, The Ruined and the Survivors

The Art Museum displays the artwork of the deportees in the camps, or of the survivors haunted by the memory of their detention.

The Mausoleum of Remembrance contains a flame that is permanently lit under the crypt – *ohel yikzor* – that holds the ashes of some of the victims brought from twenty-two concentration camps whose names are engraved on plaques.

The philosopher, Emile Fackenheim, attempted the impossible: to discuss the questions that Auschwitz raised about God, man and the world. He drew this lesson from his reflection:

Remember

Jews are forbidden to hand Hitler posthumous victories.
They are commanded to survive as Jews,
Lest the Jewish people perish.

They are commanded to remember
The victims of Auschwitz
Last their memory perish.

They are forbidden to despair of man and his world,
And to escape into either cynicism and other worldliness.
Lest they cooperate in delivering the world over
To the forces of Auschwitz.

Finally, they are forbidden to despair of the God of Israel,
Lest Judaism perish.

E. Fackenheim, *The Presence of God in the World*

The Column of Heroism rises up in a setting of devastation with this inscription: "To the martyrs of the Shoah, to the revolts of the ghettos, to the partisans in the forest, to the insurgents in the camps, to the members of the Resistance, to the soldiers in the Allied Forces, to the rescuers of their brothers in peril, to the brave of the illegal immigration, forever." Hirsch Glick, born in 1920 in Vilna, managed to escape a concentration camp in Estonia. He immediately rallied the partisans, dying at their sides. A song that he composed became the hymn of the Partisan Jews:

Never say

Never say that only death awaits you,
for gray skies can hide blue days,
and the moment we are waiting for is not far.
The ground will reverberate under our boots: here we are!

From the lands of palm-trees to far away, snow laden countries,
we will come, burdened with our anguish and with our misery,
and wherever our blood will have been spilt on the ground,
our strength and our bravery will flourish!

The sun will shine its glowing rays upon our day,
our yesterdays will vanish with our enemy,
and if it takes some time before the sun rises,
may this song be as a sign throughout the years.

This song, written with the ink of our blood, not with a pencil,
is not sung by the birds over our heads,
but by a people among smashed open barricades
riddled with bullets and grenades.

Therefore, never say that only death awaits you,
for gray skies can hide blue days,
and the moment we are waiting for is not far.
The ground will reverberate under our boots: here we are!

H. Glick

The Memorial to the Children is located in the garden that is also dedicated to perpetuating the memory of one and a half million Jewish children exterminated by the Nazis. Five candles are reflected into one and a half million stars in the most complete darkness while a grave and solemn voice recites their names one by one. Two statues await the visitor at the exit of the underground monument: one by Boris Saktsier depicts J. Korczak surrounded by the orphans in his orphanage who he chose to accompany to Auschwitz, and the other by Nathan Rapaport represents Job. These are the words of Peter Fischl, who was born on the 9th of September 1929 and who died in Auschwitz in 1944:

The habit of death

...We are accustomed to standing in a row at 7 in the morning, at noon and then again at 7 in the evening. We form a long line with a plate in hand in which they pour a little bouillon that has the taste of salt or coffee or toss some potatoes. We are accustomed to not sleeping in a bed, to systematically saluting all the uniforms, to not walking on the sidewalks and then to walking on the sidewalks. We are accustomed to the arbitrary blows of a whip, to the blows of a fist, to executions. We are accustomed to seeing people die in their excrement, the piles of coffins full of bodies, the sick laid out in the filth and decay and the powerless doctors. We are accustomed to a thousand unfortunate souls arriving here from time to time and to another thousand unfortunate souls leaving from time to time.

P. Fischl

Among the many poems written by children during this sad period, one of the most well known was left behind by Pavel Friedmann who died on June 4th, 1942:

The Butterfly

The last, the last of the last,
so rich, so brilliant, a dazzling yellow.
Perhaps the tears of the sun
singing against a white stone...

The same, the same yellow
rises lightly in the air.
It went away, I am sure of it, because it wanted
to leave this world in a kiss.

I have been here seven weeks,
confined in this ghetto,
where I have joined my people.
The dandelions call out to me
just as the white chestnut trees in the yard.
But I have not seen another butterfly again.

That butterfly was the last.
The butterflies do not live here
in the ghetto.

P. Friedmann

Yitzhak Katzenelson wrote the most poignant texts on this terrible period. In his Lament of the Martyred Jewish People, he writes:

Lamentation

They, the children of Israel, were the first in doom and disaster;
Most of them without father and mother
Were consumed by frost, starvation and lice;
Holy messiahs sanctified in pain...
Say then, how have the lambs sinned?
Why in days of doom are they the first victims of wickedness,
The first in the trap of evil are they!

The first were they detained for death,
The first into the wagons of slaughter;

They were thrown into the wagons, the huge wagons,
Like heaps of refuse, like the ashes of the earth –
And they transported them,
Killed them,
Exterminated them
Without remnant and remembrance…
The best of my children were all wiped out!
Oh woe unto me –
Doom and Desolation!

The following inscription was found engraved on the wall of a cave in Cologne where some Jews hid to escape their Nazi executioners:

I believe in the sun – even when it does not shine.
I believe in love – even when the feeling is not there.
I believe in God – even when He remains silent.

EIN KAREM

Isaiah and Jeremiah evoke the village of Ein Karem – the Vineyard Spring – declaring: "Run away, sons of Benjamin, from the midst of Jerusalem! Sound the trumpet in Tekoa! Raise the alarms in Beth Karem! For the catastrophe, the great disaster appears on the North."

The Arab inhabitants of this picturesque village that is nestled in a valley vacated it in 1948. Churches and convents, scattered upon its heights, celebrate, in their own manner, the miraculous birth of John the Baptist, the harbinger of Christianity.

A tradition that dates back to the 9th century, situates the home of his parents, Zacharias and Elisabeth, in this place:

The birth of John
Now Elisabeth's full time came that she should be delivered and she brought forth a son. Her neighbors and her cousins

had heard how the Lord had shown great mercy upon her and they rejoiced with her. And it came to pass that on the eighth day, they came to circumcise the child and they called him Zacharias like his father. But his mother responded and said: "Not so for he will be called John." They said to her: "None of your kindred is called by this name." They made signs to his father to know how he would have them call him. He asked for a writing table and wrote: "His name is John"; and they were surprised. His mouth was immediately opened and his tongue loosed and he spoke and praised God. And fear came upon all that dwelt around them and everyone spoke of these events throughout the hill country of Judea. Everyone who heard them laid them up in their hearts saying: "What manner of child will this be!" And the hand of the Lord was with him.

Luke 1: 57 - 66

An early tradition situates the birth of John on the site where the Franciscan Church of Saint John the Baptist stands today. Excavations have uncovered the vestiges of pagan sanctuaries consecrated to Venus and Adonis dating back to the Roman period. The Byzantines build a first church and the Crusaders a second church, Saint John of the Mountains, which the Arabs convert to a caravansary. In 1621, the Franciscans purchase the site with the backing of King Louis XIV, who intervenes on their behalf at the Sultan's court in Constantinople. In 1674, they settle among the ruins, which they undertake to restore. The actual building, built in the style of the Crusader's church with the assistance of the royal house of Spain, dates to the years 1857 – 1900. The bell tower housing four bells dedicated to John, Elizabeth, Zacharias as well as to the Visitation is one of the many gifts from Spain whose influence, moreover, can be seen in the fresco murals. In 1875, a new inn is built northeast of the church. A school and a seminary, which receive seminarians until 1887, are also opened.

Four columns divide the church into a nave and two aisles that face west. The dome's stained glass windows represent the four evangelists. A statue of the Virgin surrounded by those of Zacharias, Elisabeth, John and Anne are mounted over the high altar that is covered with marble of various colors. Two other statues represent Saint Francis and Saint Laura. The right aisle ends with an altar consecrated to Elisabeth. There is a rock behind iron bars that was brought in from the surrounding areas of the village, which is said to be the one that John would lean against to rest. A legend tells that in the 18th century, some Muslims cut off a piece of this rock to extract lime. The oven in which it was placed exploded and they decided to place the rock in the church to gain John's good graces – *Mar Hanna* in Arabic. John's crypt is on the left, north of the main altar, where it is said that he was born. The altar is a gift from Queen Isabel of Spain. Some white and black marble bas-reliefs reconstruct scenes from John's life. An inscription in Latin is engraved below the altar: "The messenger of God was born here." Above it, there is a painting of Mary showing the baby to Zacharias under the gaze of Elisabeth who is lying in her bed.

At the entrance of the church, a cave leads to the narthex where there are some sepulchers. An inscription on the mosaic on the floor declares: "Salvation to the martyrs of God." It is dedicated to the monks massacred in the 4th century, perhaps even to the infants massacred by Herod's soldiers in Bethlehem, and perhaps also to all the Christian martyrs. A room that is closed off by heavy wooden doors preserves the church's ancient winepress. The blessing that Zacharias pronounced eight days after John's birth is translated into many languages in the court of the church:

Zacharias' benediction

And his father, Zacharias, was filled with the Holy Ghost and prophesized saying: "Blessed be the Lord God of Israel for He has visited and redeemed his people. And he has raised a horn of salvation for us in the house of his servant, David. He spoke the words of the prophets that have been since the world began: that we should be saved from our enemies and from the hand of all who hate us to perform the mercy of our fathers and to remember his holy covenant. He swore an oath to our father Abraham: That having been delivered out of the hand of our enemies, we may serve him without fear in holiness and in righteousness before him all the days of our lives. And you, child, will be called the prophet of the Highest for you will go before the face of the Lord to prepare his way; to give knowledge of salvation to his people by the remission of their sins through the tender mercy of our God. The daystar from on high has visited us to give light to them that sit in the darkness and in the shadow of death to guide our feet along the path of peace.

Luke 1: 67 - 79

John's birth is preceded by another event that leaves its mark on the setting of Ein Karem: Mary's visit to her cousin, Elizabeth:

Mary's visit

And Mary arose in those days and went in haste into the hill country to a city of Judah. She entered the house of Zacharias and greeted Elisabeth. It came to pass that when Elisabeth heard Mary's salutation, the baby leaped in her womb and Elisabeth was filled with the Holy Ghost. And she said in a loud voice: "Blessed are you among women and blessed is the fruit of your womb. How is it that the mother of my Lord should come to me? For as soon as the voice of your greeting sounded in my ears, the baby leaped in my womb for joy. Blessed is she that believed: for that which was told to her of the Lord will be accomplished!" [...] And Mary abode with her for about three months and then returned to her own house.

Luke 1:39 - 56

According to the apocalyptic Christian literature, Elisabeth and her son also escaped from Herod's soldiers at the time that they were perpetrating the massacre of the infants. It is said that they found refuge behind or under a rock that miraculously opened for them.

The Church of the Visitation commemorates this visit between Mary and Elisabeth. It stands on a second site that is, in general, considered to be the residence of Zacharias – perhaps a second dwelling where Elizabeth is said to have hidden with John. Some ruins attest to the presence of a village on these sites prior to the Roman period. The Byzantines and the Crusaders build some churches and some outbuildings. During the first half of the 15th century, the complex is in the hands of the Armenians; during the second half, it falls into the hands of the Muslims who destroy it, preserving only the cave that provided lodging to the people of the village. In 1679, the Franciscans purchase the site; in 1862, they are authorized to undertake the first construction project. In 1938, new construction projects are undertaken that continue until 1955, enlarging the lower church of an upper church.

The first houses the cave where a miraculous spring is said to have gushed forth at the moment that Mary visited. A stone, imbedded in the wall on the right that bears the imprint of an infant's body is considered the one that served to hide Elisabeth and John. Three frescoes depict Mary's visit, Elizabeth's escape and Zacharias worshipping in the Temple. The Italian artist, Vagarini, decorated the upper church that was to be used for the services. The Magnificat, the prayer recited by Mary that is etched in forty-two languages, resonates in the courtyard of the church:

Mary's prayer

My soul magnifies the Lord,
And my spirit rejoices in God, my Savior,
For he has regarded the low estate of his handmaiden:
Henceforth, all generations will call me blessed,
for he that is mighty has done great things for me.
Holy is his name.
And his mercy is upon all those who fear him
from generation to generation.
He has shown strength with his arm;
He has scattered the proud in the imagination of their hearts.
He has brought down the mighty from their seats
and exalted the lowly.
He has filled the hungry with goods,
and the rich he has sent away empty.
He has helped his servant, Israel,
in remembrance of his mercy.
As he spoke to our fathers,
to Abraham and to his seed forever.

Luke 1: 46 - 55

A spring – the Fountain of the Virgin – flows under a mosque in the center of the village. The Virgin is said to have used these waters during her stay at her cousin's house.

HADASSAH HOSPITAL

This hospital is built during the Fifties above Ein Karem to replace the hospital on Mount Scopus, which was inaccessible until the Six Day War in 1967. The stained glass windows of the synagogue, painted by Chagall, one of the most distinguished Jewish painters of the 20th century, depicts scenes inspired by the blessing that Jacob gave to his twelve sons, the founders of the tribes that composed the Jewish people:

Jacob's benedictions

Jacob called to his sons and said: "Gather together so that I may tell you that which will befall you in the last days. Gather together and hear, you, sons of Jacob and listen to Israel, your father.

Reuven, you are my first born, my might and the beginning of my strength, the first in dignity and the first in power. But unstable as water, you will not excel because you went up to your father's bed, you defiled it and went up to my couch.

Simon and Levi are brothers; their swords are instruments of cruelty. May my soul not come into their council and may my honor not be united to their assembly; for in their anger, they slew a man and in their willfulness, they lamed an ox. Cursed be their anger for it was fierce and their wrath for it was cruel. I will separate them in Jacob and disperse them in Israel.

Yehudah, your brothers will praise you; your hand will be on the neck of your enemies; your father's children will bow down before you. Yehudah is a lion's cub when you come up with your prey. He lies down like a lion, like a lioness; who will dare rouse you? The staff will not depart from Yehudah or the scepter from between his feet until Shilo comes and the nations submit to him. Binding his foal to the vine and his ass's colt to the choice vine, he washes his garments in wine and his clothes in the blood of grapes; his eyes are red with wine and his teeth are white with milk.

Zevulun will dwell on the shores of the sea; he will be a haven for ships and his beaches will extend to Sidon.

Issachar is a strong ass lying down between the sheepfolds. He saw that rest was good and that the land was pleasant and he bowed his shoulder to bear the yoke and became a servant to tribute.

Dan will judge his people, one tribe among the tribes of Israel. Dan will be a serpent on the way, a viper on the path that bites the horse's heels so that the rider falls backwards. I count on you, Lord, for your salvation.

Gad will be attacked by his enemies, but he will strike back.

From Asher will come an abundant harvest and he will yield royal delicacies.

Naftali is a hind that dashes forward and offers good words.

Joseph is a fruitful bough by a spring whose branches overrun the others along the wall. The archers fiercely attacked him, shot at him and hated him! But his bow retained its strength and his arms were made supple by the hands of the mighty God of Jacob, from the Shepherd, the Rock of Israel. By the God of your father, who will help you, by the Almighty who will bless you and cover you with the benedictions from heaven above, from the deep that lies beneath, from the breasts and the womb! The blessings of your father are greater than those of my ancestors, exceeding the utmost boundaries of the eternal hills; they will be fulfilled upon Joseph's head, on the crown of the head of the one set apart from his brothers!

Benjamin is a ravenous wolf, devouring the prey in the morning and dividing the spoil in the evening.

All these are the twelve tribes; and this is how their father spoke to them and blessed them, each one was blessed according to his benediction.

Genesis 49: 1 - 28

The Hebrew University also has to leave Mount Scopus in 1948. Its classes continue to take place in buildings scattered throughout the city until the inauguration of the new campus of Givat Ram in 1961.

THE KNESSET

The new building of the Israeli Parliament – the Knesset – is completed in 1966. It draws its name and its composition from the Great Assembly – *ha-knesset ha-gadolah* – the representative body of the Jews following their return from captivity in Babylonia in the 5th century B.C. The Knesset has 120 deputies who are proportionally elected every four years; the number of seats allotted to each party depends on the percentage of votes gathered throughout the whole country and according to its list of candidates. This system of voting encourages the proliferation of small parties, contributing to the fragmentation of the political map. Moreover, it appears to authorize only coalition governments in which the large parties fight for the support of the small parties in order to secure a legislative majority.

One of the controversies rocking Israeli public opinion deals with the question of the need for a constitution. For the time being, the Israeli democracy makes do with a series of fundamental laws. One of them, which was passed on February 12th, 1958, defines the status of the Knesset as follows:

The Knesset
1. *The Knesset is the Parliament of the State of Israel.*
2. *The seat of the Knesset is in Jerusalem.*
3. *The Knesset is composed of 120 members.*
4. *The Knesset members will be elected through general, national, direct, equal, secret and proportional ballot elections in accordance with the Knesset Election Laws.*

5. *Every Israeli citizen of or over the age of 18 will have the right to vote in the legislative elections unless a court of justice has deprived him of this right by virtue of the law...*

6. *Every Israeli citizen, who on the day of the admission of the candidates' list containing his name is 21 years of age or over, has the right to be elected to the Knesset unless a court of justice has deprived him of this right by virtue of the law.*

7. *The following may not be candidates for the Knesset: a) the president of the State of Israel; b) the two chief rabbis; c) an incumbent judge (shofet); d) an incumbent judge (dayyan) of a religious court; e) the state comptroller; f) the chief of general staff of the Israeli Defense Forces. g) rabbis and ministers of other religions who are holding office and receiving payment from the government; h) senior state employees and senior army officers of such grades or ranks and in such functions as will be determined by law.*

8. *The term of office of the Knesset will be four years from the day it is elected.*

The Knesset elects the president of the State, which is an honorary appointment. He countersigns the laws, appoints the state comptroller and the governor of the Bank of Israel, whose candidacy is put forward by the government, and the judges based upon the recommendation of the Council of the Magistrates. He receives the credentials of the ambassadors and has the right to grant pardons and to commute sentences. He is elected for a five-year period and may be reelected only once.

The government is accountable to the Knesset. It has a four-year term unless a no confidence vote is passed or unless the prime minister resigns.

The state comptroller is responsible for monitoring the legality and the proper running of the public services. He submits an annual report to the Knesset and his term of office is five years.

The Supreme Court occupies the position of the High Court of Justice and the Supreme Court of Appeal as well as that of the State Council that is responsible for the defense of the citizen against the authorities.

The Civil Magistrate and District Courts handle civil and criminal offenses; the Religious Magistrate Courts and Court of Appeal deal with questions concerning the rights of individuals (inheritance rights, marriages, divorces...) in accordance with the religious legislation of the different communities.

THE ISRAEL MUSEUM

This national museum (1965) includes two large bodies: the Archeological and Biblical Museum and the Museum of Art. The first reconstructs eight millenniums of history, exhibiting pieces discovered on the numerous archeological sites in the country. The Museum of Art assembles rich collections of painting, sculpture, ethnography... A permanent exhibit that is devoted to Jewish art connects the two pavilions: coverings for Torah scrolls, candlesticks, tapestries, etc.: "The continuous change in the spaces", wrote one of the museum's architects, "large and small, open and closed, will offer diverse exhibition possibilities and will sharpen the sensibility of the visitor who, moreover, will be able to rest and refresh himself in the patio and the interior courtyards." Designed by the Japanese, Isamu Noguchi, the park contains the rich collection of sculptures of the American, Bill Rose.

The Shrine of the Book, located on the grounds of the museum, houses the manuscripts discovered during the Forties and the Fifties in the area near the Dead Sea as well as near Massada and in the caves of Nahal Hever. The most noteworthy manuscripts were discovered in 1947 by a Bedouin shepherd in a cave located in Qumran. This collection of books of the Old Testament – with the exception of the scroll of Esther –, translations and apocryphal books that date back to the Second Temple Period (160 B.C.? –

70 A.D.), mark a turning point in biblical and historical research and shed some light on the information provided by Josephus Flavius about the Essenes, the sect to whom researchers attribute the manuscripts.

The origins and the fate of this sect are bathed in mystery. Established about two hundred years before the destruction of the Temple (70 A.D.) by a "Master of Justice" who had gathered a handful of followers, the Romans massacred it completely during the repression that followed the Great Revolt of the Jews. At the time, the Essenes, the Pharisees and the Sadducees represented the three main streams of Judaism. Josephus Flavius, the historian of Judea, presents the last two in these terms:

Pharisees and Sadducees

The Pharisees lead a life that is neither easy nor a life of pleasure seeking, but a simple one. They are fiercely attached to their beliefs, honoring their Elders to such an extent that they dare not contradict them. They attribute everything that occurs to destiny, without, however, denying man the power to influence the course of his life in such a way that while everything happens by God's order, it, nevertheless, depends on our will, which will lead us to vice or virtue. They believe that our souls are immortal and subject to judgment in another world – rewarded or punished according to whether they were virtuous or wicked in this world. Furthermore, they believe that some souls remain in the other world for all eternity and that others return to this world. Thanks to this belief, they have such great influence over the people that the latter adhere to their views regarding everything related to the worship of God and to the official prayers that are addressed to Him. Entire cities conform to their morals, their way of life and their views.

In contrast, the Sadducees believe that the soul dies with the body and that the only thing that we are charged to uphold is the observance of the Law; it is considered to be a virtuous act to not yield to the wisdom of those who teach us. This sect has only a few members who are, in general, the most distinguished (members of society). Nevertheless, almost nothing is accomplished according to their views since once they have been raised to positions of responsibility or honor, generally against their will, they are constrained to conform to the behavior prescribed by the Pharisees, which the people will not tolerate that they shirk.

J. Flavius, *Jewish Antiquities, XVIII, 2*

The Essenes formed a monastic sect that retreated to the desert to better prepare itself for the advent of the End of Days. It was made up exclusively of men although there is archeological evidence that suggests that some communities also included women. Their doctrine often appears to be a radical version of the apocalyptic hypothesis that prevailed during this period. Humanity is divided into two opposing sides, "the Children of Light and the Children of Darkness", "those on God's side and those on Belial's side". The former are led by the "Prince of Light" or the "Spirit of Truth"; the latter by the "Angel of Darkness" or the "Spirit of Perversion". Dictated by God to the smallest detail, history is supposed to lead to a war at the end of which the Children of Light will take charge of humanity; the world will enter an era of justice and charity, and Israel will throw off the yoke of the nations. The Essenes considered themselves to be the chosen, entrusted to crystallize the humanity of the future around themselves. They denounced the impiety of the religious, social and political customs of their co-religionists, even fostering hatred towards those who did not share their views. The Thanksgiving Psalms, discovered among the Dead Sea Scrolls, emphasize the futility and the solitude in which man falls when he does not nourish his spiritual vocation and the meaninglessness of his existence in a world contaminated by evil. Researchers have identified numerous similarities between their hypotheses and those of the early Christians.

The communal life of the Essenes was dictated by a concern for unity and social cohesion. They ate together, prayed together, and submitted their questions to the deliberations of a general council: the Council of Many. They appeared to be more meticulous than the Pharisees regarding the observance of the religious commandments and they were particularly severe about ritual purity, plunging into the ritual bath, the mikveh, many times a day in order to maintain themselves in a permanent state of purity. Furthermore, the Essenes constituted a hierarchical community in which relations were governed by the stipulating principle that "the subordinates must submit to their superiors". A supervisor that bore the title of "Chief Inspector of Many" was responsible for the daily management of the community. Major decisions were discussed in a general assembly. The violation of common rules of living could result in temporary exclusion; religious transgressions as well as insubordination were liable to permanent exclusion.

The Essenes observed their own *halakha* – their interpretation of the Law of Moses – which differed on many points from that of the Pharisees, especially regarding the establishment of the calendar of religious festivals. They probably did not participate in the Temple service since they unceasingly denounced the corruption of the priests. The following passages are excerpts of the description of their life style provided by Josephus Flavius:

A charter of monasticism

Celibacy. *They are Jewish by nationality and live in tight communities; they consider sensual pleasure as something to be avoided and continence, just as the mastery of one's passions, as invaluable virtues. They refuse marriage, not that they believe that the human species must be destroyed, but to protect themselves from the intemperance of women, convinced that the latter cannot remain faithful to their husbands. Nevertheless, they do not hesitate to welcome into their communities the young children entrusted to their care whom they virtuously educate with as much attention and generosity as if they were their own children, feeding them and dressing them all in the same manner.*

Community property. *They scorn wealth and practice communal property. So rigorously do they respect equality that every new member must rid himself of his personal possessions to protect himself against wealth and to spare others the humiliation of poverty.*

The formation of the group. *They choose people who are devoted to the good of the economy to entrust with collecting* *the revenues and distributing them according to the needs of the individual. They are not concentrated in one particular city, but are dispersed in the various localities where they receive those who wish to join their society; although they do not know the newcomers, they immediately share what they own with them as if they had known them for a long time...*

Clothing. *They do not change their clothes except when they are torn or shabby. They do not sell or buy anything among themselves, but share all their possessions without demanding anything in return.*

The daily schedule. *Being very religious, they do not deal with any mundane matters until sunrise, after pronouncing the traditional prayers handed down to them by their fathers asking God to illuminate the earth. Then they go to work, each one doing the task assigned to him according to a program that was established in advance. At eleven o'clock, they gather to immerse themselves in cold water, covering themselves with cloths of linen. They then retire to their small chambers, which are off limits to anyone who does not belong to their sect. Thus purified, they go to the refectory as if to a sacred temple and there they wait, seated in silence, for someone to put a piece of bread and a small amount of food on a small plate placed before them. A priest blesses the meal, no one venturing to touch it before the prayer is finished. A second prayer will be pronounced after the meal, ending just as it began, praising God and affirming in this way that it is only through Divine generosity that the community derives its nourishment. They remove their sacred clothing and return to work. In the evening, they will prepare a similar meal, inviting guests that have arrived during the day to their tables...*

Admission requirements. *They do not immediately accept those who want to embrace their way of life. Candidates must spend a year on the outside, equipped with a pickax, the linen cloth, which we previously mentioned, and a white frock in accordance with the regulations. At the end of this period, they will begin to receive the same meals and will likewise be authorized to immerse themselves in the cold water to purify themselves; however, they will not be admitted to the refectory until after a supplementary period of two years during which time their morals will be tested just as their* *physical self-restraint had been previously tested. Judged to be worthy of joining the community, they are then fully admitted: before seating themselves at the table with the others, they must yet solemnly pledge to honor God and to serve Him with all their hearts, to carry out justice in their relations with men, to never willingly do evil and they are even ordered to dislike the wicked, to help the good with all their might and to be loyal, especially with respect to princes whose power comes from God. Furthermore, they pledge that if they are raised to the highest office, that they will not abuse their prerogative to mistreat their subordinates; that they will not have more of anything than the others, neither linen nor any other personal effects; that they will bear an unfailing love of truth, severely reprimanding liars; that they will preserve their hands and their souls pure of all theft and of all desire for dishonest gain; that they will not hide any of the most veiled mysteries of their religion from their fellow sectarians, revealing nothing to others even under the threat of death; that they will not teach any doctrine other than that which has been transmitted to them, carefully preserving the books as much as the names of those who will have transmitted it to them.*

Expulsion. *These are the solemn requirements that those who wish to embrace their way of life must fulfill, which are intended to turn them away from vice. If they transgress them by committing serious offenses, they will be expelled from the community. Because they are not permitted to eat with strangers, the majority of those excluded will be reduced to eating herbage like animals and will die in misery, consumed by hunger...*

The authority. *They will revere their lawgiver to such an extent, second to God, that those who speak about them with contempt will be punished with death. Likewise, they consider it a great obligation to obey their elders and respect their orders...*

Hygienic measures. *They observe the Sabbath even more scrupulously than the other Jews and are not satisfied with just preparing their meat the night before in order to not be obliged to light a fire on the day of rest. They are also careful not to move utensils and even abstain, to the extent that they are able, from fulfilling their natural needs. On ordinary* days, they have the habit of going off alone and digging a hole a foot deep using a pickaxe, which we previously mentioned, and then relieving themselves, covering themselves with their clothing as if they were afraid of soiling the rays of the sun that God shines upon them, and then filling up the hole; for although this is a natural function, they permit themselves to consider this activity as impure and so they must hide and then wash themselves in order to purify themselves...

Martyrdom. *They scorn calamities and disease, displaying such endurance and perseverance that they overcome their pain and prefer death to life when the stakes are high for a great cause. The war waged against the Romans demonstrated in a million ways to what extent their courage was invincible. They would suffer the sword and fire and would allow their limbs to be broken rather than speak ill of their lawmakers or eat forbidden meat and in the midst of their anguish, would not shed a single tear nor pronounce a single word to mitigate the cruelty of their executioners. On the contrary, they would mock them, encouraging each other, and would breathe their last breath with joy, hoping to attain a better life in this manner, nourishing the unwavering conviction that just as our bodies are mortal and corruptible, our souls are immortal and incorruptible. Composed of a minuscule elevated substance and being prisoners of the bodies as in a prison where a natural inclination attracts them or restrains them, they are not promptly liberated from the carnal ties that hold them in extended servitude so that when released, they rise and take flight with joy...*

Immortality. *The Essenes believe that the soul is immortal, which predisposes them to virtue and turns them away from vice. They believe that the good people become better in this life thanks to the hope of being happy after they die and that the wicked who think they can hide their evil deeds in this world will be punished in the next with eternal suffering. This is how they feel about the pre-eminence of the soul and very few of those who have been possessed by these ideas give them up. There are some among them who boast about knowing the future through the study of the holy books and the ancient prophecies as well as by the pains they take to purify themselves and their predictions are rarely wrong.*

J. Flavius, *The War of the Jews against the Romans II, 8, 1 -12*

The white dome that rises within the enclosure of the Museum of Israel symbolizes the purity of the "Children of Light"; the black wall symbolizes the blindness of the "Children of Darkness". The dome evokes the lid of the earthenware jar dating to the 2nd century in which the Qumran manuscripts were preserved. The entrance of the Museum of The Shrine of the Book evokes a crypt. Along a corridor, glass cases display fifteen of Bar Kokhba's letters – the leader of the revolt against the Romans (132 – 135) – written in Aramaic; they were discovered in a cave at Nahal Hever. A variety of documents are displayed there – a marriage certificate, a divorce certificate, a title to property – belonging to a Nabatean woman of nobility at the beginning of the 2nd century as well as some manuscript fragments discovered at Massada and Ein Gedi. The corridor leads to a cupola, whose diameter measures 25 meters, where samples of the Dead Sea Scrolls are exhibited, including a copy of the book of Isaiah, the oldest text in Hebrew of the Old Testament that is unrolled around an immense drum. The interior partition walls display some manuscripts dealing with subjects that are characteristic of the Dead Sea sects: "the war between the Children of Light and the Children of Darkness", "the disciple's manual", etc. The basement exhibits a series of tools and objects of art discovered in the cave at Nahal Hever.

THE CITY TO COME

In June 1967, a six-day war is fought between the Israelis and the Egyptians, the Syrians and the Jordanians. On the eastern front, the battles are at first concentrated in Jerusalem, lasting only three days, from Monday morning to Wednesday afternoon. Occupying the headquarters of the United Nations' forces located on the Mount of Bad Counsel, Jordan initiates the war. The Israelis counter attack, recapturing the United Nations' headquarters and cutting off the road linking Jerusalem to Bethlehem.

At the same time, heavy battles take place on Ammunition Hill[1] where the Jordanians, who take cover in the network of trenches, confront fierce resistance. The Israelis make another breach in the neighborhood of Sheikh Jarrah and the American Colony. On Tuesday, the Old City is practically encircled. On Wednesday, the paratroopers enter it through the Lions Gate. Moshe Amirav, one of the first men to reach the Western Wall[2], which Israelis had not been able to stand before in meditation for almost twenty years, recounts:

1. Ammunition Hill, a public memorial, houses a small museum that reconstructs the Israeli conquest of the Old City.

2. The Western Wall, see p.141.

Storming the Wall

I cannot help but smile when I remember how we had sought the Wall. We were a whole group of soldiers running, breathless, lost on the esplanade of the Temple Mount, seeking a wall of giant stones. We didn't even stop to look at the Mosque of Omar although it was the first time that we had seen it up close. Forward! Forward! We rushed headlong, passing through the Gate of the Maghebrians and suddenly, we stopped, astonished. It stood before us! Gray and massive, silent and contemplative! The Western Wall! I remember only once before in my life having felt the feeling that overwhelmed me in front of the wall, when my father led me to the cabinet holding the holy Torah scrolls in the synagogue – the small child was afraid that something would come out of it, something large and terrible from another world...

I approached it slowly, in fear and trembling, like a pious, officiating minister walking towards the lectern to lead the prayers. I approached it representing my father, my grandfather, my great grandfather and all the generations throughout all the exiles who were not entitled to see it and who delegated this to me in their place. Someone recited the obligatory blessing for solemn occasions like this: "Blessed are You, Eternal, our God, King of the Universe Who has kept us in life and has preserved us and has enabled us to reach this season." But I was unable to respond amen. I placed my hand on the stones and I felt that the tears that began to flow from my eyes were not my tears, but those of all of Israel, the tears of hope and of prayer, tears with a Hassidic accent, tears that burned the heavy gray stones.

M. Amirav, *Testimony*

Abraham Duvdevani, another soldier, also described the first encounter with the Wall:

Kissing the Wall

Narrow alleys, filfthy passageways, garbage at the entrances of shuttered shops, the stench of dead legionnaires – but we paid no attention. Our eyes were fixed on the golden dome which could be seen from a distance. There, more or less, it had to be! We marched faster to keep up with the beating of our hearts; we were almost running. We met a soldier from one of the forward units and asked him the way and hurried on. There was the Wall in all its grandeur and glory! We went though a gate and down some steps. I looked to the right and stopped dead. I have never seen it before but it was an old friend, impossible to mistake. Then I thought that I should not be there because the Wall belongs to the world of dreams and legends and I am real. Reality and Legend, dream and deed, all unite here. I went down and approached the Wall and stretched out my hand towards the huge, hewn stones. But my hand was afraid to touch and of itself returned to me. I closed my eyes, took a small, hesitant step forward, and brought my lips to the Wall. The touch of my lips opened the gates of my emotions and the tears burst forth. A Jewish soldier in the State of Israel is kissing history with his lips...

A. Duvdevani, *Testimony*

The journalists follow the soldiers. One of them, Yehudah ha-Ezrahi, who is among the first to run to the wall, relates:

Reuniting with a Wall

I run in turn behind a group of soldiers up to the southwest end, towards a small green gate, the Gate of the Maghebrians. It is wide open. The soldiers enter and leave with the noise of heavy boots and muffled panting. Behind the gate, a narrow passage abruptly turns towards the right, towards narrow, slippery steps – the Western Wall!

At first, I see the stones. Suddenly, in spite of a long wait that lasts interminable hours, jolted by shots and explosions... I see the holy stones and it is as extraordinary as it can be, as if I had already been there, only yesterday or the day before. They seem so familiar! Perhaps not yesterday or the day before, but generations ago. They are so old, polished by the strokes, the kisses, the tears, the supplications, the wishes and the prayers of so many generations. Perhaps even long before, beyond time, when my mother stood there, immobile, praying with dignity. In fact, for the first time, I see those stones that I knew for generations. "The stones" that whisper in my ear sound like my mother's voice. There they are lined up in a row before me. I see their fragments, their hollows and their bumps, the slightest imprint of the hand of the hewer of stones, the marks of the rain and the wind, all the crevices where strange bushes have grown their roots, the slightest flickering of shadow and light. At first, I had only seen the stones...

Some soldiers are there. Under their war gear, dusty and perspiring, covered with the smoke of the shells and stained with blood – perhaps their own, perhaps that of their comrades who were wounded in battle or died at their sides. They are wearing helmets, carrying rifles, machine guns, munitions and mines – their faces are numb. Look! One of them hesitatingly extends a black hand towards the old stones that he gently caresses. Another one plunges his hands in the stones, then his body and then his face. A third gazes at the sky. I am surprised to see tears glistening in his eyes. It must be the Divine Presence in the form of a white dove soaring above them in this piece of blue sky that is

shedding these human tears. Hardened, their faces numb,
the soldiers stand still – and cry.

Y. Ha-Ezrahi, *Testimony*

The soldier's emotions overcome the entire nation. The poet
Haim Hefer immediately composes this text to celebrate the
reunion of a people and a wall:

This Wall

This Wall has heard countless prayers.
This Wall has seen the fall of many walls.
This Wall has felt the touch of women weeping.
This Wall has felt petitions lodged between its stones.
This Wall saw Rabbi Yehudah Halevi trampled to death before it.

This Wall has seen emperors rise and fall.
But this Wall has never seen paratroopers cry.

This Wall has seen them weary and exhausted.
This Wall has seen them wounded and maimed.
Running towards it, with excitement, cries and silence,
and creeping as torn creatures in the alleys of the Old City,
covered with dust and with parched lips,
whispering: "If I forget you, if I forget you, oh Jerusalem".

They are swift as eagles and strong as lions,
and their tanks – the fiery chariots of the prophet, Elijah –
passing like thunder,
passing in anger,
remembering the terrible years,
when we didn't even have a wall upon which to shed our tears.

Here they stand before it, breathing heavily.
Here they are, contemplating it with sweet sorrow,
with tears in their eyes, gazing at it, perplexed:

Can it be, can it be that paratroopers cry?
Can it be that they touch this Wall with great emotion?
Can it be that their weeping turns to song?
Perhaps it is because these boys of nineteen were born with the State.
Perhaps it is because these boys of nineteen carry two
thousand years of exile on their shoulders.

H. Hefer

Immediately after the war, the Israeli authorities give the order to open the road going from Mount Zion to the Dung Gate to allow the Israelis to access the Wall. They also order the destruction of the hovels in the Maghrebian Quarter along the wall and the relocation of its inhabitants. In the course of a week, a first esplanade is arranged from the Mamluk building of Mahkameh to the ramp that leads to the Gate of the Maghebrians. Since then, this esplanade is constantly rearranged, stirring up on every occasion an architectural debate whose echoes move the heavens…

The current esplanade only stretches over an area of about 60 meters on the 485-meter length of the western enclosure of Herod's Temple. It is made up of seven rows of Herodian stones, of four to five rows of large stones dating to the period of the Umayyad, and of many rows of small stones at the very top. The original enclosure was made up of eight supplementary rows of Herodian stones, which can be seen through the pits hollowed out by the archeologists. In addition, nine other rows of these same stones below the paved road that skirted the enclosure constituted its foundations.

The two parts of the city are officially reunified on June 28th, 1967. The construction of new neighborhoods is immediately undertaken along the old demarcation line, as is the restoration of the Jewish Quarter in the Old City and that of the Hebrew University on Mount Scopus. Work on these projects continues until the beginning of the Eighties.

Likewise, measures are taken to assure the administrative reunification of the city. The Arab inhabitants can obtain Israeli citizenship, but few request it. They actually participate here and there in the municipal elections, but without presenting their own candidates. They are, moreover, careful not to take any steps that could be interpreted as a de facto recognition of the reunification of the city. The members of the municipal council of the eastern sector refuse to join the one of the united city; on their part, the commercial companies refuse to register themselves as Israeli companies and the Islamic courts refuse to be incorporated in the Israeli Koranic judicial system. Furthermore, a muted tension reigns between the two sectors, punctuated now and then by attacks and reprisals. The Israeli authorities, nevertheless, continue to intensify initiatives to make the Old City Jewish.

THE JEWISH QUARTER

3. The Herodian Houses, see p.84.

The architects prove their talents through the restoration projects in the Jewish Quarter. They religiously preserve the ruins, liturgically reproducing lanes and alleys. The restored quarter includes at the same time the museum – its columns, its walls, the sanctuary – its synagogues, its houses of study – and the patio. A museum about the Jewish Quarter offers a fifteen-minute, multi-media program about its history. The Museum of the Old Yishuv takes the visitor into a house in the Old City and introduces him to the customs of its inhabitants. The Burnt House and the Herodian House that date back to the Second Temple Period[3] remain the most interesting archeological sites.

4. The Hurva Synagogue, see p.172.

5. The Ramban Synagogue, see p.134.

The Hurva Synagogue, built around 1700, destroyed by the creditors of the Ashkenazim in 1720, rebuilt in 1856 and blown up by the Arab League in 1948, is not restored.[4] The arch that overlooks it, nevertheless, makes it possible to imagine its imposing architecture. The Ramban Synagogue[5] is entirely restored. Four adjoining synagogues that were destroyed in the battles of 1948 are open for services and for visits.[6] The restoration work spreads to the north-south road – the Cardo – that traversed the Roman city; 4 meters of debris is cleared and it is converted to a passageway lined with shops.[7]

6. The Yohanan ben Zakkai Synagogues, see p.140.

7. The Cardo, see p.87.

[•]

The center of the new city is demarcated by Jaffa Road, King George V St. – the King of England during the time that the Balfour Declaration announced the creation of a Jewish National Home in Palestine – and Ben Yehudah St. The first part begins at the central bus station and ends in the new neighborhood of Mamilla – from the Arabic ma min Allah, that which is from God – in front of the Jaffa Gate. King George St. continues to Keren Hayesod St. that is bordered by Independence Park – *Gan ha-Atzmaut*. This street passes in front of the Yeshurun Synagogue (1936), the building of the Jewish Agency (1929), which was considered the seat of the representative institutions of the Jewish community in Palestine under the British Mandate, and then the Great Synagogue – *Hechal Shlomo* – the seat of the Chief Rabbinate that houses the Museum of Jewish Traditions. The Square of France marks a pause in the street where the Terra Sancta Monastery is prominently located and where the Hebrew University maintains some offices and laboratories; it then continues to the Windmill, which the Jewish philanthropist, Moses Montefiore[8], built at the beginning of the century, and that provides access to the neighborhood bearing his name: Yemin Moshe. This neighborhood descends to the left towards the Sultan's Pools and to the right towards the city's Cinematheque, which overlooks the Scottish Church of Saint Anne.

8. Moses Montefiore, see p.196.

The city's wealthy neighborhoods of Talbiyeh and, especially, Rehavia, where the Prime Minister's residence, that of the President of the State, the Academy of Sciences, the Jerusalem Theater, and the Islam Museum are located, extend along the right side of Keren Hayesod St.

Since the autumn of 1987, the city is once again practically divided by the Intifada – the revolt of the Palestinians against Israeli domination. An invisible wall of violence and hate rises again in the heart of this terrible city that is so coveted that it cannot bring itself to withdraw from the history of men. A city in the open air, brooding a blessing, brooding a curse, covered with roses and thorns. The site of the most marvelous restoration, that of a sanctuary built upon the ruins of cemeteries with a wall that crosses history and a wall of wailing that is waiting to be transformed into a wall of celebration and of peace...

BIBLIOGRAPHY

Bartana, M. & Wallenstein, N. & Persky, N., Ed., *Tekoumat Israel*, Tel Aviv: Karni, 1958.

Begin, M., *The Revolt*, Jerusalem: Steimatzky, 1972.

Ben Aryeh, Y., *Ir be-Rei Tekufa*, Jerusalem: Yad Yitshak Ben Zevi, 1977.

Ben Dov, M., Naor, M., Aner, Z., Ed., *The Western Wall*, Tel Aviv: The Ministry of Defense Publishing House, 1983.

Ben Israël Avi-Oded, A., *Aggadot ha-Aretz*, Tel Aviv: Devir, 1953.

Berchet, J. C., *Le Voyage en Orient*, Paris: Robert Laffont, 1985.

Birnbaum, P., *The Daily Prayer Book*, New York: Hebrew Pub. Co, 1949.

Brody, H., *Selected Poems of Jehudah Halevi*, New York: Arno Press, 1973.

Buber, M., *On Judaism*, New York: Schocken Books, 1967.

Carmi, T., *Hebrew Verse*, London: Allan Lane, 1981.

Chartok, R. & Spencer, J., *The Holocaust Years: Society on Trial,* New York: Bantam Books, 1981.

Chateaubriand, R. *Itinéraire de Paris à Jérusalem*, Paris: GF-Flammarion, 1968.

Cohen, A. & Mendes-Flhor, P., Ed., *Contemporary Jewish Religious Thought*, New York: Scribners, 1987.

Dawidowicz, L., *A Holocaust Reader*, New York: Behrman House, 1976.

Ehrman, E. L., Ed., *Readings in Modern Jewish History*, New York: Ktav Publishing House, 1977.

Flaubert, G., *Par les Champs et par les Grèves, Voyages et Carnets de Voyages,* Paris: Club de l'Honnête Homme, 1973.

Guttmann, J., *Philosophies of Judaism*, New York: Schocken Books, 1973.

Heschel, A. J., *God in Search of Man*, Philadelphia: The Jewish Publication Society, 1955.

Heschel, A. J., *Quest of God: Studies in Prayer and Symbolism*, New York: Crossroad Publishing Company, 1986.

Heschel, A. J., *Israel: An Echo of Eternity*, New York: Noonday, 1977.

Lagerlöf, S., *Jerusalem*, London: William Heinemann, 1903.

Lamartine, *Voyage en Orient*, Paris : Hachette, 1887.

Lapierre, D. & Collins, L., *O Jerusalem*, Paris: Robert Laffont, 1971.

Levi, P., *Les Naufragés et les Rescapés*, Paris: Gallimard-Arcades, 1989.

Londres, A., *Le Juif errant est arrivé*, Paris: Union générale d'Edition, 1975.

Loti, P., *La Galilée*, Paris : Christian Pirot, 1990.

Loti, P., *Jérusalem*, Paris : Christian Pirot, 1990.

Marcus, J., R., *The Jew in the Medieval World*, New York: Atheneu, 1972.

Matthews, C. D., *Palestine – Mohamedan Holy Land*, New Haven, Yale University Press, 1949.

Mendes-Flhor, P. & Reinharz, Y., *The Jew in the Modern World*, Oxford, 1980.

Michner, J., *The Source*, New York: Fawcett, 1965.

Nahon, U., *Sir Moses Montefiore*, Jérusalem: Organisation Sioniste Mondiale, 1985.

Nahon, U., *Theodore Herzl: The Father of the Jewish State*, Tel Aviv: M. Newman, 1950.

Natanyahu, B., Ed., *Jonathan Natanyahu: Self Portrait of a Hero*, New York : Random House, 1980.

Oz, A., *In the Land of Israel*, New York: Vintage, 1984.

Ruppin, A., *Memoirs, Diaries and Letters*, London: Weidenfeld & Nicolson, 1971.

Shapira, A., Ed., *The Seventh Day*, New York: Scribners, 1970.

Scholem, G., *Sabbataï Tsevi*, Verdier, 1983.

Scholem, G., *The Messianic Idea in Judaism*, New York: Schocken Books, 1971.

Shoshuk, L., & Eisenberg, A., Ed., *Momentous Century*, New York: Cornwall Books, 1984.

Silberman, C., *A Certain People*, New York: Summit, 1986.

Silk, D., *Retrievements: A Jerusalem Anthology*, Jerusalem: Keter, 1977.

Sokolow, N., *History of Zionism*, London: Longman, 1919.

Steinsaltz, A., *The Essential Talmud*, New York: Signet, 1977.

Vilnay, Z., *Legends of Judea and Samaria: The Sacred Land*, Philadelphia : Jewish Publication Society of America, 1978.

Vilnay, Z., *Legends of Galilee, Jordan and Sinai: The Sacred Land*, Philadelphia : Jewish Publication Society of America, 1978.

Vogüé, M. de, *Jérusalem hier et aujourd'hui*, Paris: Plon, 1912.

Volney, *Voyage en Égypte et en Syrie*, Paris: Mouton, 1959.